If...Then

Oxford Studies in Digital Politics

Series Editor: Andrew Chadwick, Professor of Political Communication in the Centre for Research in Communication and Culture and the Department of Social Sciences, Loughborough University

If...Then

ALGORITHMIC POWER AND POLITICS

TAINA BUCHER

OXFORD
UNIVERSITY PRESS

Oxford University Press is a department of the University of Oxford.
It furthers the University's objective of excellence in research, scholarship,
and education by publishing worldwide. Oxford is a registered trade mark of
Oxford University Press in the UK and certain other countries.

Published in the United States of America by Oxford University Press
198 Madison Avenue, New York, NY 10016, United States of America.

Library of Congress Cataloging-in-Publication Data

Names: Bucher, Taina, author.
Title: If... then : algorithmic power and politics / Taina Bucher.
Description: New York : Oxford University Press, [2018] | Includes
    bibliographical references and index. |
Identifiers: LCCN 2017054909 (print) | LCCN 2018008562 (ebook) |
ISBN 9780190493042 (Updf) | ISBN 9780190493059 (Epub) |
    ISBN 9780190493035 (pbk. : alk. paper) | ISBN 9780190493028 (hardcover : alk. paper)
Subjects: LCSH: Information technology—Social aspects. | Information
    society—Social aspects. | Algorithms—Social aspects. | Big data—Social aspects. |
Artificial intelligence—Social aspects.
Classification: LCC HM851 (ebook) | LCC HM851 .B798 2018 (print) |
DDC 303.48/33—dc23
LC record available at https://lccn.loc.gov/2017054909

Contents

Acknowledgments

I enjoyed writing this book. The initial idea behind this book started taking shape as a dissertation at the University of Oslo, but soon evolved into something else entirely, as most things do. I therefore owe a sense of gratitude toward all the efforts I put into my PhD project. Memories of past struggles greatly lessened the burden of undertaking and writing my first book. The encouragement and the generosity of series editor Andrew Chadwick and editor Angela Chnapko at Oxford University Press were also huge contributions to that end, as well as fundamental in developing this project. Thanks to both of you for believing it would make a valuable contribution to the Oxford Studies in Digital Politics series. The book is a product of various encounters with people, things, and places. It was written in the libraries, offices, homes and cafés of Copenhagen, Oslo, Berlin, and New York. Writing allowed me to explore these places in new ways. I'd also like to acknowledge the sunlight, coffee, sounds, views, connectivity, and solitude that these places helpfully offered. The University of Copenhagen has provided a rich academic community, and I am grateful to all my colleagues at the Centre for Communication and Computing for the intellectual discussions and support. Thanks to Shannon Mattern for hosting me at the New School in New York for my sabbatical. A number of people have provided valuable feedback on the book as it emerged: Anne-Britt Gran, Michael Veale, Angèle Christin, Ganaele Langlois, and Fenwick McKelvey. Thanks for your insightful comments. My appreciation also goes to all people involved in the editorial process, copyediting, transcription services, and to all the anonymous referees whose work and critical remarks have greatly improved the final product. There are countless other scholars and students met at conferences and seminars to thank as well for their keen interest in my work and their astute suggestions. I hope a collective word of thanks will be accepted. This book also benefited from insightful interviews and conversations with media leaders, producers, and social media users. I am grateful to all the people who generously agreed to be interviewed and for giving up their time to help me understand the world of algorithms a bit better.

Fragments of this text have been previously published, but are all freshly milled here. Chapter 4 takes parts from "Want to be on the top?" (*New Media & Society*). Chapter 5 builds on pieces from "The algorithmic imaginary" (*Information, Communication & Society*) and chapter 6 has adapted sections from "Machines don't have instincts" (*New Media & Society*). Probably there are many more fragments to be acknowledged, but the boundaries of a text are never easily delineated. Chapter 5 and 6 also benefited from financial support from the Digitization and Diversity project funded by the Research Council of Norway. Thanks to friends and family for their patience and support, and especially to my mom who never forgot to mention that there is more to life than writing a book. More than anyone I am grateful to Georg Kjøll for his unconditional love, superb editorial skills, music playlists, daily home-cooked dinners, and companionship; you make living and writing so much fun each and every day.

If...Then

1

Introduction

Programmed Sociality

Let us for a moment consider the following scenario: Copenhagen on a rainy November day. The semester is coming to a close. Students and professors alike are stressed, but it is nonetheless a sociable time of the year. Conference trips, essays to be graded, dinner plans, and Christmas presents in the pipeline. In other words: buying plane tickets, surfing the Web for restaurant tips, streaming music, coordinating dinner plans with friends, shopping for Christmas gifts, preparing lectures, watching a movie after work. Besides describing a random day in an academic life, all these activities imply using the Internet. I found some cheap tickets using a meta-search engine, discovered a nice restaurant through a collaborative filtering system, listened to a music playlist suggested to me by a music-streaming site, bought a gift for my mother at an online designer store, chatted with friends on a social-networking site to find a suitable time for a pre-Christmas dinner, and, finally, watched an episode of my favorite TV series on a movie-streaming site.

It is not just a story about the good life of a Scandinavian academic. It suggests a life deeply entwined with media. Following media theorist Mark Deuze (2012), we might say that life is not only lived in and through media but in and through specific types of media. What these activities have in common is a high degree of interaction with algorithmic media, media whose core function depends on algorithmic operations. This book starts from the premise that life is not merely infused with media but increasingly takes place in and through an algorithmic media landscape. Key to this premise is the notion of the co-production of social life, practices, and technology. While people interact with specific media companies and platforms, these platforms interact with people as well. Users do not simply consult websites or talk to their friends online. Social media and other commercial Web companies recommend, suggest, and provide users with what their algorithms have predicted to be the most relevant, hot, or interesting news, books, or movies to watch, buy, and consume. Platforms act as performative intermediaries that participate in shaping the worlds they only purport to represent. Facebook is not simply a social networking site that lets users "connect with friends and the world around you."[1] As media scholar José van Dijck has argued, "Social media are inevitably automated systems that engineer and manipulate connections" (2013: 12). By the same token, Netflix is not a website that lets users "see what's next and watch anytime, cancel anytime."[2] It can't be seen as a neutral platform that merely queries its vast database about a user's request to show the movies they explicitly want to watch. Relying on vast amounts of data, Netflix algorithms are used to analyze patterns in people's taste, to recommend more of the same. Popularity is not only a quantifiable measure that helps companies such as Facebook and Netflix to determine relevant content. User input and the patterns emerging from it are turned into a means of production. What we see is no longer what we get. What we get is what we did and that is what we see. In the case that Netflix suggests we watch *House of Cards*, it is largely a matter of consumers getting back their own processed data. When the show was released in 2013 it quickly became a cornerstone for data-driven programming, the idea that successful business decisions are driven by big data analytics.

Of course, there is nothing inherently wrong with this form of data-driven media production. After all, it seems, many people enjoy watching the show. The interesting and potentially troubling question is how reliance on data and predictive analytics might funnel cultural production in particular directions, how individual social media platforms code and brand specific niches of everyday life (van Dijck, 2013: 22). Starting from the basic question of how software is shaping the conditions of everyday life, this book sets out to explore the contours and implications of the question itself. In what ways can we say that software, and more specifically algorithms, shape everyday life and networked communication? What indeed, are algorithms and why should we care about their possible shaping effects to begin with?

Let us quickly return to my rainy November day. While chatting with friends on Facebook about the pre-Christmas dinner, two rather specific ads appeared on the right-hand side of my Facebook news feed. One was for a hotel in Lisbon, where I was going to travel for the conference, and the other was for a party dress. How did Facebook *know* about my upcoming trip, or that I had just bought my mother a Christmas gift from that shop? My musings were only briefly interrupted by one of my friends asking me about a concert I had recently been to. She had seen a picture I posted on Facebook from the concert a few days earlier. My other friend wondered, why hadn't she seen the picture? After all, as she remarked, she checks her Facebook feed all the time. While these connections might be coincidental, their effects are not incidental. They matter because they affect our encounters with the world and how we relate to each other. While seeing ads for party dresses in a festive season might not appear strange, nor missing a picture posted from a concert for that matter, such programmed forms of sociality are not inconsequential. These moments are mediated, augmented, produced, and governed by networked systems powered by software and algorithms. Understood as the coded instructions that a computer needs to follow to perform a given task, algorithms are deployed to make decisions, to sort and make meaningfully visible the vast amount of data produced and available on the Web. Viewed together, these moments tell the story of how our lives are networked and connected. They hint at the fundamental question of who or what has power to set the conditions for what can be seen and known with whatever possible effects. To address this important question, this book proposes to consider the power and politics of software and algorithms that condense and construct the conditions for the intelligible and sensible in our current media environment.

The ideas of power and politics I have in mind are both very broad, yet quite specific. For one, this book is not going to argue that algorithms *have* power. Sure, algorithms are powerful, but the ways in which this statement holds true cannot simply be understood by looking at the coded instructions telling the machine what to do. Drawing on the French philosopher Michel Foucault's (1982; 1977) understanding of power as exercised, relational and productive, I intend to show how the notion of "algorithmic power" implies much more than the specific algorithm ranking e.g. a news feed. What I am going to argue is that the notion of algorithmic power may not even be about the algorithm, in the more technical sense of the term. Power always takes on many forms, including not only the ways in which it is exercised through computable instructions, but also through the claims made over algorithms. As such, we might say that algorithmic systems embody an ensemble of strategies, where power is immanent to the field of action and situation in question. Furthermore, following Foucault, power helps to produce certain forms of acting and knowing, ultimately pointing to the need for examining power through the kinds of encounters and orientations algorithmic systems seem to be generative of.

Neither are the "politics" of this book about politics with a capital P. I will not be discussing parliamentary politics, elections, campaigns, or political communication in the strictest sense. Rather, politics is understood in more general terms, as ways of world-making—the practices and capacities entailed in ordering and arranging different ways of being in the world. Drawing on insights from Science and Technology Studies (STS), politics here is more about the making of certain realities than taking reality for granted (Mol, 2002; Moser, 2008; Law, 2002). In chapter 2 I will describe this form of politics of the real, of what gets to be in the world in terms of an "ontological politics" (Mol, 2002). In ranking, classifying, sorting, predicting, and processing data, algorithms are political in the sense that they help to make the world appear in certain ways rather than others. Speaking of algorithmic politics in this sense, then, refers to the idea that realities are never given but brought into being and actualized in and through algorithmic systems. In analyzing power and politics, we need to be attentive of the way in which some realities are always strengthened while others are weakened, and to recognize the vital role of non-humans in co-creating these ways of being in the world. *If… Then* argues that algorithmic power and politics is neither about algorithms determining how the social world is fabricated nor about *what* algorithms do per se. Rather it is about *how* and *when* different aspects of algorithms and the algorithmic become available to specific actors, under what circumstance, and who or what gets to be part of how algorithms are defined.

Programmed Sociality

Increasingly, we have come to rely on algorithms as programmable decision-makers to manage, curate, and organize the massive amounts of information and data available on the Web and to do so in a meaningful way. Yet, the nature and implications of such arrangements are far from clear. What exactly is it that algorithms "do" and what are the constitutive conditions necessary for them to do what they do? How are algorithms enlisted as part of situated practices, and how do they operate in different settings? How can we develop a productive and critical inquiry of algorithms without reducing it to a question of humans versus the machine?

Let's begin a tentative answer with a conceptual understanding of how software induces, augments, supports, and produces sociality. Here, I suggest the concept of programmed sociality as a helpful heuristic device. Through this we might study algorithmic power and politics as emerging through the specific programmed arrangements of social media platforms, and the activities that are allowed to take place within those arrangements. Facebook and other software systems support and shape sociality in ways that are specific to the architecture and material substrate of the medium in question. To do justice to the concept of programmed sociality, it is important to highlight that it does not lead us down a pathway of technological determinism. In using the term "programmed," I draw on computer scientist John von Neumann's notion of "program," for which the term "to program" means to "assemble" and to "organize" (Grier, 1996: 52). This is crucial, as it frames software and algorithms as dynamic and performative rather than as fixed and static entities. Regarding "sociality," I refer to the concept of how different actors belong together and relate to each other. That is, sociality implies the ways in which entities (both human and non-human) are associated and gathered together, enabling interaction between the entities concerned (Latour, 2005). To be concerned with programmed sociality is to be interested in how actors are articulated in and through computational means of assembling and organizing, which always already embody certain norms and values about the social world. To exemplify how algorithmic media prescribe certain norms, values, and practices, let me describe how programmed sociality plays out in the specific context of Facebook, by focusing on friendships as a particularly pertinent form of being together online.

As Facebook has become an integral part of everyday life, providing a venue for friendships to unfold and be maintained, it is easy to forget just how involved Facebook is in what we often just take to be interpersonal relationships. Everything from setting up a profile and connecting with other users to maintaining a network of friends entails an intimate relation with the software underlying the platform itself. As van Dijck has pointed out, "what is important to understand about social network sites is how they activate relational impulses" (2012: 161). It is important to understand *that* relationships are activated online, but also *how* and *when* they are activated: by whom, for what purpose, and according to which mechanisms.

With nearly two billion users, many of whom have been members of the platform for many years, most people have long forgotten what it felt like to become a member, how they became the friend that Facebook wanted them to be. Upon first registering with the site, the user is instantly faced with the imperative to add friends. Once a user chooses to set up an account, he is immediately prompted to start filling in the personal profile template. Users' identities need to be defined within a fixed set of standards to be compatible with the algorithmic logic driving social software systems. If users could freely choose what they wish to say about themselves, there would be no real comparable or compatible data for the algorithms to process and work with. Without this orderly existence as part of the databases, our connections would not make much sense. After all, "data structures and algorithms are two halves of the ontology of the world according to a computer" (Manovich, 2001: 84). Being part of databases means more than simply belonging to a collection of data. It means being part of an ordered space, encoded according to a common scheme (Dourish, 2014). As Tarleton Gillespie (2014) points out, data always need to be readied before an algorithm can process them. Categorization is a powerful mechanism in making data algorithm-ready. "What the categories are, what belongs in a category, and who decides how to implement these categories in practice, are all powerful assertions about how things are and are supposed to be" (Bowker and Star, in Gillespie, 2014: 171). The template provided by Facebook upon signing in constitutes only one of many forms of categorization that help make the data algorithm-ready. The politics of categorization becomes most pertinent in questions concerning inclusion and exclusion. The recurring conflicts over breastfeeding images and Facebook's nudity-detection systems—comprising both algorithms and human managers—represent a particularly long-lasting debate over censorship and platform policies (Arthur, 2012). The politics of categorization is not just a matter of restricting breastfeeding images but one that fundamentally links database architecture and algorithmic operations to subjectification.

To understand how sociality is programmed—that is, how friendships are programmatically organized and shaped, let us consider the ways in which the platform simulates existing notions of friendship. As theorists of friendship have argued, shared activity and history are important aspects of considering someone a friend (Helm, 2010). Simulating and augmenting the notion of a shared history, Facebook provides several tools and techniques dedicated to supporting memory. As poorly connected or unengaged users pose a threat to the platform's conditions of existence, programming reasons for engagement constitutes a key rationale from the point of view of platforms. On Facebook, connecting users to potential friends provides the first step in ensuring a loyal user base, because friendships commit. Functioning as a memory device, algorithms and software features do not merely help users find friends from their past, they play an important part in maintaining and cultivating friendships, once formed. As such, a variety of features prompt users to take certain relational actions, the most well-known being that of notifying users about a friend's birthday. While simulating the gesture of phatic communication represented in congratulating someone on his or her birthday, the birthday-reminder feature comes with an added benefit: The birthday feature is the most basic way of making users return to the platform, by providing a concrete suggestion for a communicative action to be performed. As I've described elsewhere, platforms like Facebook want users to feel invested in their relationships, so they are continually coming up with new features and functionalities that remind them of their social "obligations" as friends (Bucher, 2013).

While the traditional notion of friendship highlights the voluntary and durational aspects of becoming friends and becoming friends anew (Allan, 1989), the software, one may claim, functions as a suggestive force encouraging users to connect and engage with the people in ways that are afforded by and benefit the platform. From the point of view of critical political economy, sociality and connectivity are resources that fuel the development of new business models. Platforms do not activate relational impulses in an effort to be nice. Ultimately, someone benefits financially from users' online activities. This is, of course, a familiar story and one that many scholars have already told in illuminating and engaging ways (see Andrejevic, 2013; Couldry, 2012; Fuchs, 2012; Gehl, 2014; Mansell, 2012; van Dijck, 2013). From the perspective of companies like Facebook and Google, but also from the perspective of legacy news media organizations (discussed in chapter 6), algorithms are ultimately folded into promises of profit and business models. In this sense, a "good" and well-functioning algorithm is one that creates value, one that makes better and more efficient predictions, and one that ultimately makes people engage and return to the platform or news site time and again. The question then becomes: What are the ways in which a platform sparks enough curiosity, desire, and interest in users for them to return?

The subtle ways of software can, for example, be seen in the manner in which Facebook reminds and (re)introduces users to each other. When browsing through my Facebook news feed it is almost as if the algorithm is saying, "Someone you haven't spoken to in five years just liked this," or, "This person whom you haven't heard from in ages, suddenly seems to be up to something fun." Somehow, I am nudged into thinking that these updates are important, that I should pay attention to them, that they are newsworthy. Rather than meaning that friendships on Facebook are less than voluntary, my claim is that the ways in which we relate to each other as "friends" is highly mediated and conditioned by algorithmic systems. People we do not necessarily think about, people we might not remember, or people we might not even consider friends continue to show up on our personalized news feeds, as friend suggestions, in birthday reminders, and so forth. While it is often difficult to recognize how Facebook "actively steers and curates connections" (van Dijck, 2013: 12), moments of everyday connectivity provide a glimpse into the ways in which the effects of software might not necessarily *feel* as incidental as they might appear to be.

The programmed sociality apparent in Facebook is about more than making people remember friends from their past with the help of friend-finding algorithms. From the very beginning, a friendship is *formed* and the friendship is "put to test." From a political economic standpoint, this is very important, as not every friendship is equally valuable. Some relations are more "promising" and "worthwhile" than others. With more friends than the news feed feature allows for, friendships are continuously monitored for affinity and activity, which are important measures for rendering relations visible. Friendships in social media are programmed forms of sociality precisely because they are continuously measured, valued, and examined according to some underlying criteria or logic. As this book will show in more detail, the news feed algorithm plays a powerful role in producing the conditions for the intelligible and sensible, operating to make certain users more visible at the expense of others. The Facebook news feed displays an edited view of what one's friends are up to, in an order of calculated importance with the most important updates at top of the feed. Every action and interaction connected to Facebook, be it a status update, comment on someone's photo, or "like button" clicked, may become a story on someone's news feed. Not every action, however, is of equal importance, nor is every friend for that matter. Friendships are put to test, because friendships need to be nurtured and maintained to stand the "test of time." Algorithms decide which stories should show up on users' news feeds, but also, crucially, which friends. Rachel, a 24-year-old journalist from New York City, whom I interviewed for this book about her perceptions of algorithms, exclaimed that "Facebook ruins friendships." With more than seven hundred friends, Rachel says that she is constantly taken aback by all the information and people Facebook seems to be hiding from her feed:

> So, in that sense, it does feel as if there is only a select group of friends I interact with on the social network, while I've practically forgotten about the hundreds of others I have on there. An example of this is a friend from high school, who liked one of my posts a few weeks back. I'd totally forgotten she was even on Facebook until she liked it and we started chatting.

Rachel's experience is reminiscent of what I mean by programmed sociality, the notion that social formations and connections are algorithmically conditioned and governed by the sociotechnical and political-economic configurations of specific media platforms. Rachel's worry about Facebook ruining friendship should also remind us that algorithms need to be understood as powerful gatekeepers, playing an important role in deciding who gets to be seen and heard and whose voices are considered less important. Programmed sociality, then, is political in the sense that it is ordered, governed, and shaped in and though software and algorithms. If we want to consider everyday life in the algorithmic media landscape, we need to pay attention to the ways in which many of the things we think of as societal—including friendship—may be expressed, mediated and shaped in technological designs and how these designs, in turn, shape our social values. As we will see throughout the book, such considerations, however, do not stop with values in design, but exceed the purely technical (whatever that is taken to mean) in important ways.

A key argument of this book is that the power and politics of algorithms stems from how algorithmic systems shape people's encounters and orientations in the world. At the same time, I claim that this shaping power cannot be reduced to code. Specifically, I argue for an understanding of algorithmic power that hinges on the principle of relational materialism, the idea that algorithms "are no mere props for performance but parts and parcel of hybrid assemblages endowed with diffused personhood and relational agency" (Vannini, 2015: 5). Thus, it is important to acknowledge that while we start with the question of how software and algorithms shape sociality by looking at materiality in the more conventional sense as "properties of a technology," the answer cannot be found *in* these properties alone, but rather the ways in which programmed sociality is realized as a function of code, people, and context.

Computable Friendships

The concept of friendship provides an apt example for the understanding of programmed sociality and algorithmic life, because it shows the discrepancies between our common-sense notions of friendship and the ways in which friendship becomes embedded in and modeled by the algorithmic infrastructures. Friendships are deeply rooted in the human condition as a fundamental aspect of being together with other people, and which is always already contested based on cultural and historical contexts. Traditionally, friendship has been thought of as an exclusive social relation, a private and intimate relation between two persons (Aristotle, 2002; Derrida, 2005; Hays, 1988). For this reason, true friendship has been regarded as something that one cannot have with many people at the same time, simply because it requires time to build, nurture, and maintain. Compared to Aristotle's conception of friendship as something rather precious that one cannot have with many people at once (Aristotle, 2002), Facebook seems to promote the completely opposite idea.

The way the platform puts friendships at the center of a business model is no coincidence, of course, and is probably one of the core reasons Facebook has evolved into an unprecedented media company during the past decade. In a patent application filed by Facebook concerning the People You May Know (PYMK) feature, no doubt is left as to the value of friendships for Facebook: "Social networking systems value user connections because better-connected users tend to increase their use of the social networking system, thus increasing user-engagement and corresponding increase in, for example, advertising opportunities" (Schultz et al., 2014). Software intervenes in friendships by suggesting, augmenting, or encouraging certain actions or relational impulses. Furthermore, software is already implicated in the ways in which the platform imagines and performs friendships. Contrary to the notion that "friendship clearly exists as a relation between individuals" (Webb, 2003: 138), friendship on Facebook exists as a relation between *multiple actors,* between humans and non-humans alike. As Facebook exemplifies in another patent document:

> [T]he term friend need not require that members actually be friends in real life (which would generally be the case when one of the members is a business or other entity); it simply implies a connection in the social network. (Kendall and Zhou, 2010: 2)

The disconnect between how members usually understand friendship and the ways in which Facebook "understands" friendship becomes obvious in the quote above. According to Facebook, a user can be "friends" with a Facebook page, a song, a movie, a business, and so on. While it might seem strange to consider a movie a friend, this conception of friendship derives from the network model of the Web in which users and movies are considered "nodes" in the network and the relationship that exists between them an "edge" or, indeed, a friend. Indeed, "the terms 'user' and 'friend' depend on the frame of reference" (Chen et al. 2014). It is exactly the different and sometimes conflicting frames of reference that are of interest in this book. A core contention is that media platforms and their underlying software and infrastructures contain an important frame of reference for understanding sociality and connectivity today. If we accept that software can have a frame of reference, a way of seeing and organizing the world, then what does it mean to be a friend on Facebook or, more precisely, what are friends for, if seen from the perspective of the platform?

Facebook friendships are, above all, computable. In an age of algorithmic media, the term *algorithmic,* used as an adjective, suggests that even friendships are now subject to "mechanisms that introduce and privilege quantification, proceduralization, and automation" (Gillespie, 2016a: 27). Measuring the performance of individuals and organizations is nothing new, though. As sociologists Espeland and Sauder (2007) suggest, social measurements and rankings have become a key driver for modern societies during the past couple of decades. According to philosopher Ian Hacking, "society became statistical" through the "enumeration of people and their habits" (1990: 1). Hacking connects the emergence of a statistical society to the idea of "making up people," meaning that classifications used to describe people influence the forms of experience that are possible for them, but also how the effects on people, in turn, change the classifications:

> The systematic collection of data about people has affected not only the ways in which we conceive of a society, but also the ways in which we describe our neighbour. It has profoundly transformed what we choose to do, who we try to be, and what we think of ourselves. (1990: 3)

If we accept Hacking's notion of "making up people," it becomes necessary to interrogate the ways in which counting, quantification, and classification limits the condition of possibility for subjects on Facebook. The manner in which the categories and classifications are constituted is not arbitrary or neutral; nor are the implications incidental. Here, I want to suggest that Facebook friends are "made-up people" in the sense described by Hacking. Friends are not natural kinds but, rather, constructions that serve specific purposes in a specific historical and cultural context. As has already been pointed out, the category "friend" as used by the Facebook platform does not even require members of that category to be human beings. While all Facebook users may belong to the set of "friends," subsets of "friends" or "users" are dynamically being made up to serve different purposes. As exemplified in a Facebook patent application detailing the idea of adaptive ranking of news feed: "The social networking system divides its users into different sets, for example, based on demographic characteristics of the users and generates one model for each set of users" (Gubin et al., 2014). In other words, sets are powerful classification devices implying a politics in terms of demarcating who or what belongs and what does not, "what the set 'counts' in, what counts as members in the set" (Baki, 2015: 37). Subsets are "made up" based on demographic information, attributes of connections, frequency of interaction, and other factors affecting the features used for modeling what users can see or not see (we will return to the politics of visibility in chapter 4). If friends are not of a natural kind, what kinds of friends or, rather, subsets are there? Again, we might turn to Facebook patent applications for some tentative answers. According to a document describing a technique for optimizing user engagement, some friends seem more valuable than others (Chen et al., 2014). Particularly useful friends are called "top friends," defined as persons having the highest measures of relatedness to a specific user (Chen et al., 2014). The determinants of relatedness are generated using a so-called coefficient module. These, in turn, depend on a variety of factors (as is the case with all of Facebook's computations)—for example, "based on how many times or how frequently interactions occurred within the last 30 days, 60 days, 90 days, etc." (Chen et al., 2014). Top friends are used for a number of purposes and in a variety of contexts such as:

To identify participants to play online games; to identify relevant connections to the user for inclusion in her social network; to display a listing of
photos of persons having highest relevance to the user; to otherwise display or list an identification of persons having highest relevance to the
user; to identify persons with whom the user can engage in an instant message or chat session; etc. (Chen et al. 2014)

Above all, top friends are used to prioritize information associated with them above
others. Top friends are made-up people insofar as "those kinds of people would not
have existed, as a kind of people, until they had been so classified, organized and taxed"
(Hacking, 2007: 288). The subset of algorithmic top friends can be seen as a new
category of people, emerging in the age of programmed sociality and algorithmic life.
There are many more. As the notion of top friends shows, computable friendships
hinge on measuring and evaluating users in order to be able to determine their
friendship status. While friendships have always been qualitatively determined, as
the notion of "best friend" suggests, the extent to which Facebook now quantifiably
produces and classifies friendships works to dehumanize sociality itself by encouraging an empty form of competitiveness. Like most social media platforms, Facebook
measures social impact, reputation, and influence through the creation of composite
numbers that function as a *score* (Gerlitz & Lury, 2014: 175). The score is typically
used to feed rankings or enhance predictions. The computing of friendships is no
different. In another patent application Facebook engineers suggest that the value of
friendship is not confined to users but also serves an essential role in sustaining the
social networking system itself. As Schultz et al. (2014) suggest, better-connected
users tend to increase their use, thereby increasing advertising opportunities. A so-
called friendship value is not only computed to determine the probability of two users
"friending" but also to make decisions as to whether to show a specific advertising
unit to a user. The higher the score, the "better" Facebook deems the friendship to
be, increasing the likelihood of using the connection to help promote products. The
value of a friendship is produced as a composite number based on a "friendship
score, sending score, receiving score or some combination of the scores as determined by value computation engine" (Schultz et al., 2014). According to Schultz et al.,
"the sending and receiving scores reflect the potential increase in the user's continued
active utilization of the social networking system due to a given connection" (2014:
2). From a computational perspective, friendships are nothing more than an equation geared toward maximizing engagement with the platform.

Far from loving the friend for the friend's own sake, which would be exemplary
of the Aristotelian notion of virtue ethics and friendship, Facebook "wants" friendships to happen in order to increase engagement with the social network, ultimately serving revenue purposes. The quantification and metrification of friendship
are not merely part of how connections are computed by Facebook's algorithmic
infrastructure but increasingly make up the visuals of social networking systems

through the pervasive display of numbers on the graphical user interface. With more than 3 billion likes and comments posted on Facebook every day, users are both expressing their sentiments and engagement and reminded and made aware of these actions and affects through the visual traces thereof. As the software artist Ben Grosser notes, "A significant component of Facebook's interface is its revealed enumerations of these 'likes,' comments and more" (Grosser 2014: 1). Grosser questions whether people would add as many friends if they were not constantly confronted with how many they have or whether people would "like" as many ads if they were not always told how many others have liked them before them. Grosser's artwork *The Demetricator* is a software plugin that removes all metrics from the Facebook interface and critically examines these questions. According to Grosser, Facebook draws on people's "deeply ingrained 'desire for more' compelling people to reimagine friendship as a quantitative space, and pushing us to watch the metric as our guide" (Grosser, 2014). The pervasive enumeration of everything on the user interface function as a rhetorical device, teaching users that more is better. More is also necessary if we consider the operational logics of the platform. The drive toward more is evident when considering the value of friendship, given that more friends increases the likelihood of engaging with the site. Friends are suggested based on mutual friends, but also on factors such as low activity or few friends. The idea is that, by suggesting friends with low activity level, Facebook "can enable those users to likely have more friends as a result of being suggested [...] and thereby likely increasing the candidate user's engagement level with the social networking system" (Wang et al., 2012: 6). Friendships, then, are variously made and maintained by humans and non-humans alike. The specifics of how friendships are susceptible to computation is immeasurable in and of itself. The purpose, however, of explicating the term "programmed sociality" as core to understanding algorithmic life is to draw attention to software and computational infrastructure as conditions of possibility for sociality in digital media.

Guilt by Association

Whereas "friend" in the sociological sense signifies a voluntary relationship that serves a wide range of emotional and social aims, "friends" as seen from the perspective of the platform are highly valuable data carriers that can be utilized for a variety of reasons. One of the core principles underlying networked media is that information is derived as much from the edges (connections) as it is from the nodes (users, businesses, objects). This means that users do not just provide data about themselves when they fill out profiles, like things, or comment on posts; in doing so, they simultaneously reveal things about the people and things they are interacting with. If data are missing from a user's personal profile or that user is not as engaged as the platforms would prefer, the best way to extract more information about the user is through his or her various connections. From a platform perspective, friends are in the data delivery business. This becomes particularly evident when looking at the patent documents by Facebook describing techniques related to advertising. For example, given the insufficient personal information provided by a particular member, ads are tailored and targeted based on friends. Facebook calls this "guilt by association" (Kendall & Zhou, 2010: 2). While the authors of the patent document acknowledge that they are "giving credence to an old adage," the word "guilt" is worth pondering. Guilt evokes notions of responsibility, autonomy, and accountability. Who or what is responsible for the content shown on Facebook, and who might be held accountable? While it might be easier to understand how users' own actions determine what content they see online, it seems more difficult to come to terms with the notion that users also play a crucial role in determining what their friends see on their feeds. Guilt by association, as Facebook uses the term, implies that users are made "complicit" in their friends' ad targeting, which seems highly problematic. While it is now commonplace to say users are the product, not the media platforms they are using, the extent to which users are *used* to promote content and products—often, without their explicit knowledge—is unprecedented in the age of algorithmic media. If the classical notion of friendship is political in the sense that it assumes gendered hierarchy through the notion of brotherhood (Derrida, 2005), the politics of algorithms suggests hierarchies of a different sort— of what is "best," "top," "hot," "relevant," and "most interesting."

When examining the contours and current state of algorithmic life, it is important to understand the mechanisms through which algorithmic media shaping sociality is deeply intertwined with power and politics. This book is not just about highlighting the role of algorithms as a core governing principle underlying most online media platforms today, but also about showing how algorithms always already invoke and implicate users, culture, practice, ownership, ethics, imaginaries, and affect. It means that talking about algorithms implies asking questions about how and when users are implicated in developing and maintaining algorithmic logics, as well as asking questions about governance, who owns the data, and to what end it is put to use? While friends have always been valuable for advertisers, algorithms seem to lessen the autonomy and intentionality of people by turning *everything* they do into a potential data point for the targeting of ads and news feed content. Such is the network logic, which users cannot escape. For neoliberalism, "friendship is inimical to capital, and as such, like everything else, it is under attack" (Cutterham, 2013: 41). Moreover, as Melissa Gregg holds, "'friendship' *is* labour in the sense that it involves constant attention and cultivation, the rewards of which include improved standing and greater opportunity" (2007: 5). As Langlois and Elmer point out, "social media seek to mine life itself" (2013: 4). That is, social media platforms "do much more than just sell users' attention to advertisers: they actually help identify the very strategies through which attention can be fully harnessed" (Langlois & Elmer, 2013: 4). Algorithms are key to this end. If we want to understand the ways in which power and politics are enacted in and through contemporary media, we need to look more closely at the ways in which information, culture, and social life are being processed and rendered intelligible. In this book, I set out to do so.

Examining algorithmic media and the ways in which life is increasingly affected by algorithmic processing, means acknowledging how algorithms are not static things but, rather, evolving, dynamic, and relational processes hinging on a complex set of actors, both humans and nonhumans. Programmed sociality implies that social relations such as friendships are not merely transposed onto a platform like Facebook but are more fundamentally *transduced*. The concept of transduction names the process whereby a particular domain is constantly undergoing change, or *individuation,* as a consequence of being in touch or touched by something else (Mackenzie, 2002; Simondon, 1992). Rather than maintaining an interest in what friendship *is*, transduction and the related term "technicity" help to account for how domains such as friendship come into being because of sociomaterial entanglements. Using Facebook to access a social network transduces or modulates how a person connects with friends. When using Facebook, the technicity of friendship unfolds as conjunctions between users and algorithms (e.g., the PYMK feature), coded objects (e.g., shared video), and infrastructure (e.g., protocols and networks). As Kitchin and Dodge point out: "This power to affect change is not deterministic but is contingent and relational, the product of the conjunction between code and people" (2005: 178). Transduction and technicity become useful analytical devices in exemplifying the concept of programmed sociality as they point toward the ways in which software has the capacity to produce and instantiate modalities of friendship, specific to the environment in which it operates. The productive power of technology, as signified by the concept of technicity, does not operate in isolation or as a unidirectional force. Algorithms and software, in this view, do not determine what friendships are in any absolute or fixed sense. Rather, technicity usefully emphasizes the ways in which algorithms are entities that fundamentally hinge on people's practices and interaction, in order to be realized and developed in the first place. Taking such a perspective allows us to see friendship and other instances of programmed sociality as emerging sociomaterial accomplishments.

Back to the rainy November day introduced at the beginning of the chapter: The question of what categories were used to determine the specific ads or the content of my and my friends' news feeds persists. Was it my clicking behavior, my age and gender, pages that I have liked, the cookies set by the online design store where I bought the gift for my mom, my friends' clicking behavior, the friends of my friend, everything or nothing of the above? Whatever the exact reason might be, online spaces are always computed according to underlying assumptions, norms, and values. Although we simply do not know and have no way of knowing how exactly our data and the algorithmic processing are shaping our experiences online, a critical perspective on sociotechnical systems, along with personal encounters and experiences with algorithmic forms of connectivity and sociality, might help to illuminate the ways in which "categorization is a powerful semantic and political intervention" (Gillespie, 2014:171). Judging solely by the content and ads served up on my news feed, I am perceived as having children, being overweight, and single— none of which is true, at least for the time being. While the case of Facebook and programmed friendship provides a useful entry point to questions of how information is governed and organized online, an understanding of algorithmic power and politics cannot simply be reduced to a single social media platform. As this book will show, how we come to know others, the world, and ourselves as mediated through algorithms is the result of complex sociomaterial practices that exceed the specific coded instructions. Facebook and the notion of programmed sociality are but one way in which algorithmic arrangements bring new possibilities, realities, and interventions into being. And there are many more.

By now, I hope to have instilled enough curiosity in the reader to keep you exploring the power and politics of algorithms in the contemporary media landscape with me throughout the next chapters. The goal of the book is for readers to not simply be the subjects of algorithmic judgment but, rather, to be in a position to critically judge the workings of the algorithmic apparatus for themselves.

Outline of the Book

The overall aim of this book is to sketch the contours of an algorithmic media landscape as it is currently unfolding. While algorithms and software are starting to catch the interest of social scientists and humanities scholars, having become somewhat of a buzzword in media and communication studies during the past years, we are only at the beginning of understanding how algorithms and computation more broadly are affecting social life and the production and dissemination of knowledge as we know it. This book seeks to contribute to these discussions by offering conceptual, theoretical, and empirical analyses of the ways in which algorithms produce the conditions for the sensible and intelligible.

In the chapters 2 and 3, which comprise the conceptual framework of the book, I focus on the ontological, epistemological, and methodological dimensions of algorithms. Chapter 2 provides an outline for understanding what algorithms are and how they are conceptualized in different manners. While the chapter functions as a conceptual introduction to the interdisciplinary field of critical algorithms studies, merging perspectives from computer science, social sciences and the humanities, it mainly does so for analytical reasons. I argue that these are not simply different perspectives on a static object called an algorithm, but rather, following insights from STS (Law, 2002; Mol 2002), provide different *versions* of what an algorithm is. Even if we assume that we are talking about the same algorithm (say, *the* "Facebook algorithm" or "K-nearest neighbor"), the algorithm is always "many different things. It is not one, but many" (Law, 2002: 15).

Chapter 3 tackles the question of how algorithms can be known, proposing an epistemology of algorithms that moves beyond the popular conception of the algorithm as a black box. I draw on the concept of the black box as a heuristic device to discuss the nature of algorithms in contemporary media platforms, and how, we might attend to and study algorithms, despite, or even because of, their seemingly secret nature. The chapter develops a conceptual repertoire that moves beyond the textbook definition of algorithms as step-by-step instructions for solving a computational problem. It does so to better account for the fundamental interlinking or entanglement of the social and material implicated by algorithms. To support such a view, chapter 3 builds on insights from relational materialism and process-relational philosophy (e.g., Barad, 2007; Mol, 2002; Whitehead, 1978). Here, I suggest a conceptual vocabulary that allows for investigating algorithms as *eventful,* understood as constituents that co-become, and their power and politics as tied to the ways in which these configurations have the capacity to produce certain orderings and disorderings of the world. In chapter 2 I introduced the notion of "ontological politics" (Mol, 2002) to convey how realities are never given but shaped and emerge through interactions. In chapter 3 I expand on these ideas by suggesting, perhaps somewhat paradoxically, that algorithms are not always important. Rather, their agency emerges as important only in particular settings or constellations. The argument is made that by shifting attention away from asking *what* and *where* agency is, to *when* agency is and *to whom* it belongs in specific situations, we see how the notion of algorithms as black boxes is a political claim. The chapter concludes by offering some possible methodological routes for the study of algorithms premised on their eventfulness, which are operationalized in the chapters that follow.

Having outlined the ontological and epistemological contours of algorithms, the chapters 4–6 turn to specific constellations of algorithmic power and politics as it materializes is the contemporary media landscape. Each chapter presents a case study that is meant to get at two related concerns: the ways in which algorithmic systems govern the possible field of action of others, and how these possibilities are made more or less available or unavailable to certain actors in specific settings. Taken together, these case studies are concerned with the world-making capacities of algorithms, questioning how algorithmic systems shape encounters and orientations of different kinds, and how these systems are endowed with diffused personhood and relational agency.

Chapter 4 pays attention to the mechanisms of power that work as a concerted distribution of people, information, actions, and ways of seeing and being seen. It uses Facebook's news feed as a case study to develop the argument that algorithms now play a fundamental role in governing the conditions of the intelligible and sensible. The chapter looks at how the news feed operates algorithmically to govern the "distribution of the sensible [. . .] defining what is visible or not in a common space" (Ranciere, 2004: 12–13). While users feed Facebook with data, the techniques and procedures to make sense of it, to navigate, assemble, and make meaningful connections among individual pieces of data are increasingly being delegated to various forms of algorithms. The question raised in this chapter is, how does this kind of algorithmic intervention into people's information-sharing practices takes place? What are the principles and logics of Facebook's algorithmic form of editing the news feed? What implications do these algorithmic processes have for users of the platform? Through an analysis of the algorithmic logics structuring the flow of information and communication on Facebook's news feed, I argue that the regime of visibility constructed, imposes a perceived "threat of invisibility" on the part of the participatory subject. As a result, I reverse Foucault's notion of surveillance as a form of permanent visibility, arguing that participatory subjectivity is not constituted through the imposed threat of an all-seeing vision machine, but by the constant possibility of disappearing and becoming obsolete. The intention is not so much to offer a definite account of the role played by Facebook in capturing the world in code, but to open avenues for reflection on the new conditions through which in/visibility is constructed by algorithms online.

Chapter 5 considers the barely perceived transitions in power that occur when algorithms and people meet, by considering how social media users perceive and experience the algorithms they encounter. While it is important to interrogate the operational logics of algorithms on an infrastructural level, materiality is only half the story. To do the topic of algorithmic power and politics full justice, there is a need to understand how people make sense of and experience the algorithms with which they persistently interact. Technical systems and infrastructure alone do not affect use. Users' perceived knowledge of how the systems work might be just as significant. The questions raised in chapter 5 are: How do social media users imagine algorithms, and to what extent does their perception and knowledge affect their use of social media platforms? The chapter reports findings from an exploratory study of 35 social media users who were asked about their perceptions of and experiences with algorithms online. The chapter examines the specific situations in which users notice algorithms and start reflecting and talking about them. Focusing on a few of these user-reported situations, the chapter shows how users respond to and orient themselves differently toward algorithms as. Moving beyond a call for intensified code literacy, I argue that these personal algorithm stories provide important insight into the ways in which algorithms are currently imagined and understood, and how users negotiate and resist algorithms in their everyday life.

Chapter 6 looks at how algorithms acquire the capacity to disturb and to compose new sensibilities as part of situated practices, particularly in terms of how they become invested with certain political and moral capacities. While the previous chapters considered how algorithms are publicly imagined and how they work to produce impressions of engagement, chapter 6 looks at how algorithms materialize in the institutional setting of the news media. More specifically, in this chapter we continue to consider how algorithms are not just matters of fact but also an important matter of concern (Latour, 2004). By taking the field of journalism as a case in point for understanding the politics and power of algorithms as they are manifested in the current media landscape, I aim to illuminate how algorithms are always differently materialized—how they are made out and carved into existence at the intersection of technology, institutional practice, and discourse. I make an argument to the effect that the ontology of algorithms is up for grabs. Based on 20 interviews with digital editors and managers at leading Scandinavian news organizations, as well as on field observations at the Swedish news app *Omni,* chapter 6 explores how institutional actors are responding to the proliferation of data and algorithms. If algorithms have an audience or are otherwise consumed, as previous chapters have highlighted, they are also produced and variously put to work, which is the focus of this chapter. The question is how and when algorithms come to matter and whom they matter for. On the one hand, news organizations feel the pressure to reorient their practices toward the new algorithmic logic governing the media landscape at large, and often with a close eye to what's perceived as one of their biggest competitors—Facebook. On the other hand, the interview data suggest that algorithms work to disturb and question established boundaries and norms of what journalism is and ought to be. In order to understand the power and politics of algorithms in the contemporary media landscape, my claim is that it is vital to understand how algorithms are neither given nor stable objects, but rather made and unmade in material-discursive practices. Sometimes algorithms are rendered important, at other times, they are deemed insignificant. Knowing more about processes of mattering, I suggest, enables us to understand the multiple realities of algorithms, and how these relate and coexist.

Taken together, the chapters offer different versions of how and when algorithms are made present and important to individual and institutional actors. An important suggestion here is that power and politics are never reducible to question of materiality *or* perception, but rather about making algorithms matter in specific ways and for specific purposes. In the concluding chapter, I revisit the core arguments of the book, and suggest that there's a need to blend an understanding of the material substrates of algorithmic media with an understanding of the multiple ways on perceiving, feeling, acting, and knowing which coalesce around algorithms as an object of social concern. Here, I revisit some of the initial questions asked at the beginning of the book (including this introduction), and look at how algorithmic power and politics can be understood if power and politics are not necessarily about imposing force from above (or below for that matter, if understood as code). Ultimately, this chapter serves to summarize the key contributions of the book in terms of: (1) providing an understanding of algorithms that is not committed to one ontological position, but instead sees algorithms in terms of a multiple and variable ontology; (2) helping to identify forms of algorithmic power and politics; and (3) offering a theoretical framework for the kinds of work that algorithms do and the landscapes they help to generate.

2

The Multiplicity of Algorithms

Consider the following descriptions of what an algorithm is: "a step-by-step instruction of how to solve a task," "a recipe," "a form of programmed logic," "made of people," "code that tries to accommodate personal interests," "an application that determines what you see," "a type of technology," "an automated filtering mechanism," "what platforms use to guarantee the best user experience possible," "an appetizer to make you crave for more of the same," "magical." You may already recognize some of these descriptions from standard computer science textbooks, common language, media reports, or from the way in which platforms market their algorithms. Indeed, these descriptions are the accounts of computer scientists, marketers, lay people, critics, journalists, or media users. These are the textbook definitions, tropes, PR slogans, tweets, folk theories, and popular descriptions of algorithms. Yet you may wonder, are these people describing the same thing? What does magic have to do with a recipe? Can something both determine what you see and accommodate your own interests?

This chapter suggests that algorithms are multiple in the sense that there is more than one kind of thing that we call "algorithm." Not only is this true in the technical sense of there being many different types of algorithms but also in the social sense. When people speak of algorithms they often have different things in mind, different concerns, worries, conceptions, and imaginations. In a more theoretical and philosophical sense, one can talk of such multiplicity as "manyfoldedness, but not pluralism" (Mol, 2002: 84). Whereas plurality assumes that there is one stable thing and different perspectives one can take on that thing, to speak of manyfoldedness implies the idea that algorithms exist on multiple levels as "things done" in practice. In other words, algorithms can be magical *and* concrete, good *and* bad, technical *and* social. Yet, the notion of multiplicity also reminds us that putting it in such binary terms risks perpetuating an overly simplistic understanding of what algorithms are and what they can be. What is at stake, then, is the meaning of a variable existence for the ways in which we understand algorithmic power and politics. While I want to stress a view on algorithms that sees it not as one object (or subject, for that matter) but many, I shall first need to say a few things about the ways in which algorithms are commonly understood.

This chapter offers the conceptual groundwork I believe is necessary to appreciate the multiple levels at which algorithms exist and operate, both technically and theoretically. The first part of this chapter explains what algorithms are in a more technical sense, particularly with regards to machine learning, as most of the algorithms operating in the media landscape depend on systems that are able to learn from data and make predictions. This should provide readers with enough background knowledge to appreciate the question of how algorithms intersect with power and politics on a more philosophical and sociological scale—the concern of the second part of this chapter. While I do not mean to suggest that algorithms can be understood from either a technical or a sociological perspective—as if there exists one single object called an "algorithm" that we might understand from different perspectives—the aim is to show how dynamic both the notion of an algorithm and the concerns they foster are in order to introduce readers to the complexities of algorithmic power and politics. The third part of this chapter uses Foucault's conceptualizations of power to map how power and politics intersect with algorithms as an emerging social concern. I make the argument that algorithms do not merely *have* power and politics; they are fundamentally productive of new ways of ordering the world. Importantly, algorithms do not work on their own but need to be understood as part of a much wider network of relations and practices. The view to which I am subscribing in this book (and which I will further elaborate on in the next chapter), sees algorithms as entangled, multiple, and eventful and, therefore, things that cannot be understood as being powerful in one way only.

A Beginning

HISTORIES AND TECHNICALITIES

Let's take a step back. What exactly do (most) people mean when they invoke the term "algorithm"? According to standard computer science definitions, an algorithm is a set of instructions for solving a problem or completing a task following a carefully planned sequential order (Knuth, 1998). Although the algorithm is a key concept in computer science, its history dates back to the medieval notion of "algorism," understood as a way of performing calculations with natural numbers. Algorism goes as far back as the 9th century when the Persian astronomer and mathematician Abdullah Muhammad bin Musa al-Khwarizmi (circa 780–850) was indirectly responsible for coining the term. When his scripts were translated into Latin in the 12th century, his name was rendered as "Algorithmi."[1] These scripts described the basic methods of arithmetic in the Hindu-Arabic numeral system, which much later formed the basic operations of computer processors (Miyazaki, 2012). As Wolfgang Thomas describes, many paragraphs of the scripts translated from al-Khwarizmi's text "Computing with the Indian Numbers" started with the phrase "Dixit Algorizmi," where algorithm referred to a "process of symbol manipulation"

(2015: 31). During the 17th century, the German philosopher Gottfried Wilhelm Leibniz (1646–1716) added a new dimension to symbolic computation by developing "the vision of calculating truths (true statements)" (Miyazaki, 2012).[2] As far as a the prehistory of algorithms goes, Leibniz provided the groundwork for what later became known as Boolean algebra by "arithmetizing logic" and using if/then conditionals for calculating truth (Thomas, 2015). In Thomas' account, the origin can be traced to Boole (1847) and his theory of Boolean algebra and continues with Frege's 1879 introduction of a formal language in which mathematical statements could be expressed (see Thomas, 2015). For many historians, however, the history of algorithms proper starts with David Hilbert and what is called the *Entscheidungsproblem*, the challenge of whether an algorithm exists for deciding the universal validity or satisfiability of a given logical formula (Sommaruga & Strahm, 2015: xi). In 1936, Alan Turing famously solved this problem in the negative by reducing the problem to a notion of symbolic computation, which later became known as the Turing machine. Although Turing himself scarcely made direct reference to the term "algorithm," contemporary mathematicians such as Alonzo Church (1903–1995) or Stephen C. Kleene (1909–1994) did (Miyazaki, 2012). In tracing the historical origins of the term "algorithm" and its role in the history of computing, Shintaro Miyazaki (2012) suggests that "algorithm" first entered common usage in the 1960s with the rise of scientific computation and higher-level programming languages such as Algol 58 and its derivatives. By the mid 20th century, then, "an algorithm was understood to be a set of defined steps that if followed in the correct order will computationally process input (instructions and/or data) to produce a desired outcome" (Kitchin, 2017: 16).

Perhaps the most common way to define an algorithm is to describe it as a recipe, understood as a step-by-step guide that prescribes how to obtain a certain goal, given specific parameters. Understood as a procedure or method for processing data, the algorithm as recipe would be analogous to the operational logic for making a cake out of flour, water, sugar, and eggs. Without the specific instructions for *how* to mix the eggs and flour or *when* to add the sugar or water, for instance, these ingredients would remain just that. For someone who has never baked a cake, step-by-step instructions would be critical if they wanted to bake one. For any computational process to be operational, the algorithm must be rigorously defined, that is, specified in such a way that it applies in all possible circumstances. A program will execute a certain section of code only if certain conditions are met. Otherwise, it takes an alternative route, which implies that particular future circumstances are already anticipated by the conditional construct of the "if…then statement" upon which most algorithms depend. The "if…then statement" is the most basic of all control flow statements, tasked with telling a program to execute a particular section of code only if the condition is deemed "true." However, in order to be able to test and compute a "false" condition, the "if…then" statements needs to include an "else" statement, which essentially provides a secondary path of executing. In other words, while the "if...then" statement can only compute "true" statements, the "if...then...else" construct will be able to execute an alternate pathway as well.[3] An algorithm essentially indicates *what* should happen *when*, a principle that programmers call "flow of control," which is implemented in source code or pseudocode. Programmers usually control the flow by specifying certain procedures and parameters through a programming language. In principle, the algorithm is "independent of programming languages and independent of the machines that execute the programs" (Goffey, 2008: 15). The same type of instructions can be written in the languages C, C#, or Python and still be the same algorithm. This makes the concept of the "algorithm" particularly powerful, given that what an algorithm signifies is an inherent assumption in all software design about order, sequence, and sorting. The actual steps are what is important, not the wording per se.

Designing an algorithm to perform a certain task implies a simplification of the problem at hand. From an engineering perspective, the specific operation of an algorithm depends largely on technical considerations, including efficiency, processing time, and reduction of memory load—but also on the elegance of the code written (Fuller, 2008; Knuth, 1984).[4] The operation of algorithms depends on a variety of other elements—most fundamentally, on *data structures*.[5] Tellingly, Niklaus Wirth's (1985) pioneering work on "structured programming" is entitled *Algorithms + Data Structures = Programs*. To be actually operational, algorithms work in tandem not only with data structures but also with a whole assemblage of elements, including data types, databases, compilers, hardware, CPU, and so forth.[6] Explaining why he starts his book with data structures and not algorithms, Wirth writes: "One has an intuitive feeling that data precede algorithms: You must have some objects before you can perform operations on them" (2004: 7). Furthermore, Wirth's book title suggests that algorithms and programs are not the same. A program, or software, is more than its algorithms. Algorithms alone do not make software computable. In order to compute, the source code must be transformed into an executable file, which is not a one-step process. The transformation usually follows multiple steps, which include translation as well as the involvement of other software programs, such as compilers and linkers. The "object file" created by the compiler is an intermediate form and not itself directly executable. In order for a program to be executed, another device called a linker must combine several object files into a functional program of executable (or ".exe") files.[7] Software is quite literally the gathering or assembling of different code files into a single "executable." While software might appear to be a single entity, it is fundamentally layered and dependent on a myriad of different relations and devices in order to function. To compute information effectively, then, algorithms are based on particular representations and structures of data. Despite the mutual interdependence of algorithms and data structures, "we can treat the two as analytically distinct" (Gillespie, 2014: 169). Given that my primary interest lies in the *operations* performed on data—what

Wirth defines as algorithms– and the social and cultural implication those operations have, the focus in this book will almost exclusively be on algorithms.

While no agreed-upon definition of algorithm exists, a few aspects have been described as important characteristics. For Donald Knuth (1998), who has written one of the most important multivolume works on computer programming, algorithms have five broadly defined properties: finiteness, definiteness, input, output, and effectiveness. What is generally asked of an algorithm is that it produce a correct output and use resources efficiently (Cormen, 2013). From a technical standpoint, creating an algorithm is about breaking the problem down as efficiently as possible, which implies a careful planning of the steps to be taken and their sequence.

Take the problem of sorting, which is one of the most common tasks algorithms are deployed to solve. A given sorting problem may have many solutions; the algorithm that eventually gets applied is but one possible solution. In other words, an algorithm is a manifestation of a proposed solution. Just as there are multiple ways of sorting a bookshelf in some well-defined order—for example, according to alphabetical order by the author's surname, by genre, or even by the color of the book jacket, different sorting algorithms (e.g., selection sort, merge sort, or quicksort) can be applied for the same task. Anyone who has ever tried to arrange a bookshelf according to the color of the book jacket will probably be able to understand how this specific organizational logic might have an aesthetically pleasing effect but also come with the added practical challenge of finding a particular book by a certain author (unless you have an excellent color memory). This is to say that algorithms, understood as forms of organizational logic, come with specific affordances that both enable and constrain. To use a well-known insight from science and technology studies (STS), such orderings are never neutral. Algorithms come with certain assumptions and values about the world on which they are acting. Compared to the archetypical example used in STS about the inherent politics of engineering and urban planning in the example of Robert Moses' low-hanging bridges described by Langdon Winner (1986), the politics and values of algorithms are a really blatant example of that same logic as they explicitly decide, order, and filter the world in specific ways. Why some people still think of algorithms as neutral, given they are a relatively easy example of an STS value-laden technology, is a different question altogether. Ultimately, algorithms and the models used have consequences. In the example of the bookshelf, a color coding scheme might, for instance, imply that I might become less inclined to read books by the same author simply because I did not facilitate my thinking or decision-making process in terms of genre or author in the first place.

THE LEARNING TYPE OF ALGORITHM

An important distinction needs to be made between algorithms that are preprogrammed and behave more or less deterministically and algorithms that have the ability to "learn" or improve in performance over time. Given a particular input, a deterministic algorithm will always produce the same output by passing through the same sequence of steps. The learning type, however, will learn to predict outputs based on previous examples of relationships between input data and outputs. Unlike a deterministic algorithm that correctly sorts an alphabetized list, many of the algorithms that run the Internet today do not necessarily have one easily definable, correct result. The kinds of algorithms and techniques to which I am referring here are called *machine learning*, which is essentially the notion that we can now program a computer to learn by itself (Domingos, 2015). In contrast to the strict logical rules of traditional programming, machine learning is about writing programs that learn to solve the problem from examples. Whereas a programmer previously had to write all the "if...then" statements in anticipation of an outcome herself, machine learning algorithms let the computer learn the rules from a large number of training examples without being explicitly programmed to do so. In order to help reach a target goal, algorithms are "trained" on a corpus of data from which they may "learn" to make certain kinds of decisions without human oversight. Machines do not learn in the same sense that human do, although many of the algorithms used are based on artificial neural networks are inspired by the structure and functional aspects of the brain's deep architecture (Hecht-Nielsen, 1988). The kind of learning that machines do should be understood in a more *functional* sense: "They are capable of changing their behavior to enhance their performance on some task through experience" (Surden, 2014: 89).

Machine learning algorithms come in many different flavors. Similar to humans, the machine itself learns in different ways.[8] One of the most common ways in which algorithms learn is called *supervised learning*. Essentially an inductive approach to learning, algorithms are given a training set comprising the characteristics that engineers want the algorithm to detect and compare with new data (Flach, 2012). Importantly, the training set includes data about the desired output. When the training data do *not* include data about desired outputs, the approach is called *unsupervised learning*. Often, machine learning algorithms may fall somewhere in between: The data only contain a few desired outputs, which is also called *semi-supervised learning* (Domingos, 2015).[9] Before an algorithm can be applied to learn from data, *models* have to be constructed that formalize the task and goals, so that it can be processed by a computer. For instance, before an algorithm can perform the task of finding the most important news feed stories, models have to be created to represent the relationship between news and relevance. As Mackenzie puts it:

> The techniques of machine learning nearly all pivot around ways of transforming, constructing or imposing some kind of shape on the data and using that shape to discover, decide, classify, rank, cluster, recommend, label or predict what is happening or what will happen. (2015: 432)

In data-intensive environments such as social media, machine learning algorithms have become a standard way of learning to recognize patterns in the data, to discover knowledge, and to predict the likelihood of user actions and tastes. Put another way, machine learning is largely enabled by proliferating data from which models may learn. In the age of so-called big data, having the biggest pool of data available from which to detect patterns is often seen as a competitive necessity. The bigger the database, so the story goes, the better the conditions for algorithms to detect relevant patterns.

Models are central to the understanding of machine learning as "they are what is being learned from the data, in order to solve a given task" (Flach, 2012: 20). The way it works is that a pool of data is first mined (automatically processed) to identify regularities upon which subsequent decision-making can rely. The accumulated set of discovered relationships, then, produce the model, which subsequently "can be employed to automate the process of classifying entities or activities of interest, estimating the value of unobserved variables, or predicting future outcomes" (Barocas & Selbst, 2016: 7). As Joaquin Quiñonero Candela, Director of Applied Machine Learning at Facebook, says about the company's machine learning philosophy:

> 1. Get as much data as you can and make sure it is of highest quality 2. Distill your data into signals that will be maximally predictive—a process called feature-engineering 3. Once you have the most awesome data and tools for feature engineering, keep raising the capacity of your algorithms. (Candela, 2016)

Machine learning, then, is about using data to make models that have certain features. Feature engineering, or the process of extracting and selecting the most important features from the data, is arguably one of the most important aspects of machine learning. While feature extraction is usually performed manually, recent advances in deep learning now embed automatic feature engineering into the modeling process itself (Farias et al, 2016). If the algorithm operates on badly drawn features, the results will be poor, no matter how excellent the algorithm is.

How would feature engineering work in calculating such an abstract notion as relevance? One option might be to consider the frequency and types of content on which a specific user has clicked. However, we might also imagine a scenario in which "most important" is not about the frequency of clicks but, rather, the time spent watching or reading certain content. The point here is that the problem of determining what is "most important" depends on the data and the outcome you want to optimize. As Gillespie suggests, "All is in the service of the model's understanding of the data and what it represents, and in service of the model's goal and how it has been formalized" (2016a: 20). The understanding of data and what it represents, then, is not merely a matter of a machine that learns but also of humans who specify the states and outcomes in which they are interested in the first place.[10] In the case of supervised learning, humans (the data miners and machine learning specialists) first need to specify the target variables (desired states and outcomes), which are then used to define "class labels"—"the different classes between which a model should be able to distinguish" (Barocas & Selbst, 2016: 8). Take the task of filtering spam, an area in which machine learning is commonly applied: The goal of the algorithm is to build an internal computer model that will ultimately allow the machine to make automated, accurate classification decisions (Surden, 2014: 91).[11] However, learning tasks are far from alike. Classifying spam is one of the "easier" tasks as it typically merely operates on binary categories. Either something is classified as spam or it is not. But most of the tasks with which we are concerned in this book have to do with ranking and recommendations that cannot be broken down into binary categories. For example, the question of what constitutes newsworthiness or relevancy is not a straightforward task. As we shall see—particularly in chapters 4 and 6—there is no way to measure newsworthiness directly because the notion is a function of the particular way in which the respective industries and platforms have constructed their systems.[12] Whether it is about ranking content in a feed or classifying email as spam, a useful model depends on the ongoing input of new data to optimize its performance.

The bottom line is that there are many different algorithms that can be used to "impose a shape on the data," as Mackenzie put it. For predictive modelling, for example, well-known algorithmic techniques include: logistic regression models, the Naive Bayes classifier, k-nearest neighbors, support vector machines, random forests and neural networks (Mackenzie, 2015). However, as Bernhard Rieder (2017) points out, something like the Naive Bayes classifier is not yet an algorithm in a more restrictive understanding of the term. Rather, it outlines a common method—an "algorithmic technique"—used to solve specific computational problems. If we want to make it into an algorithm that can be run, we have to further specify it. For random forests, for example, you would have to specify the number of trees, and the number of splits to try in each tree. For neural networks you would have to specify the depth of the hidden layers. So in some sense, we are far away from an algorithm. Yet there are also algorithmic techniques for specifying these so-called hyperparameters.[13] Many pieces of software also come with default parameters. Once you specify these parameters, and you have the data, then it is an "algorithm" in a narrow computational sense, whereas without them it is incomplete. What determines whether to use one technique over another "depends upon the domain (i.e., loan default prediction vs. image recognition), its demonstrated accuracy in classification, and available computational resources, among other concerns" (Burrell, 2016: 5). Take, for example, the problem of face recognition. With more than 350 million photos uploaded onto Facebook every day, face recognition is an important area in which Facebook is using machine learning.[14] Algorithms are trained on a variety of existing data sets to learn how to detect faces in the wild. Depending on the specific task of recognition, however, different algorithms can be deployed. One of the simplest and fastest learning algorithms for this purpose is the nearest neighbor (Domingos, 2015: 179). In order to determine whether an image contains a face, the nearest neighbor algorithm works by finding the image most similar to it in Facebook's entire database of labeled photos. "If" it contains a face, "then" the other one is presumed to contain a face as well. This approach is used, for example, in Facebook's auto-tagging functionality. Given Facebook's vast data pool, the company's engineers are able to train algorithms to detect faces in ways that most photo-sharing sites cannot. Facebook's artificial intelligence team has recently developed a system called *DeepFace*, which is supposedly able to identify faces at a 97.25% accuracy level, which is just slightly worse than the average human score of 97.53% (Taigman et al., 2014). This system uses what is called "deep learning," a technique that currently constitutes one of the leading and most advanced machine learning frameworks available. Deep learning is based on neural networks, a model most widely used in image and speech recognition. Modeled to emulate the way in which the human brain works, neural networks "use different layers of mathematical processing to make ever more sense of the information they are fed" (Condliffe, 2015).[15] In terms of image recognition, a system powered by neural networks, for example, would analyze pixel brightness on one layer, shapes and edges through another layer, actual content and image features on a third layer, and so on. Using different algorithms on every layer to process the information, the system would gain a more fine-grained understanding of the image.[16]

As recent cases of image recognition failures have shown, machine learning is not without its problems, and there is much to be learned from cases in which machine learning goes awry. For example, in May 2015, Google was accused of having a "racist" algorithm when its newly launched Photos app tagged two black people in a photograph as "gorillas" (Barr, 2015). A similar incident happened when the photo-sharing service Flickr, powered by Yahoo's neural network, labeled a person as an "ape" due to the color of his skin. While incidents like these are perfect examples of how the results of machine learning can be very problematic, they are also good examples of how the media, which often neglect to explain why certain inferences were made, frequently reports on algorithms, thus catering to an often shallow understanding of how these systems actually work. My hope is to show how we might better understand the power and politics of algorithms if we try to take a more holistic approach by acknowledging the complexity and multiplicity of algorithms, machine learning and big data. Incidents such as these failed image-recognition tasks point to a core concern about dealing with algorithms, namely, the question of agency, responsibility, and accountability to which I shall return in the next chapter. Suffice it to mention at this point the importance of the training data as another element for understanding the possibilities and limits of machine learning. As Barocas and Selbst point out, "what a model learns depends on the examples to which it has been exposed" (2016: 10). This raises an important question with regards to accusations of a "racist" algorithm: What was the initial data set that Google used to train its image recognition algorithms, and whose faces did it depict? What generalizable signals/patterns was it picking up on?

Understood as sets of instructions that direct the computer to perform a specific task, algorithms are essentially used to control the flow of actions and future events. Sometimes, the flow of events is more or less known in advance, as in the case of algorithms sorting an alphabetized list. More often than not in the world of machine learning, however, the outcome of events remains uncertain. Machine learning algorithms reduce this uncertainty by making predictions about the *likelihoods* of outcomes. Put differently, machine learning is about strengthening the probability of some event happening, based on evolving information. This is also the principle of Bayes' theorem: the "simple rule for updating your degree of belief in a hypothesis when you receive new evidence" (Domingos, 2015: 144).[17] Following Wendy Chun, then, we might understand an algorithm as a "strategy, or a plan of action— based on interactions with unfolding events" (2011: 126). This implies that algorithms do not simply change with the event but are always *in becoming* since events are not static but unfolding. In the case of algorithmically driven sites such as Facebook, users are crucial to the development and maintenance of the underlying coding systems as they constantly feed the system with new data. As Mukund Narasimhan, a software engineer at Facebook, tellingly suggests: "Everything in Facebook is a work in progress." The models Facebook uses to design the system are evolving because the data is changing. This means that the exact ways in which the algorithms work are also constantly tweaked by employees because of the fact that everything else changes (Narasimhan, 2011).

Algorithms do not simply change *with* the event; they also have the ability to change the event. In the era of big data and data mining, algorithms have the ability performatively to change the way events unfold or, at the very least, change their interpretation. A good example of this is the failed Google Flu Tracker, which was operative from September 2011 to August 2013. Often heralded as the prime example of what big data could do, Google's Flu Tracker was designed to predict outbreaks of flu before they happened, based on mining data from their vast troves of search queries. According to Google, they "found a close relationship between how many people search for flu-related topics and how many people actually have flu symptoms" (Walsh, 2014). However, in February 2013, the Flu tracker made headlines because it turned out that it had predicted "more than double the proportion of doctor visits for influenza-like illness than the Centers for Disease Control and Prevention," which had been used as a *de facto* predictor until then (Lazer et al., 2014: 1203). The fact that the tracker was dependent upon Google's search algorithms played a significant part in skewing the results for flu trends. By recommending search terms to its users through its autocomplete feature, Google itself was producing the conditions it was trying to merely describe and predict. As Walsh (2014) put it: "If the data isn't reflecting the world, how can it predict what will happen?"

Algorithms as a Social Concern

Incidents like the Google Flu tracker or the more recent examples of data and algorithmic discrimination outlined above have arguably encouraged many more social scientists and humanities scholars to explore the ethical, political, and social implications that these digital infrastructures and systems have. Since the first cycle of hype and optimism concerning the rise of big data seems to be fading gradually, we are now seeing a growing scholarly interest in what Tarleton Gillespie and Nick Seaver have termed "critical algorithm studies." Over the past decade or so, work spanning sociology, anthropology, science and technology studies, geography, communication, media studies, and legal studies has started to focus critical attention not just on software but algorithms more specifically (Amoore, 2009; Ananny, 2016; Beer, 2009; Cheney-Lippold, 2011, Diakopoulos, 2015; Gillespie, 2014; Introna, 2016; Karppi & Crawford, 2016; Lenglet, 2011; Mackenzie, 2015; McKelvey, 2014; Seaver, 2013; Striphas, 2015; Wilf, 2013; Ziewitz, 2016). Whereas computer scientists typically focus on designing efficient algorithms, a sociological or cultural approach to algorithms is starting to emerge, focusing on what algorithms are actually doing as part of situated practices. Indeed, an algorithmic logic of information processing and dissemination has become pervasive in such fields as finance (Mackenzie, 2015; Pasquale, 2015), transportation (Kitchin & Dodge, 2011), the travel sector (Orlikowski & Scott, 2015), higher education (Introna, 2011; Williamson, 2015), journalism (Anderson, 2013; Diakopoulos, 2015; Dörr, 2016), security (Amoore, 2013; Cheney-Lippold, 2016), surveillance (Braverman, 2014; Introna & Wood, 2004), popular culture (Beer, 2013), and the media industry more generally (Hallinan & Striphas, 2016; Napoli, 2014).[18] Social scientists and humanities scholars are not primarily concerned with the technical details of algorithms or their underlying systems but, rather, with the meanings and implications that algorithmic systems may have. As Gillespie (2016a) suggests, critical algorithm scholars are often more concerned with the algorithm as an *adjective*, understood as the social phenomena that are driven by and committed to algorithmic systems.

While the growing concern over algorithms may be a relatively recent phenomenon in the context of the social sciences and humanities—in part, spurred by the rise of big data—the underlying social concerns have a much longer history. The more pervasive use of algorithms in a wide range of societal sectors and institutions should be seen along a much longer continuum of scholarship concerned with the intersection of technology and society, the social history of computing, and related fields such as new media studies, software studies, platform studies, STS, and human-computer interaction (HCI). Work in these domains has contributed knowledge about the power and politics of computing technologies, software systems, and information infrastructures relevant to our present concern with the role of algorithms in the contemporary media landscape. Take, for example, the growing interest in software as a cultural object of study investigated in the field of software studies (Fuller, 2008). During the past decade or so, social scientists and humanities scholars have called for an expanded understanding of code that extends significantly beyond its technical definitions (Berry, 2011; Fuller, 2008; Kitchin & Dodge, 2011; Mackenzie, 2006). Software studies can be understood as a cultural studies approach to the "stuff of software" (Fuller, 2008), where what counts as "stuff" remains relatively open to interpretation. This conceptual openness is, perhaps, what distinguishes software studies from computer science approaches since what counts as software is seen as a "shifting nexus of relations, forms and practices" (Mackenzie, 2006: 19). This is not to say that scholars interested in software as a cultural object of study dismiss the importance of materiality or technical operations, quite the contrary. While calling for an expanded understanding of the meaning and significance of software as part of everyday life, scholars within software studies also maintain a high level of sensibility toward the technical and functional dimensions of software. In his book *Protocol*, Alexander Galloway makes the case that "it is not only worthwhile, but also necessary to have a technical as well as theoretical understanding of any given technology" (2004: xiii). In order to understand power relationships at play in the "control society," Galloway argues that it is crucial to start with the questions of how technology (in this case, protocols such as HTTP) works and who it works for. In fact, *not* addressing the technical details of software or algorithms as part of a sociological or critical inquiry is seen as problematic (Rieder, 2017: 101). While media scholars differ in their assessment of how necessary coding skills are to a critical understanding of software and algorithms, some technical knowledge is clearly desirable.[19]

If an expanded understanding of software and algorithms does not necessarily mean discarding technical details from analysis, what does it mean? One view, inspired by actor network theory and similar perspectives, takes software and algorithms to be complex technical systems that cannot merely be described as technological alone because their ontological status remains unclear. As Mackenzie argues, software has a "variable ontology," suggesting "that the essential nature of the entity is unstable" (2006: 96). The variable ontology of software means that "questions of when and where it is social or technical, material or semiotic cannot be conclusively answered" (2006: 96). Similarly, Gillespie suggests that "'Algorithm' may, in fact, serve as an abbreviation for the sociotechnical assemblage that includes algorithm, model, target goal, data, training data, application, hardware—and connect it all to a broader social endeavour" (2016a: 22). Moreover, as Seaver points out, "algorithmic systems are not standalone little boxes, but massive, networked ones with hundreds of hands reaching into them, tweaking and tuning, swapping out parts and experimenting with new arrangements" (2013: 10). Another way of answering the question of what algorithms are beyond their technical definition is to see them as inscriptions of certain ideologies or particular ways of world-making (Goodman, 1985). For example, scholars have analyzed the algorithmic logic underpinning search engines and high-frequency trading in terms of how they can be said to advance a capitalist ideology (Mager, 2012; Snider, 2014). Another option, not unlike the networked view, is to emphasize the ways in which algorithms are "entangled in practice" (Introna, 2016; Gillespie, 2014; Orlikowski & Scott, 2015). This is the notion that algorithms do things as part of what else they are entangled with. As Gillespie writes, "algorithms are built to be embedded into practice in the lived world that produces the information they process" (2014: 183). Researchers have drawn on notions of sociomateriality, performativity, or ideas of entanglement to focus their attention not on what algorithms do in technical terms but on what they do in terms of constituting and being constituted in and through practice. What matters is not so much the precise instructions or the theorem underlying the algorithm, but how it is incorporated within specific sociomaterial practices (Introna, 2016).

The notion of algorithm as adjective suggests that, when social scientists and humanities scholars invoke the term "algorithmic," what they are really concerned with "is not the algorithm per se but the insertion of procedure into human knowledge and social experience" (Gillespie, 2016a: 25). The insertion of procedurality and quantification into human experience has been noted in various recent accounts on culture, aesthetics, and knowledge production. Cultural theorist Ted Striphas (2015), for example, writes about the emergence of an "algorithmic culture," which he takes to be the ways in which platforms such as Netflix and Amazon are seen to alter the way in which culture has traditionally been practiced, experienced, and understood.[20] Furthermore, Mark Lenglet (2011) describes how the financial world has become algorithmic not only by having algorithmic procedures inserted into trading but also through the ways in which algorithms now occupy the minds of traders, making them act and react in certain ways. As I will discuss in chapter 5 and 6, this is not unique to the financial world but is evident in everything from social media users orientation toward platforms through to the institutional contexts of journalism where algorithms are inserted into both journalistic practices and discourse. Even identity seems to have become algorithmic, as evidenced by the "shift from offline to online marketing" (Cheney-Lippold, 2011: 175). As seen from the perspective of many sociologists, cultural theorists, and media scholars, what is interesting about algorithms is not necessarily the same as what interests a computer scientist or an engineer. While an algorithm is still a set of instructions used to solve a computational problem, the valences of the term obviously differ in mathematics and sociology. However, as Gillespie points out, "to highlight the mathematical quality is not to contrast algorithms to human judgement. Instead it is to recognize them as part of mechanisms that introduce and privilege quantification, proceduralization, and automation in human endeavors" (2016a: 27).

The social concerns voiced about algorithms today are not necessarily new. As mechanisms of quantification, classification, measurement, and prediction, algorithms are as much imbued in the history of computation and software engineering as they are in the history of statistics, accounting, and bureaucratization. As such, the historical and cultural contexts of algorithms intersect with the social history of calculation and ordering of various types, including the history and politics of statistical reasoning and large numbers (Desrosieres & Naish, 2002; Foucault, 2007; Hacking, 2006; Power, 2004); practices of quantification, numbering and valuation (Callon & Law, 2005; Espeland & Stevens, 2008; Verran, 2001); the cultural logic of rankings and ratings (Espeland & Sauder, 2007; Sauder & Espeland, 2009); and ideas of critical accounting and auditing (Power, 1999; Strathern, 2000b). Moreover, contemporary concerns about the power of algorithms can also be seen as an "extension of worries about Taylorism and the automation of industrial labor" (Gillespie, 2016a: 27) or "the century long exercise by media industries to identify (and often quantify) what's popular" (Gillespie, 2016b). Clearly, algorithms need to be understood as part of a historical lineage. Indeed, we might say that the "avalanche of numbers" (Hacking, 1991, 2015), which occurred as nation-states started to classify and count their populations in the 19th century, forms a general backdrop for an understanding of algorithms in the era of big data. This specific historical lineage, however, if we were to carry it all the way through, would also require us to travel a complex and disjunctive route via the social history of census, punch cards, bureaucratization and the rise of industrial society and factory work, wartime machinery and the rise of computers, databases and the automated management of populations, before arriving at the contemporary milieu of "making up people" (Hacking, 1999) through data mining and machine learning techniques. This is the genealogy that tells the story of managing populations—most notably theorized by Michel Foucault in his *College de France* lectures (Foucault, 2007, 2008). As Foucault (2007: 138) points out, statistics means etymologically "knowledge of the state." The task for those who govern, then, is to determine what one needs to know in order to govern most effectively and how that knowledge is to be organized. If the collection of data through the numbering practices of statistics and the corporate data mining of recent years makes algorithmic operations possible, the algorithms themselves (understood in the technical sense) give shape to otherwise meaningless data. While the significant power and potential of big data (the quantity of information produced by people, things, and their interactions) cannot be denied, its value derives not from the data themselves but from the ways in which they have been brought together into new forms of meaningfulness by the associational infrastructure of the respective software systems in which algorithms play a key role.

Power of Algorithms

The starting premise for the book is the observation that algorithms have become a key site of power in the contemporary mediascape. During the past decade or so, social scientists and humanities scholars have started to explore and describe the increased presence of algorithms in social life and the new modes of power that these new "generative rules" entail (Lash, 2007; Beer, 2009; Cheney-Lippold, 2011; Gillespie, 2014; Diakopoulos, 2015). As Scott Lash argues, "[a] society of ubiquitous media means a society in which power is increasingly in the algorithm" (2007: 71). To say that algorithms *are* powerful, *have* power, animate, exert, or produce power needs some qualification and explanation. The concept of power is one of the most contested and important terms there is. While it is difficult to provide a short answer to the fundamental question of what power is, Michel Foucault's scholarship provides one of the most comprehensive avenues for a nuanced and multifaceted understanding of the term. For Foucault, power was never just one thing but, fundamentally, about different forms of relations. Throughout his career, Foucault changed and modified his ideas of what power is, coining analytically distinct conceptions of power sensitive to specific contexts, institutions, objects of knowledge, and political thought.[21] Generally speaking, Foucault identified three levels of power relations, which he termed strategic games between liberties, domination, and governmental technologies. As Foucault elaborates in an interview:

> It seems to me that we must distinguish the relationship of power as strategic games between liberties—strategic games that result in the fact that some people try to determine the conduct of others—and the states of domination, which are what we ordinarily call power. And, between the two, between the games of power and the states of domination, you have governmental technologies. (Bernauer & Rasmussen, 1988: 19)

The first level—strategic games between liberties—is a ubiquitous feature of society and human interaction. From this very broad conception, it follows that there is nothing outside power relations because power conditions the very existence of society. Although Foucault is mostly associated with conceptualizing power as immanent to the modern social productive apparatus, he also maintained a notion of power that acknowledged the asymmetrical relationships of the subordinate position of certain individuals and groups. Yet, domination was never seen as default form of power but rather the exception. The third notion of power relations—government—refers to a more systematized and regulated form of power that follows a specific form of rationality. Foucault's notion of government demarcates power from domination by seeing power, first and foremost, as a form of guidance and "shaping the field of possible action of subjects" (Lemke, 2012: 17). In many ways, these three levels of power can be seen in the various ways in which the power of algorithms has recently been framed within the literature. While most authors do not explicitly frame their notion of algorithmic power in Foucauldian terms, connecting the discussion back to Foucault might help analytically to distinguish what is at stake in making a claim about the powerful role that algorithms have in society today.

Like the immanent form of power described by Foucault, Scott Lash sees new forms of capitalist power as "power *through* the algorithm" (Lemke, 2012: 17, emphasis mine). This is a form of power that works from below, not a power-over as it were. As such it becomes indistinguishable from life itself by sifting into "the capillaries of society" (Lash, 2007: 61). In his seminal article on algorithmic power in the age of social media, Beer builds on Lash's notion of "post-hegemonic" forms of power to argue that the algorithms underpinning social media platforms "have the capacity to shape social and cultural formations and impact directly on individual lives" (2009: 994). Drawing on the example of Last.fm, a music-sharing platform, Beer argues that the power of the algorithm can be seen in the ways that the platform provides users with their own taste-specific online radio station. Power, in others words, stems from the algorithm's capacity to "shape auditory and cultural experiences" (2009: 996). This notion of power through the algorithm does not treat power as hierarchical or one-directional but, rather, as immanent to life itself. Algorithmic power in this sense can be understood as a force, energy, or capacity of sorts (Lash, 2007). This way of understanding power as immanent is, perhaps, most famously reflected in Foucault's notion of power as an omnipresent feature of modern society in which power relations are not seen as repressive but as productive (Lemke, 2012: 19).[22]

Others have argued that algorithms have an intrinsic power to regulate social lives through their "autonomous decision-making" capacity (Diakopoulos, 2015: 400). Here, power seems to be located *in* the mechanics of the algorithm. According to Nick Diakopoulos, algorithmic power stems from the "atomic decisions that algorithms make, including *prioritization, classification, association*, and *filtering*" 2015: 400, emphasis in the original). As such, algorithms exert power by making decisions about the ways in which information is presented, organized, and indicated as being important. As filtering devices, algorithms make decisions about what information to include and exclude, constituting a new form of gatekeeping (Bozdag, 2013; Helberger et al., 2015; Napoli, 2015).[23] In contrast to the rhetoric surrounding the early days of the Web, which often heralded the Internet's potential for doing away with hierarchy by giving everyone a voice, scholars now worry that algorithms are assuming gatekeeping roles that have a significant effect on the way public opinion is formed (Just & Latzer, 2016). Worries about algorithms diminishing the democratic potential of the public sphere—for example, by creating filter bubbles (Pariser, 2011; Zuiderveen et al., 2016) or manipulating what information is shown to the public in the first place (Tufekci, 2015)—are frequently framed in more traditional terms as forms of domination or power seen as hierarchical and top-down. In this sense, algorithms are seen as *having power over* somebody or something. As Frank Pasquale writes in his recent book *The Black Box Society*, search engines and social networks, by way of their capacity to include, exclude, and rank, have "the power to ensure that certain public impressions become permanent, while others remain fleeting" (2015: 14). In Foucault's terms, this would be power seen as a form of political, social and economic domination, where one entity prevents another from seeing or doing something. As Pasquale puts it, "we have given the search sector an almost unimaginable power to determine what we see, where we spend, how we perceive" (2015: 98). However, framing algorithms as having power over someone or something risks losing sight of the human decision-making processes and programming that precedes any algorithmic operation. When Pasquale notes that we have given power to the search sector, he does not simply mean the algorithms running Google. Yet, there is a tendency to use algorithm as a placeholder for a much more distributed form of power. As I argue in this book, critical inquiry into algorithmic forms of power and politics should always extend any claim of algorithms *having* power. As I will elaborate in in the next chapter, the question of whom or what power most obviously belongs to cannot be conclusively answered. Instead, what can be examined are algorithms *in* practice, the places and situations through which algorithms are made present and take on a life of their own.

Claims about algorithmic decision-making, which are often accompanied by subsequent calls for greater accountability and regulation (Diakopoulos, 2015; Pasquale, 2015), are part of a much longer continuum of concerns about the ways in which technology can be said to have politics. According to this view, technology is never neutral but always already embedded with certain biases, values, and assumptions. At least since Winner's (1986) influential arguments about Moses' low-hanging bridges, scholars have followed suit in advocating the necessity to consider the politics of artifacts, particularly by attending to the values in design and the moral import of those design choices.[24] Introna and Wood (2004), for example, argue that facial recognition systems are political in the sense that these algorithmic forms of surveillance carry certain assumptions about designated risks in the very design of the system. As Introna and Wood explain, the politics is mostly implicit, "part of a mundane process of trying to solve practical problems" (2004: 179). Every artifact implicating human beings, including algorithms, always carries certain assumptions and values about how the world works. Take the design of an ATM: "if you are blind, in a wheelchair, have problem remembering, or are unable to enter a PIN, because of disability, then your interest in accessing your account can be excluded by the ATM design" (2004: 179). The point is not that designers of ATM machines consciously or deliberately exclude people in wheelchairs from using an ATM but that the ways in which systems are designed always involve certain exclusionary practices that sometimes appear to be a more or less coherent and intentional strategy despite nobody "authoring" it as such (Introna and Nissenbaum, 2000).

The question of intentionality—whether someone explicitly authors an artifact to function in a particular way or whether its functioning is emergent—gets even more complicated with respect to machine learning algorithms. These algorithms are able to improve performance over time based on feedback. In addition, machine learning algorithms "create an internal computer model of a given phenomenon that can be generalized to apply to new, never-before-seen examples of that phenomenon"

(Surden, 2014:93) without being explicitly programmed to do so. How should we think about the politics of artifacts when the design of the system is continuously performed by the system itself? Returning to the example of the failed image recognition in the case of Google's Photos app, the nature of the training data might be just as important to consider as the algorithm itself. As Gillespie points out:

> The most common problem in algorithm design is that the new data turns out not to match the training data in some consequential way [...] Phenomena emerge that the training data simply did not include and could not have anticipated [...] something important was overlooked as irrelevant, or was scrubbed from the training data in preparation for the development of the algorithm. (2016a: 21)

Indeed, as Introna and Wood contend, it seems "we cannot with any degree of certainty separate the purely social from the purely technical, cause from effect, designer from user, winners from losers, and so on" (2004: 180). This does not mean, however, that taking a "value in design" approach in the study of machine learning algorithms is not a viable option. To the degree that algorithms are, in fact, capable of labeling black people as "gorillas" or to score black people as predominantly high-risk in committing a future crime (Angwin et al., 2016), they ought to be scrutinized for the kinds of values and assumptions underlying their function. While many scholars and policymakers have worried about the discriminatory capabilities of algorithms, calling for more transparency on part of the companies involved is only part of the solution. What many of the "algorithms gone awry" cases suggest is the importance of seeing the results as reflections of more fundamental societal biases and prejudices. This is to say that, if the machine that is supposed to compute the likelihood of future crimes is fed statistical data tainted by centuries of racial bias materialized in police reports, arrests, urban planning, and the juridico-political systems, it would be misleading only to talk about the power of algorithms in producing such risk assessments. Instead of locating predictive power *in* the algorithm (narrowly defined), we may think of algorithms as what Foucault calls governmental technologies (Lemke, 2001; Miller & Rose, 1990).

Foucault used the notions of government and governmentality to analyze the forms of power and politics involved in the shaping and structuring of people's fields of possibility. While Foucault used the terms government and governmentality somewhat interchangeably, especially in his later writings, "government" broadly refers to the "conduct of conduct," whereas governmentality refers to the modes of thought, or rationalities, underlying the conduct of conduct (Foucault, 1982; 2007; 2010; Lemke, 2001; Rose, 1999).[25] As Lemke remarks, "the problematic of government redirects Foucault's analytics of power" (2012: 17). It is a notion of power that moves beyond relations of consent and force and, instead, sees power relations in the double sense of the term "conduct" as both a form of leading and "as a way of behaving within a more or less open field of possibilities" (Foucault, 1982: 789). Government is about "the right disposition of things" (Foucault, 2007: 134), which concerns "men in their relationships, bonds, and complex involvements with" various things such as resources, environment, habits, ways of acting and thinking (Foucault, 2007: 134).[26] By way of example, Foucault asks what it would mean to govern a ship?

> It involves, of course, being responsible for the sailors, but also taking care of the vessel and the cargo; governing a ship also involves taking winds, reefs, storms, and bad weather into account. What characterizes government of a ship is the practice of establishing relations between the sailors, the vessel, which must be safeguarded, the cargo, which must be brought to port, and their relations with all those eventualities like winds, reefs, storms and so on. (Foucault, 2007: 135)

Extending the analytics of government to an understanding of algorithmic power implies a concern for the ways in which things are arranged and managed to guide people in a certain way. For Foucault, this organizing power has a crucial technological dimension since the conduct of conduct is achieved through various technical means.[27] Introna (2016), for example, explores this dimension of algorithmic power by considering how plagiarism algorithms are used to govern academic writing practices. He makes the argument that algorithms have the power to enact particular governed subjects, exemplified in the way that the plagiarism software enacts "a particular understanding of originality and plagiarism, as well as subjects who conceive of 'good' writing practice as the composition of undetectable texts" (Introna, 2016: 20). As with Foucault's earlier notion of disciplinary power, a concept that will be further discussed in chapter 4, the notion of government and governmentality strongly hinges on subjectivation as a core principle of power. The making of subjects and subject positions in Foucault's work, frames power as something that is productive and generative.

Power as such does not exist; it only exists "when it is put into action" (Foucault, 1982: 788). For an understanding of algorithmic power, this implies that algorithms do not *have* or possess power. Instead, algorithms enact "the possibility of conduct and putting in order the possible outcome" (Foucault, 1982: 789). "Governmentality" does not "force people to do what the governor wants" but, rather, works by assuring "coercion and processes through which the self is constructed or modified by himself" (Foucault, 1993: 204).[28] I want to suggest that we conceive of government and governmentality as particularly helpful concepts in understanding the power of algorithms. Algorithms do not simply have power in the possessive sense; they constitute "technologies of government." Just as statistics enabled the governing of populations in Foucault's account of security, algorithms operate as instruments of government to direct the flow of information and the practices of users "to this or that region or activity" (Foucault, 2007: 141).

To conceive of algorithms as *technologies* of government in the Foucauldian sense, however, is not to restrict analysis of algorithms to the material domain. As Lemke writes, "an analytics of government operates with a concept of technology that includes not only material but also symbolic devices" (2012: 30). Discourses and narratives are "not reduced to pure semiotic propositions; instead they are regarded as performative practices" and part of the mechanisms and techniques through which the conduct of conduct is shaped. Throughout the book, the different ways in which algorithms operate as technologies of government will be both explicitly and implicitly addressed. In chapter 4, Facebook's news feed algorithm is explicitly framed as an architectural form that arranges things (relationships between users and objects) in a "right disposition." Chapter 5 highlights the ways in which narratives and beliefs about algorithms constitute a double articulation, shaping both the conduct of individuals and the algorithm through feedback loops. Chapter 6, meanwhile, considers how algorithms are used to govern journalism in a digital age, looking at how algorithms do not just enact a particularly understanding of journalism but also through the ways in which algorithms now occupy the minds of news professionals, making them act and react in certain ways.

Targeting the Algorithm as the Target

A final word needs to be said about the choice of making the algorithm the target in the first place. While I maintain a broad conception of algorithms throughout the book as a way of talking about the imbrication of computer rules and instructions on everyday life, it is worth noting that using the algorithm as the target is not without its problems. As Ian Bogost has argued, there is a certain danger of theologizing the algorithm by singling it out as the target for describing contemporary culture. While I agree with Bogost (2015) that algorithms are not simple, singular systems but, rather, multipart and complex, involving a "varied array of people, processes, materials, and machines," it does not discredit algorithms as objects of study and phenomena of interest, quite the contrary. Precisely *because* of their entangled and complex nature, there is an obvious need to disentangle their meanings and ways of acting in the world.

What I want to do in this book is to explore and understand better what it means to have algorithms interwoven in the social fabric of the contemporary media landscape. Targeting the algorithm is primarily about developing a better understanding of the rhetorical registers that these mechanisms of proceduralization have. That is, precisely because the "algorithm has taken on a particularly mythical role in our technology-obsessed era" (a "sloppy shorthand" for something much more complex, as Bogost puts it), not-so-sloppy descriptions are called for. When platforms such as Twitter and Instagram publicly announce that they are introducing an "algorithmic timeline" or when the media are repeatedly reporting on incidents of "algorithmic discrimination" and bias, there is also an increasing need to examine not just what the term means but, more importantly, how and when "algorithms" are put to use as particularly useful signifiers and for whose benefit. In the way Katherine Hayles (2005: 17) sees computation as connoting "far more than the digital computer" and "not limited to digital manipulations or binary code," this book sees algorithms as much more than simply step-by-step instructions telling the machine what to do.[29] When a London bookstore labels a bookshelf containing employees' book recommendations their "human algorithm" or when the BBC starts a radio show by announcing that "humans beat robots," there is clearly something about the notion of an algorithm that seems to inform the way we think and talk about contemporary culture and society that is not just strictly confined to computers.[30]

Algorithms, I want to suggest, constitute something of a cultural logic in that they are "much more than coded instruction," drifting into the ways in which people think and talk about everything from the economy to knowledge production to culture. Algorithms exist on many scales, ranging from the operationality of software to society at large. However, in this book, I am less interested in asserting what algorithms are, as if they possess some essence that can be clearly delineated. What is of interest is the "ontological politics" of algorithms, the sense that "conditions of possibility are not given" but shaped in and through situated practices (Mol, 1999: 75). Algorithms are seen as multiple. This is to say that there is no one way in which algorithms exist as a singular object. By positing the multiple nature of algorithms, the intention is to take their manyfoldedness seriously.[31]

Drawing on Mol's work in *The Body Multiple* (2002) in which she argues that there is no essence to what the disease arthrosclerosis is—only ever different *versions* that are enacted in particular settings, I argue that algorithms never materialize in one way only. This does not mean, however, that there cannot be a singular object called an algorithm or that algorithms are nothing but relations. Like the diseases studied by Mol or the aircraft studied by John Law, algorithms oscillate between multiplicity and singularity. As Law puts it: "Yes, atherosclerosis. Yes, alcoholic liver disease. Yes, a water pump [...] And yes, an aircraft. All of these are more or less singular but also more or less plural" (2002a: 33). Similarly, we might say: Yes, a neural network. Yes, a code written in C++. Yes, PageRank. Yes, a conversation about how we organize our lives. All of which are more or less singular, more or less plural. In contrast to Mol and Law, however, this book is not about a specific object such as one specific aircraft (Law is specifically concerned with the military aircraft TSR2), disease (i.e., anemia), or algorithm (i.e., PageRank). The singularity and multiplicity in question are the result of analytical cuts. Sometimes, the algorithm might appear as a singular entity—for example, in chapter 4 on the Facebook news feed algorithm.

At other times, the algorithm is less identifiable; yet, the question of what and where it is looms large. What is at stake, then, in addressing the ontological politics of algorithms is not so much an understanding of what exactly the algorithm is or the moments in which it acts (although this is important, too) but, rather, those moments in which they are *enacted* and made to matter as part of specific contexts and situations.

3

Neither Black nor Box

(Un)knowing Algorithms

The power of algorithms can be felt in all spheres of society. Algorithms do not merely filter news or arrange people's social media feeds, they also are routinely used to help law enforcement, financial institutions, and the health sector make decisions that may have a profound impact on individual lives (Pasquale, 2015). Yet algorithms are not the kinds of objective and neutral decision makers that they are frequently held out to be. Examples of bias in algorithmic decision-making now abound, and scholars and policymakers are trying to figure out the best ways to govern and make these systems more accountable. A major obstacle to holding algorithms accountable, however, is to know them in the first place. Many of the algorithms that we are most concerned with and interested in—for example, those that underlie popular media platforms—are often governed by trade-secret protection. The algorithms running Facebook and Google are the "secret sauces" that give shape to the information and data flowing online. Algorithms are made to be opaque—not just to protect businesses but due to the technical necessity of handling the complexity of the system. Knowing algorithms, then, is severely burdened by their often "black-box" nature. As Frank Pasquale writes, knowing what algorithms do matters because authority is increasingly expressed through them: "Decisions that used to be based on human reflection are now made automatically" by encoded rules that are "hidden within black boxes" (2015: 8). Algorithmic decision-making is often described as impenetrable and secretive, concealed behind a "veil of code" and trade law (Perel & Elkin-Koren, 2017). The story often goes that, if only we could make algorithms more transparent, we would stand a better chance of governing the big corporations that make these automatic decisions on our behalf.

While "transparency is not just an end in itself," transparency is still seen as a necessary condition for greater intelligibility (Pasquale, 2015: 8). As Barack Obama (2009) famously stated in the opening of a memorandum of the Freedom of Information Act: "A democracy requires accountability, and accountability requires transparency." The question remains as to what exactly it is that should be made transparent and what transparency is believed to help reveal. In her review of

Pasquale's *The Black Box Society*, Dewandre (2015) instructively connects the recent calls for greater algorithmic transparency to what feminist scholar Susan H. Williams has called the "Enlightenment Vision." For Williams, "the liberal model of autonomy and the Cartesian model of truth are deeply connected. The autonomous liberal is the Cartesian knower" (2004: 232). According to the Enlightenment Vision, transparency is what makes rationality, autonomy, and control possible. When something is hidden, the Enlightenment impetus says we must reveal it because knowing leads to greater control.[1] But what if the power believed to emanate from algorithms is not easily accessible simply because the idea of origins and sources of actions that come with the Cartesian assumption of causality are problematic to begin with? By thinking around the cusp of sensibility and knowledge, I take up in this chapter the challenge of formulating an epistemological stance on algorithms that is committed to the notion of algorithm as multiple introduced in the previous chapter. That is, how to know algorithms when the algorithm is both multiple, "concealed behind a veil of a code," and seemingly "impenetrable"?

In this chapter, I use the concept of the black box as a heuristic device to discuss the nature of algorithms in contemporary media platforms and how we, as scholars and social actors interested in them, might attend to algorithms despite, or even because of, their seemingly secret nature. Moving beyond the notion that algorithms *are* black boxes, this chapter asks, instead, what is at stake in framing algorithms in this way and what such a framing might possibly distract us from asking. The questions that I want to pose in going forward have to do with the limits of using the black box as a functional analogy to algorithms. To what extent are algorithms usefully considered as black boxes? What could we possibly see if efforts to illuminate algorithms are not directed as the source code or details of its encoded instructions but elsewhere, and what would this elsewhere be? The chapter unfolds as follows: First, I address the trope of algorithms as black boxes, arguing that algorithms are neither as black nor as boxed as they are sometimes made out to be. Next, I unpack this claim more by conceptualizing algorithms in terms of a relational ontology. This implies a shift in focus from the question of what algorithms are to what they do. The argument is made that, in order to address the power and politics of algorithms, questions concerning the agency of algorithms should be focused not on *where* agency is located but *when*. Finally, I point to three methodological tactics around which to orient ways of making sense of algorithms.

Black Box

THE PROBLEMATIC OF THE UNKNOWN

The concept of the black box has become a catch-all for all the things we (seemingly) cannot know. Referring to an opaque technical device about which only the inputs and outputs are known, the figure of the black box is linked to the history of secrecy—to trade secrets, state secrets, and military secrets (Galison, 2004: 231).[2] The black box is an object whose inner functioning cannot be known—at least not by observation, since the blackness of the box obscures vision. Historically, the black box refers, quite literally, to a physical black box that contained war machinery and radar equipment during World War II. In tracing the genealogy of the black box, von Hilgers (2011) describes how the black box initially referred to a "black" box that had been sent from the British to the Americans as part of the so-called Tizard Mission, which sought technical assistance for the development of new technologies for the war effort. This black box, which was sent to the radiation lab at MIT, contained another black box, the Magnetron. During wartime, crucial technologies had to be made opaque in case they fell into enemy hands. Conversely, if confronted with an enemy's black box, one would have to assume that the box might contain a self-destruct device, making it dangerous to open. As a consequence, what emerged was a culture of secrecy or what Galison (1994) has termed "radar philosophy," a model of thought that paved the way for the emergence of cybernetics and the analysis and design of complex "man-machine" systems. The black box readily became a metaphor for the secret, hidden, and unknown. In everyday parlance, everything from the brain to markets to nation-states is now conceptualized as a black box. Algorithms are no different.

When algorithms are conceptualized as black boxes, they are simultaneously rendered a problem of the unknown.[3] As unknowns, algorithms do not simply signify lack of knowledge or information. The black box notion points to a more specific type of unknown. What the pervasive discourses on transparency and accountability surrounding algorithms and trade secrecy suggest is that algorithms are considered *knowable known unknowns* (Roberts, 2012)—that is, something that, given the right resources, might be knowable in principle. All that is needed, according to popular discourse, is to find a way of opening up the black box. Indeed, a key mantra in science and technology studies, "opening up the black box," implies disentangling the complexities and work that goes into making a technical device appear stable and singular.[4] The impetus for opening up the black box can also be seen in calls for greater transparency and accountability characteristic of the "audit society" (Power, 1999). In a climate of auditing, organizations are increasingly asked to be transparent about their dealings and ways of operating. Universities, for example, are asked to produce more and more paper trails, including assessment records, numbers of research outputs, and lists of funding received. As Marilyn Strathern (2000a) puts it, axiomatic value is given to increased information. Today, scholars have extended the notion of auditing to the field of algorithms, arguing for the need to conduct audit studies of algorithms in order to detect and combat forms of algorithmic discrimination (Sandvig et al., 2014). While such efforts are certainly admirable, what I want to examine critically as part of this chapter is precisely the hope of intelligibility attached to calls for more transparency. There are many ways of knowing algorithms (broadly understood) besides opening the black box and reading the exact coded instructions that tell the machine what to do. Indeed, while some things are "fundamentally not discoverable" (von Hilgers, 2011: 42), the widespread notion of algorithms as black boxes constitutes something of a red herring—that is, a piece of information that distracts from other (perhaps, more pressing) questions and issues to be addressed. The metaphor of the black box is often too readily used as a way of critiquing algorithms without critically scrutinizing the metaphor itself. What is gained and what is lost when we draw on the metaphor of the black box to describe algorithms? To what extent does the metaphor work at all?

To say that something is a black box may not simply be a statement of facts. As I will discuss in this chapter, declaring something a black box may serve many different functions. Unlike the Socratic tradition, which sees the unknown as a fundamental prerequisite to wisdom, the black box renders the unknown an epistemological problem. The unknown—including the black box—is deemed problematic because it obscures vision and, ultimately, undermines the Enlightenment imperative *aude sapere*: " 'dare to know,' 'have the courage, the audacity, to know' " (Foucault, 2010: 306). For Kant, the Enlightenment philosopher par excellence, not knowing is characterized by immaturity, the notion that people blindly accept someone else's authority to lead (Foucault, 2010: 305). Alas, if something is willfully obscured, the task for any enlightened mind would be to find ways of rendering it visible. Critics of the Enlightenment vision have often raised flags against the notion of exposing or decoding inner workings, as if there were a kernel of truth just waiting to be revealed by some rational and mature mind (a mind that is quite often seen as specifically male) (Chun, 2011; Foucault, 1980; Harding, 1996). In the Kantian tradition, the audacity to know is not just explicitly linked to rationalism but to the quest for the conditions under which true knowledge is possible. On the face of it, then, black boxes threaten the very possibility of knowing the truth.

While threatening access to a seemingly underlying truth, the very concept of the black box also denotes a device that releases rational subjects from their obligation, as Kant would see it, to find a "way out" of their immaturity (Foucault, 2010: 305). As Callon and Latour suggest, "[a] black box contains that which no longer needs to be reconsidered" (1981: 285). In discussions on technical or commercial black boxes and transparency, one of the arguments often raised in defense of the black box is the necessity to keep details closed and obscured. In writing about trade secrets, historian of science Peter Galison (2004) makes the point that secrecy is legitimized as a form of "antiepistemology," knowledge that must be covered and obscured in order to protect a commercial formula or the like.[5] Indeed, it seems that the entire figure of the black box is premised on the notion of antiepistemology. Without secrecy, systems would cease to work properly. From a more technical standpoint, making the inner workings obscure helps to remedy attempts at gaming the system. As Kroll et al. write, "Secrecy discourages strategic behavior by participants in the system and prevents violations of legal restrictions on disclosure of data" (2016: 16). Finally, from an engineering point of view, concealing or obfuscating large portions of code is a necessary feature of software development. As Galloway points out, "obfuscation, or 'information hiding,' is employed in order to make code more modular and abstract and thus easier to maintain" (2006a: 323). Black boxing code, in other words, reduces both the cognitive load of programmers and enables the writing of new portions of the code, or the design new features or functionalities without having to think about every little detail of how the systems work.

When algorithms are positioned as black boxes in current discourses, it is usually to problematize the fact that many have harmful or discriminatory effects. Particularly within legal circles, repeated calls have been made for opening up the black box of algorithms. As Pasquale argues, "without knowing what Google actually does when it ranks sites, we cannot assess when it is acting in good faith to help users, and when it is biasing results to favor its own commercial interests" (2015: 9). For Pasquale, what is worrisome is the knowledge asymmetry inherent in the black box society or what he calls the "one-way mirror" of knowledge: "Important corporate actors have unprecedented knowledge of the minutiae of our daily lives, while we know little to nothing about how they use this knowledge to influence the important decisions that we—and they—make" (2015: 9). This knowledge asymmetry impinges new power relations—not just between corporations knowing more and more about the people it monitors but also between corporations themselves, ultimately undermining robust competition (Pasquale, 2015: 83). Thus, legal scholars (especially, in the US context) are now intensifying calls for greater transparency, asking corporations to make their workings more transparent (see, for example, Balkin, 2016; Benjamin, 2013; Citron & Pasquale, 2014; Cohen, 2016; Mehra, 2015).[6] As Pasquale provocatively puts it, "you can't form a trusting relationship with a black box" (2015: 83).

What, then, are some of the proposed solutions to the pervasive black boxing of technical details in the "algorithmic society" (Balkin, 2016)? For Pasquale, black boxes must be revealed in order to counteract any wrongdoings, discrimination, or bias these systems may contain: "algorithms should be open for inspection—if not by the public at large, at least by some trusted auditor" (2015: 141). Here, opening up may simply involve making source code accessible. As Citron and Pasquale argue in the context of detecting bias in credit-scoring systems, "To know for sure, we would need access to the source code, programmers' notes and algorithms at the heart of credit-scoring systems to test for human bias, which of course we do not have" (2014: 14). Others are more skeptical about the demands for transparent source code, pointing out that such calls are not taking account of the many adequate reasons for not making every detail fully transparent (Kroll et al., 2016). However, opening up the black box of algorithms may also imply opening up the conditions under which algorithms can be legally audited from the outside. As a recent lawsuit filed in US federal court by researchers Sandvig and colleagues attest, the law may constitute an additional barrier to access—in this case, "preventing researchers from collecting data to determine whether online algorithms result in discrimination" (Grauer, 2016). While the many calls for greater transparency certainly hold merit, what I want to argue in the following is that knowing algorithms need not necessitate opening the black box. In fact, the black box may not even be the most adequate notion to use when thinking about the ontology and epistemology of algorithms.

UNKNOWING ALGORITHMS

While it is true that proprietary algorithms are hard to know, it does not make them *unknowable*. Perhaps paradoxically, I want to suggest that, while algorithms are not unknowable, the first step in knowing algorithms is to *un-know* them. By unknowing, I mean something akin to making the familiar slightly more unfamiliar. In the previous chapter, we saw how algorithms mean different things to different stakeholders and people from different disciplines. This is not to say that a computer scientist needs to dismiss her knowledge of algorithms or that social scientists should somehow dismiss their ways of seeing algorithms as objects of social concern. "Unknowing" also does not imply "blackboxing" the black box even more. Rather, "unknowing" means seeing differently, looking elsewhere, or not even looking at all. As much as calls for transparency attempt to make the object of concern *more* visible, visibility, too, may conceal. As Strathern notes, "there is nothing innocent about making the invisible visible" (2000a: 309). Too much information may blind us from seeing more clearly and, ultimately, from understanding (Strathern, 2000a; Tsoukas, 1997). Unknowing does not foreclose knowledge but challenges it. In this sense, the kind of unknowing I have in mind can be likened to Bataille's notion of "nonknowledge" as "a form of excess that challenges both our thinking and our ethics" (Yusoff, 2009: 1014). For Bataille, nonknowledge is not something that must be eradicated but embraced as an enriching experience (1986, 2004).[7] Baudrillard develops the distinction between "obscenity" and "seduction" in response to Bataille's thinking about the knowledge/nonknowledge divide, stating how "nonknowledge is the seductive and magical aspect of knowledge" (Juergenson & Rey, 2012: 290). In other words, we might think of "unknowing algorithms" as a form of distancing or a form of engaging with the seductive qualities of algorithms that cannot always be explained in fully rational terms. On a practical level, unknowing algorithms may simply imply opening the black box of one's own assumptions about knowing algorithms. For a computer scientist, this may imply knowing more about the social dynamics impinging on the data that algorithms are designed to process. Conversely, for social scientists and humanities scholars, it might imply knowing more about how computers and algorithms make decisions (Kroll et al., 2016: 14). On a more theoretical and conceptual level, unknowing algorithms implies confronting the limits of the metaphor of the black box itself. Grappling with what Karin Knorr-Cetina calls *negative knowledge*, the task is to identify the limits and imperfections of the black box metaphor. For Knorr-Cetina:

> [N]egative knowledge is not nonknowledge, but knowledge of the limits of knowing, of the mistakes we make in trying to know, of the things that interfere with our knowing, of what we are not interested in and do not really want to know. (1999: 64)

Unknowing algorithms as a first step in knowing them would be to engage more actively in addressing the things that seem to interfere with or keep us from knowing. Indeed, what I want to argue is that the metaphor of the black box itself constitutes such interference. In our attempts to open the black box, what frequently gets ignored is the question of whether the metaphor of the black box holds at all. It might be easier and more tangible to think of algorithms *as* black boxes because it allows the analyst, policymaker, or outside critic to call for more transparency and openness as a practical means for making powerbrokers accountable. For all its alleged blackness, the box not only conceals the code the critics want to reveal, it also conceals the fact that algorithms may not even be as black or as boxy as they are often held out to be.

Multiple, Processual, Heterogeneous
RELATIONAL ONTOLOGY AND ALGORITHMS

The central focus in this chapter has to do with the possibilities and challenges of knowing algorithms that are commonly described as black boxes. What I have argued so far is that the metaphor of the black box conceals its own limitations as an epistemic device. By encouraging the Enlightenment impetus of unveiling—of opening—the black box positions visibility as a conduit for knowledge and control. Algorithms, though, are not stand-alone boxes but always part of complex systems. They often operate as a collection of algorithms in what are, ultimately, networked systems. This is particularly true for the algorithms underlying platforms such as Facebook, Twitter, Netflix, or YouTube. These systems do not contain one algorithm but a collection of algorithms, working together to create a unified experience. As product owners at Netflix, Gomez-Uribe and Hunt write, "our recommender system consists of a variety of algorithms that collectively define the Netflix experience" (2015: 2). To give an impression of the many algorithms at play in designing this overall Netflix experience, Gomez-Uribe and Hunt list at least eight different algorithms, including the personalized video ranker (PVR), which orders the entire catalogue of videos for each member in a personalized way; the Top-N Video ranker, which produces the recommendations in the Top Picks; and the page generation algorithm, which works to construct every single page of recommendations. Similarly, YouTube's video recommendation system is not powered by one single algorithm but many, including the related/recommended video suggestion algorithm, search algorithms, and Content ID (Davidson et al., 2010). Facebook is no exception. As technology reporter Will Oremus (2016) writes in *Slate*: "the algorithm is really a collection of hundreds of smaller algorithms solving the smaller problems that make up the larger problem of what stories to show people."

Their multiplicity, moreover, pertains to their constantly changing nature. As we saw in the previous chapter, Facebook is routinely described as *a work in progress*. This is not just to be understood as innovation speak but, quite literally, as an integrated business plan constantly to improve its algorithms in order to retain users. This ethic of continuous change is by no means unique to Facebook: It is part and parcel of how most online platforms now develop their products. So-called A/B testing is integral to the culture of experimentation that governs platforms as a means for assessing and comparing how well different versions of the algorithm perform.[8] A/B tests basically work like focus groups in which people are asked for their opinion on a certain product—with the important difference that most people participating in an A/B test are not aware of it. As *Wired* reporter Brian Christian (2012) explains:

> Without being told, a fraction of users are diverted to a slightly different version of a given web page and their behavior compared against the mass of users on the standard site. If the new version proves superior—gaining more clicks, longer visits, more purchases—it will displace the original; if the new version is inferior, it's quietly phased out without most users ever seeing it.

These "invisible" experimentations have now become such an important part of product development on the Web that, for a company like Netflix, A/B test results are seen as their "most important source of information for making product decisions" (Gomez-Uribe & Hunt, 2015: 11). Typically performed as a test of two variants and on two user groups, A/B tests epitomize the logic of constant change. At any given time, multiples of these tests are executed in parallel. At Netflix, these tests are not just performed on two variants but often include 5 to 10 versions of the algorithm and, typically, run for a period of 2 to 6 months (Gomez-Uribe & Hunt, 2015: 9-12). As a result, there is not one "Netflix" to speak of but many different permutations (Seaver, 2013). The culture of experimentation complicates any effort to know algorithms, as the question inevitably arises as to *which version*, what test group, or what timeframe we are talking about. What I want to suggest, then, is that the algorithms operating in contemporary media platforms are simply neither black nor box but *eventful*. For a conceptualization of algorithms, this implies a rejection of essences and permanence and an ontological shift towards a world of process and relations.

THE EVENTFULNESS OF ALGORITHMS

Theoretically, this ontological shift is indebted to diverse but interrelated perspectives, including actor-network theory and post-ANT (Latour, 2005; Mol, 1999; Law; 1999), process-relational philosophy (Deleuze & Guattari, 1987; Simondon, 2011; Whitehead, 1978), agential realism (Barad, 2003; 2007), and new materialism (Bennett, et al., 2010; Braidotti, 2006).[9] While these perspectives do not represent a homogeneous style of thought or a single theoretical position, even among the thinkers referenced here as belonging to a specific category, they all, in one way or another, emphasize a relational ontology and the extension of power and agency to a heterogeneity of actors, including non-humans or the more-than-human.[10]

In arguing for an understanding of algorithms as eventful, I am drawing on a Whiteheadian sensibility that puts emphasis on processes of *becoming* rather than being. For Whitehead (1978), *actual entities* or actual occasions (such as algorithms) are combinations of heterogeneous elements (or what he calls *prehensions*).[11] Actual entities are only knowable in their becoming as opposed to their being. As Whitehead suggests, "how an actual entity becomes constitutes what that actual entity is. Its 'being' is constituted by its 'becoming'. This is the 'principle' of process" (1978: 23). This view of entities as processes breaks with the more traditional view of entities as substance and essence. Indeed, "'actual entities' are the final real thing of which the world is made up. There is no going behind actual entities to find anything more real" (Whitehead, 1978: 18). This has important consequences for the analytical treatment of algorithms, since there is nothing "more real" behind the ways in which they actualize to form novel forms of togetherness.[12] It is not enough simply to state that algorithms are eventful, understood as constituents that co-become. Analytical choices have to be made as to *which* relations and *which* actors to include in the study of actual entities. As Mike Michael suggests, the value of studying processes or events "rests not so much on their empirical 'accuracy' as on their capacity to produce 'orderings and disorderings' out of which certain actualities (such as practices, discourses and politics) emerge" (2004: 9, 19).[13] What this means for an understanding of algorithms is a shift in attention away from questions of what algorithms are to *what they do* as part of specific situations.

At the most basic level, algorithms do things by virtue of embodying a command structure (Goffey, 2008: 17). For the programmer, algorithms solve computational problems by processing an input toward an output. For users, algorithms primarily do things by virtue of assistance—that is, they help users find something they are searching for, direct attention to the "most important" content, organize information in a meaningful way, provide and limit access to information, or make recommendations and suggestions for what to watch or buy. The doing of algorithms can also be seen in the various ways they shape experience and make people feel a certain way—for example, in how they animate feelings of frustration, curiosity, or joy (see chapter 5). As Introna suggests, "the doing of algorithms is not simply the execution of instructions (determined by the programmers)," algorithms "also enact the objects they are supposed to reflect or express" (2016: 4). The notion of performativity that Introna draws on here posits that algorithms, by virtue of expressing something, also have the power to act upon that world.[14] When algorithms become part of people's everyday lives, incorporated into financial markets or entangled in knowledge production, they do something to those domains.

What algorithms do in these cases, however, cannot simply be understood by opening up the black box, as it were. This is not because, as Winner (1993) suggests, we risk finding it empty when we open the box; but, rather, as Latour (1999) reminds us, all black boxes are black boxes because they obscure the networks and assemblages they assume and were constituted by. For Latour, all scientific and technical work is made invisible by its own success through a process of blackboxing. In a much-cited example of an overhead projector breaking down, Latour suggests that the black box reveals itself as what it really is—not a stable thing but, rather, an assemblage of many interrelated parts (1999: 183). When a machine runs smoothly, nobody pays much attention, and the actors and work required to make it run smoothly disappear from view (Latour, 1999: 34). For Latour, the black box ultimately hides its constitution and character as a network, while blackboxing refers to the process in which practices become reified. If the metaphor of the black box is too readily used as a way of critiquing algorithms, Latour's notion of blackboxing reminds us that we might want to scrutinize critically the ways in which algorithms *become*.

A core tenet of a relational ontology is the principle of relational materialism, the idea that "objects are no mere props for performance but parts and parcel of hybrid assemblages endowed with diffused personhood and relational agency" (Vannini, 2015: 5). Concepts such as sociotechnical and sociomateriality are often used to express the idea of a radical symmetry between human and nonhuman actors.[15] According to this view, the social and technical are not seen as separate entities that can be considered independently of each other. The social and technical are always already engaging in symbiotic relationships organized in networks, assemblages, or hybrids.[16] What is important on a relational account is that the enactive powers of new assemblages or composite entities cannot merely be reduced to its constituent parts. Rather, these new composite entities are able to "produce new territorial organisations, new behaviours, new expressions, new actors and new realities" (Müller, 2015: 29). This agential force is, perhaps, most explicitly expressed in the concept of assemblage or, more specifically the French term *agencement*. As Callon points out, "agencement has the same root as agency: agencements are arrangements endowed with the capacity of acting in different ways depending on their configuration" (2007: 320).

These discussions, of course, raise the tricky question of how we should think about agency in the first place. After all, it is not for nothing that agency has been called "the most difficult problem there is in philosophy" (Latour, 2005: 51). If algorithms are multiple and part of hybrid assemblages or even hybrid assemblages themselves, then *where* is agency located? Who or what is acting when we say that algorithms do this or that? Although scholars committed to a relational ontology may differ in terms of the ontological status they ascribe to entities and relations, the general answer would be to see agency as *distributed*.[17] For a theory of the agential capacities of algorithms, adopting a relational view implies discarding any "neatly ordered flow of agency" (Introna, 2016: 9). As Karen Barad puts it, agency is not an attribute that someone or something may possess but, rather, a name for the process of the ongoing reconfiguration of the world (2003: 818). In a similar vein, actor-network theory sees agency as a mediated achievement, brought about through forging associations (Müller, 2015: 30). Anything—whether human or nonhuman—can potentially forge an association. As Barad emphasizes, "agency is not aligned with human intentionality or subjectivity" (2003: 826). According to Latour: "*any thing* that does modify a state of affairs by making a difference is an actor"; one needs simply to ask whether something "makes a difference in the course of some other agent's action or not" (2005: 71). At the core of a relational ontology lies the importance of acknowledging the relationality and agential capacities of nonhumans. Perhaps more so than any other concept, the notion of assemblage has served as way to account for the ways in which relations are assembled for different purposes. Deleuze and Parnet view assemblage as a "multiplicity which is made up of many heterogeneous terms and which establishes liaisons, relations between them," where the only unity "is that of co-functioning" (2007: 69). This notion of co-functioning usefully describes "how different agents within the assemblage may possess different resources and capacities to act" (Anderson et al., 2012: 181). Viewed in these terms, the agency of algorithms cannot be located in the algorithm as such but in the "ever-changing outcome of its enactment" (Passoth et al., 2012: 4).

The implications of viewing agency as distributed are far from trivial. When we hear that "algorithms discriminate" (Miller, 2015) or that "discrimination is baked into algorithms" (Kirchner, 2015), it may easily be understood as saying algorithms possess the agency to discriminate. While cases such as the Google "gorilla" incident (see chapter 2), Amazon's exclusion of predominately black ZIP codes from their same-day deliveries, or Google's display of ads for arrest records when distinctively black names are searched (Sweeney, 2013) leave much to be desired in terms of algorithmic fairness and performance, the question of who or what is actually discriminating in these cases is not as straightforward to answer as the media headlines seem to suggest.

Take the controversy over Facebook's trending feature. In May 2016, Facebook hit the news (again) after it became clear that their trending feature was not, in fact, "the result of a neutral, objective algorithm" but, partly, the accomplishment of human curation and oversight.[18] Facebook had employed journalism graduates to keep checks on algorithmically produced trending topics, approving the topics and writing headlines to describe them. The problem was that the human editors employed to oversee the trending topics happened to lean to the political left, and this, according to the news stories, could be seen in the kinds of stories that were made to "trend." As the Gizmodo article first reported, "In other words, Facebook's news section operates like a traditional newsroom, reflecting the biases of its workers and the institutional imperatives of the corporation" (Nunez, 2016). Shortly after the story broke, Tom Stocky, a Facebook executive, wrote that "there are rigorous guidelines in place for the review team to ensure consistency and neutrality" (Stocky, 2016). The incident also prompted a letter from the US Senate to Mark Zuckerberg, demanding more transparency about how Facebook operates. The letter, signed by Republican Senator John Thune, asked Facebook to elaborate on questions such as: "Have Facebook news curators in fact manipulated the content of the Trending Topics section" and "what steps will Facebook take to hold the responsible individuals accountable?" As Thune later told reporters, any level of subjectivity associated with the trending topics would indeed be "to mislead the American public" (Corasaniti & Isaac, 2016).

What remained puzzling throughout the ordeal was the apparent lack of vocabulary available to talk about what it is that algorithms do or are even capable of doing, as exemplified in the repeated attribution of bias either to *the* algorithm or to the humans involved. Words such as bias, neutrality, manipulation, and subjectivity abound, making the controversy one of locating agency in the right place. The prevailing sense in the discourse surrounding the event seemed to be that Facebook should not claim to use algorithms to make decisions when, in fact, humans make the decisions. Of course, what was being slightly overlooked in all of this was the fact that algorithms are always already made, maintained, and sustained by humans. Yet, if only the responsible *people* could be held accountable, the story went, it would make it easier to control or regulate such "manipulations" and "subjective orderings" in the future. From a relational perspective, however, determining the origin of action as if it belonged to one source only would be misleading. After all, as Latour puts it, "to use the word 'actor' means that it's never clear who and what is acting when we act since an actor on stage is never alone in acting" (2005: 46). The stage in this case was clearly composed of a myriad of participants, including journalism graduates, professional culture, political beliefs, work guidelines, the trending product team, Facebook executives and management, algorithms, users, news agencies, and so on.

So, then, what about the supposed bias of algorithmic processes? As John Naughton, professor of the public understanding of technology, writes in an op-ed in the *Guardian*, bias or, human values, is embedded in algorithms right from the beginning simply because engineers are humans:

> Any algorithm that has to make choices has criteria that are specified by its designers. And those criteria are expressions of human values. Engineers

may think they are 'neutral', but long experience has shown us they are babes in the woods of politics, economics and ideology. (Naughton, 2016)

Of course, with machine-learning algorithms, some would, perhaps, be tempted to argue that, because the engineers or designers of the system are not necessarily human, concerns over the influence of human values or bias becomes less of a problem. However, just as algorithms may "inherit the prejudices of prior decision-makers," they may "reflect the widespread biases that persist in society at large" (Barocas & Selbst, 2016: 1). To understand where bias might be located in the case of the Facebook trending topic controversy, it certainly helps to know something about *how* the trending topic algorithm works. It helps to know, for instance, that, at the time of the controversy, Facebook relied on a few news outlets to determine whether "a subject is newsworthy or not" (Statt, 2016). This meant that heavy hitters such as the *New York Times* and CNN—traditional media institutions—played a significant part in determining whether something would actually be considered a trend or not. As suggested by the leaked internal documents used by Facebook to guide the work of its trending topic editors, "The document designates 10 outlets as particularly central, and instructs editors to only label a topic as a 'National Story' or 'Major Story' based on how many of those publications placed the news on their front page" (Brandom, 2016). These guidelines and the information about the work practices of editors and the types of decisions they have to make when faced with labeling something as particularly newsworthy or not sheds important light on the different values, mechanisms, and ideologies at play in a seemingly neutral and objective decision-making process. Furthermore, it helps to know how central a role users have in shaping algorithmic outcomes. As reporter Ezra Klein puts it, the *user* is "Facebook's most biased curator" (Klein, 2016). Users matter because it is their data, their clicking behavior, preferences, network relations, and communicative actions that provide the data for algorithms to act on.

Although Facebook's news feed is often heralded as a prime example of algorithmic finesse, the feed is far from simply automatic or without human intervention. As with the trending section, Facebook enlists human intervention of the news feed as well. During the summer of 2014, Facebook set up a "feed quality panel," a group of several hundred people located in Knoxville, Tennessee, whom the company paid to provide detailed feedback on what they were seeing in their news feed (Oremus, 2016). Later, Facebook took its panel nationwide, paying a representative sample of users to rate and review their feeds on a daily basis. They even expanded the panel overseas. More recently, Facebook has been running a survey asking a subset of users to choose between two posts that are shown side-by-side and pick the one that appeals to them the most. Facebook is not the only platform that "humanizes" its algorithmic systems. Netflix, for example, employs a wide range of "taggers," whose responsibility it is to assess the genre, tone, and style of a film's content to help determine what users might want to watch next. Humans are also in the loop when it comes to music recommendations in which music is often presented as belonging to a special category of content that computers cannot necessarily "understand." One of the selling points of Apple Music, the music-streaming service developed by Apple and launched in the summer of 2015, was the fact that it relied heavily on human curators and radio hosts to provide the recommendations as opposed to mere algorithms. In an interview with the *Wall Street Journal*, Apple CEO Tim Cook claimed, "People love the human curation" aspect of the streaming service (WSJ, 2015). Similarly, Ajaj Kalia, product head of Taste Profiles at Spotify, thinks that for "something as emotional as music […] it is crucial to keep humans in the loop" (Popper, 2015). Because computers "cannot truly appreciate music," Spotify employs a team of 32 music experts around the world to curate playlists that are updated on a weekly basis (Knight, 2015). Around the same time that Apple Music was launched, Spotify introduced Discover Weekly, an algorithmically generated playlist that would get closer to cracking the emotional standard of human taste. The algorithms behind Discover Weekly provide users with a recommended playlist every Monday, based on the user's unique taste profile, compiled by comparing her tastes to the playlists of other users who have featured the same songs and artists that she liked (Heath, 2015; Pasick, 2015). Then, the algorithm goes through the other songs that the related people have added to their playlists but the target user has not yet heard, based on the assumption that there is a good chance she might like them, too (Popper, 2015). Matthew Ogle, who oversees Discover Weekly, describes this process as one of "magic filtering" (Pasick, 2015). However, algorithms are just one aspect to this magic. As the majority of media reports on Discover Weekly emphasize, the main ingredient is other people and their curated playlists. Reminiscent of what seems to be a broader rhetorical strategy surrounding big data and algorithms on part of media platforms, Ogle insists that thinking of Discover Weekly in terms of algorithms misses the point since the "whole thing is built on data created by humans— it's just that algorithms are connecting the dots on a massive scale […] Discover Weekly is *humans all the way down*" (Heath, 2015, my emphasis). These examples do not merely show how humans are always already implicated in algorithms, whether as end-users providing the data input from which algorithms learn or the human experts employed to help algorithms compute things such as musical taste or the tone of a film, they are also meant to illustrate the pothole of attributing agency to either an algorithm or a human. The point here is not that we need to choose to whom or what agency most obviously belongs. It is not that agency is with the designers, the users or the algorithm. A relational perspective precisely "disavows any essentialist or isolated explanation of either human or nonhuman agency" (Schubert, 2012: 126). Rather, it is a matter of accounting for the manner in which the assemblage or coming together of entities becomes more or less human, more or less nonhuman. As it was suggested in the previous chapter, algorithms have a variable ontology, meaning that the question of where agency operates cannot be conclusively answered. What needs explaining, then, is the continuum of variation. In the following, I want to suggest that one way of answering what makes an algorithm more or less technical/nonhuman or more or less social/human can be done by shifting attention away from questions of *where* agency is located to questions of *when* agency is mobilized and on whose behalf.

When Is an Algorithm?

The case of Facebook's trending controversy and other instances of "humanizing algorithms" do not merely call the source of agency into question but suggest that the more politically poignant question to ask is *when* agency is located, on whose behalf and for what purpose? The real controversy was not the fact that Facebook employs journalism graduates to intervene in an algorithmic decision-making process by adding their editorial human judgments of newsworthiness to the mix. The controversy lies in the selective human and nonhuman agency. What became apparent in the public reaction to the Facebook trending controversy was the fact that algorithms only matter sometimes. This, I want to suggest, constitutes an important dimension of thinking around the politics of algorithms—politics not as *what* algorithms do per se but *how* and under what circumstances different aspects of algorithms and the algorithmic are *made* available—or *un*available—to specific actors in particular settings.[19] By shifting attention away from the proper source of action toward the practices of mobilizing sources of action in specific circumstances, we might be able to understand both how and when algorithms come to matter (the mattering of algorithms is taken up again in chapter 6).[20] Why is it that, sometimes, an algorithm is blamed for discrimination when, on a similar but different occasion, a human is "accused" of bias? Why is it contentious that Facebook employs journalism graduates in the process of curating the trending feature when, in the context of news organizations, the opposite seems to be considered problematic? Put differently, why is it OK for Facebook to use algorithms when doing the same thing is considered problematic for a news organization? These and similar questions cannot simply be answered by adhering to a vocabulary of essences. Algorithms are not given; they are not either mathematical expressions *or* expressions of human intent but emerge as situated, ongoing accomplishments. That is, they emerge as more or less technical/nonhuman or more or less social/human because of what else they are related to. In the case of the Facebook trending topic incident, the algorithms shifted its configuration as a result of controversy. In the face of widespread accusations against the subjective biases of the human editors, Facebook decided to fire the 26 journalism graduates contracted to edit and write short descriptions for the trending topics module. In a bid to reduce bias, Facebook announced, instead, that they would replace them with robots. While still keeping humans in the loop, "a more algorithmically driven process," according to Facebook, would "allow our team to make fewer individual decisions about topics" (Facebook, 2016). What is of interest in this case is not whether algorithms or humans govern Facebook's trending topic but how the different categories were enlisted and made relevant in the context of the controversy. That is, the "algorithm" emerged as objective and neutral while humans were seen as subjective and biased. The point is that there is nothing inherently neutral about algorithms or biased about humans, these descriptive markers emerge from particular contexts and practices. It could have been otherwise.[21]

From the perspective of relational materialism, the questions that matter the most are "not philosophical in character, but political" (Mol, 2013: 381). Returning to the notion of ontological politics introduced at the end of the previous chapter, engaging with the question of how algorithms come to matter in contemporary society is not about trying to define what they are or at what points they act but, rather, about questioning the ways in which they are enacted and come together to make different versions of reality. I think what the many contrasting examples of controversies involving the algorithm-human continuum show is how algorithms are not inherently good or bad, neutral or biased, but are made to appear in one way or the other, depending on a whole range of different factors, interests, stakeholders, strategies and, indeed, politics. The term "ontological politics" is precisely meant to highlight how realities are never given but shaped and emerge through interactions.[22] Instead of determining *who* acts (or discriminates, for that matter), the interesting question is *what* and *when* an actor becomes in the particular ways in which the entity is active (Passoth et al., 2012: 4).

By shifting attention away from asking *what* and *where* agency is to *when* agency is and *to whom* agency belongs in specific situations, we may begin to see how the notion of algorithms as black boxes may not just be an ontological and epistemological claim but, ultimately, a political one as well. As I said in the beginning of this chapter, positioning something as a black box serves different functions. The black box of algorithm is not simply an unknown but, in many cases, constitutes what Linsey McGoey (2012) has called a *strategic unknown*, understood as the strategic harnessing of ignorance. As McGoey asserts, strategic unknowns highlight the ways in which "cultivating ignorance is often more advantageous, both institutionally and personally, than cultivating knowledge" (2012: 555). In the case of disaster management, for example, experts' claims of ignorance soften any alleged responsibility for the disaster or scandal in question. By mobilizing unknowns strategically, organizations and individuals can insist that detection or prior knowledge was impossible. These forms of ignorance are frequently mobilized in discourses on algorithms and software as well.

In fact, it seems that machine learning and the field of artificial intelligence often appear as entire fields of strategic unknowns. At the most fundamental level, the operations of machine-learning algorithms seem to preclude any form of certainty. Because the machine learns "on its own" without being explicitly programmed to do so, there is no way of knowing what exactly caused a certain outcome. As Dourish reflects on the advent of machine learning. "During my years of computer science training, to have an algorithm was to know something. Algorithms were definitive procedures that lead to predictable results. The outcome of the algorithmic operation was known and certain" (2016: 7). Machine-learning techniques, on the other hand, produce unknowns:

> When my credit card company deems a particular purchase or stream of purchases "suspicious" and puts a security hold on my card, the company cannot explain exactly what was suspicious–they know that there's something odd but they don't know what it is. (2016: 7)

Indeed, in context of machine learning, the decisional rule emerges "from the specific data under analysis, in ways that no human can explain" (Kroll et al., 2016: 6). While this fundamental uncertainty may be disgruntling to those interested in knowing algorithms, it can also be used to restore what McGoey calls *knowledge alibis*, "the ability to defend one's ignorance by mobilizing the ignorance of higher-placed experts" (2012: 563-564). As McGoey writes:

> A curious feature of knowledge alibis is that experts who *should* know something are particularly useful for *not* knowing it. This is because their expertise helps to legitimate claims that a phenomenon is impossible to know, rather than simply unknowable by the unenlightened. If the experts didn't know it, nobody could. (2012: 564, emphasis in the original)

People routinely defend their lack of knowledge of algorithms by alluding to the notion that they could not have known because no one else can, either. As the title of a recent article in *The Atlantic* tellingly puts it: "Not even the people who write algorithms really know how they work" (LaFrance, 2015). To what extent does this notion of unknowability hold true? While it might indeed be difficult to explain what patterns in the data are being caught by the model of a machine learning algorithm as the above statements seem to suggest, the general principles and operational logics of these systems are very well-known. That's why they are used in the first place. The claim that no human can really explain the working of an algorithm or the decisional rules emerging from pattern recognition might be more about the organizational construction of software than the algorithm itself. As discussed in the previous chapter, machine learning systems of massive scale are really networked sets of machine-learning algorithms that are wired together to compute some emergent property (e.g., search). When we are dealing with a newsfeed or a search engine we never deal with single algorithms that train single models from a table of data. They are machine learning systems pieced together and layered like Lego. Often, several machine-learning systems are doing the same task, but a user will only see the results aggregated from the top-three performing ones. If any of the top three start to perform poorly, they will fall out and be replaced automatically.

What we need to remember is that all of these layers and structures are built by people in teams, and so the ability for one person to understand everything is very much the same challenge as understanding how the University of Copenhagen works. Yet at the same time teams can build heuristic understanding of their algorithmic systems, feelings of what might cause it to break or what is causing the bottleneck, which allow them to work and do their job.[23]

The ignorance of higher-placed experts, however, should not detract us from knowing differently. Now, if the exact configuration of the algorithmic logic cannot be easily traced—say, for example, by examining what the machine learned at different layers in a neural net, it should not keep us from interrogating the oddity itself, particularly since the allusion to ignorance often comes in handy for the platforms themselves. As Christian Sandvig (2015) suggests, "platform providers often encourage the notion that their algorithms operate without any human intervention, and that they are not designed but rather 'discovered' or invented as the logical pinnacle of science and engineering research in the area." When things do not go exactly as planned and platforms are accused of censorship, discrimination or bias, the algorithm is often conveniently enlisted as a strategic unknown. Of course, as Callon and Latour aptly remind us, "black boxes never remain fully closed or properly fastened [. . .] but macro-actors can do as if they were closed and dark" (1981: 285). It is certainly odd that a particular purchase is deemed suspicious, or that a credit card company cannot explain why an algorithm came to this or that conclusion. However, the knowledge of an algorithmic event does not so much hinge on its causes as it does on the capacity to produce certain "orderings and disorderings" (Michael, 2004). As an event whose identity is uncertain, there is an opportunity to ask new questions. In the case of the credit card company, the question might not necessarily be phrased in terms of why the algorithm came to a certain conclusion but what that conclusion suggests about the kinds of realities that are emerging because people are using algorithms and what these algorithmic practices do to various people.

In terms of transparency, questions also need to be asked of functions and expectations. When the Norwegian newspaper *Aftenposten* and Norway's Prime Minister Erna Solberg called out Facebook in September 2016, accusing its algorithms of censoring the iconic Pulitzer Prize image "Terror of War," they did so because they expected the algorithm to behave in a specific way. An algorithm, they suggested, should have been able to distinguish between an award-winning iconic image and "normal nudity." Not only was this incident, to which I shall return later in chapter 6, yet another example of the differential enactment of agency as exemplified in the question of whether the fault was with the algorithms or the humans: It also shows that, sometimes, what there is to know about algorithms may not be about the algorithm itself but, rather, our own limits of understanding. Should we, perhaps, not just worry about algorithms being wrong but also ask whether they do what they are supposed to do? Why was Facebook called out on censoring an image of a naked girl

when, in fact, this is what is expected of them? Knowing algorithms, I want to suggest, may be just as much about interrogating "negative knowledge" in Knorr-
Cetina's sense as it is about trying to peel the layers of a neural network or getting
access to the actual source code. In other words, when trying to know algorithms we
also have to take into account what things interfere with our knowing, what we are
not interested in, what we do not want to know and why.

What the figure of the black box conceals is not just the inner workings of algorithms but also the ways in which the unknown can be used strategically as a resource to maintain control or deny liability in certain situations. In suggesting, as
I have done, that the black box metaphor constitutes a red herring of sorts, the
metaphor itself becomes a strategic unknown, enabling knowledge to be deflected
and obscured. What needs to be critically scrutinized, then, is not necessarily the
hidden content of the box but the very political and social practices that help sus-
tain the notion of algorithms as black boxes. The question is not simply whether
we *can* know algorithms but *when* the realm of its intelligibility is made more or
less probable. That is, when are algorithms framed as unknowns, for whom and for
what purpose?

Three Methodological Tactics

Despite the obvious epistemological limits addressed so far, I want to finish this
chapter by offering three methodological tactics for (un)knowing algorithms.
Broadly construed, these tactics correspond to the different kinds of ignorance discussed throughout this chapter and focus on tackling the seemingly black-boxed
nature of algorithms. These tactics are not meant as an exhaustive list but as a few
possible methodological routes that scholars may take when they examine algorithms as objects for cultural analysis.

"REVERSE ENGINEERING" KNOWN UNKNOWNS

Instead of following the Enlightenment impetus seeking to reveal the origin of
actions, one way to proceed would be to follow the cybernetic lead. Cybernetics
is the science of control and communication, in the animal and the machine
(Wiener, 1948). It is concerned with understanding the relationship and feedback
mechanisms between a system and its environment. As the neuropsychiatrist Ross
Ashby put it in *An Introduction to Cybernetics*, cybernetics is not concerned with
what things are but what they do (1999 [1956]: 1). In the book, Ashby dedicated a
whole chapter to the problem of the black box, presented as a challenge to the engineer who had "to deduce what he can of its contents" (1999 [1956]: 86). For Ashby,
the black box was not necessarily an obstacle but simply part of everyday life. The
black box is not an exception but the norm. Lots of things are seemingly hidden and

inaccessible—that is, until we find the leaks, cracks, and ruptures that allow us to see into them.

The first step in knowing algorithms is not to regard the "impossibility of seeing inside the black box" as an epistemological limit that interrupts any "futile attempts at knowledge acquisition" (von Hilgers, 2011: 43). As Ashby recognized: "In our daily lives we are confronted at every turn with systems whose internal mechanisms are not fully open to inspection, and which must be treated by the methods appropriate to the Black Box" (1999: 86). Because opacity, secrecy, and invisibility are not epistemic anomalies but a basic condition of human life, the black box is not something to be feared but something that "corresponds to new insights" (von Hilgers, 2011: 32) When confronted with a black box, the appropriate task for the experimenter, as Ashby saw it, is not necessarily to know exactly what is inside the box but to ask, instead, which properties can actually be discovered and which remain undiscoverable (Ashby, 1999). Because what matters is not the thing but what it does, the cybernetic lead does not ask us to reveal the exact content of the box but to experiment with its inputs and outputs.

What can be discovered and described about algorithms differs from context to context with varying degrees of access and availability of information. However, even in the case of seemingly closed and hidden systems such as Facebook or Google, there are plenty of things that can be known. Speculative experimentation and playing around with algorithms to figure out how they work are not just reserved for hackers, gamers, spammers and search engine optimizers (SEO). In the spirit of reverse engineering—"the process of extracting the knowledge or design blueprints from anything man-made" (Eilam 2005: 3)—we might want to approach algorithms from the question of how they work and their general "operational logics" (Wardrip-Fruin, 2009). There are already some very instructive examples of "reverse engineering" algorithms within the domain of journalism and journalism studies (Angwin et al., 2016; Diakopoulos, 2014) and in related academic calls for "algorithm audits" (Hamilton et al, 2014; Sandvig, et al., 2014).

Mythologizing the workings of machines, however, does not help, nor should we think of algorithmic logics as somehow more hidden and black-boxed than the human mind. While we cannot ask the algorithm in the same way we may ask humans about their beliefs and values, we may indeed attempt to find other ways of making it "speak." Similar to the way ethnographers map people's values and beliefs, I think of mapping the operational logics of algorithms in terms of *technography*.[24] As Latour puts it, "specific tricks have to be invented to make them [technology] talk, that is, to offer descriptions of themselves, to produce scripts of what they are making others—humans or non-humans—do" (2005: 79). Technography, as I use the term, is a way of describing and observing the workings of technology in order to examine the interplay between a diverse set of actors (both human and nonhuman). While the ethnographer seeks to understand culture primarily through the meanings attached to the world by people, the technographic inquiry starts by asking what algorithms are suggestive of. Although he does not use the term himself, I think Bernhard Rieder's (2017) way of scrutinizing diverse and general algorithmic techniques could be thought of as an attempt to describe the "worldviews of algorithms" I have in mind when I use the term "technography." Rieder offers a particularly instructive account of how different technical logics—in this case, the Bayes classifier—entail certain values and assumptions that inevitably have consequences for the operational logics of specific systems.

Following Ashby's cybernetic lead, what is at stake in a technographic inquiry is not to reveal some hidden truth about the exact workings of software or to unveil the precise formula of an algorithm. Instead the aim is to develop a critical understanding of the mechanisms and operational logic of software. As Galloway states, the question is "how it works" and "who it works for" (2004: xiii). Just as the ethnographer observes, takes notes, and asks people about their beliefs and values, Ashby's observer and the technographer describe what they see and what they think they see. The researcher confronted with the black box algorithm does not necessarily need to know much about code or programming (although it is certainly an advantage). As Ashby points out, "no skill is called for! We are assuming, remember, that nothing is known about the Box" (1999: 89).

In general, we might say that a good way to start is by confronting known unknowns in terms of one's own limits of knowledge. What, for example, is there to know about key concepts in computer science, mathematics, or social sciences that would be useful for understanding a specific algorithmic context? Then, we also have the option of tracing the many "semiotic systems that cluster around technical artefacts and ensembles" (Mackenzie, 2002: 211): patent applications and similar documents that detail and lay out technical specifications, press releases, conference papers on machine learning techniques, recorded documents from developer and engineering conferences, company briefs, media reports, blog posts, Facebook's IPO filing, and so on. Finally, we might want to experiment with systems as best we can or even code them ourselves. As the next chapter will show, a technography of algorithms need not imply elaborate experimentation or detailed technical knowledge but, above all, a readiness to engage in unknown knowns, seeing the black box not as an epistemological obstacle but as a playful challenge that can be described in some ways (but not all).

PHENOMENOLOGICAL ENCOUNTERS WITH UNKNOWN KNOWNS

The second tactic suggests another way of knowing algorithms, which is to bring sense to what we do not know but know nonetheless. From a phenomenological perspective, approaching algorithms is about being attentive to the ways in which social actors develop more or less reflexive relationships to the systems they are using and how those encounters, in turn, shape online experience. Drawing on concepts such as "tacit knowledge," "nonknowledge," and "practical knowledge," a phenomenological approach to algorithms is concerned with understanding how algorithms are perceived and made sense of by the actors in a given situation. Positing the algorithm as an unknown known in this case is meant to highlight the productive force of personal forms of knowledge, knowledge that is gained through experience and practical engagement with one's lived-in environments (Ingold, 2000). Although algorithms, in the strict technical and mathematical sense of the term, may remain unknowns, there are tacit forms of knowledge that linger in the background and which may have as much of an impact on the ways in which life with algorithms take shape as the coded instructions themselves. When long-lost friends suddenly show up on your Facebook news feed or a hotel that you have been looking at on a booking site materializes as an ad and seems to follow you wherever else you go on the Web, or Netflix just seems to be "reading your mind" in terms of the kind of movie you are in the mood to watch, algorithms become locally available for analysis in terms of the kinds of experiences and affects they engender.

Here, the notion of the black box is tackled by claiming that what there is to know about algorithms may not even be inside the box. As we have seen, for Ashby and the early cyberneticians, the black box was not an obstacle but a means for play and exploratory experimentation (Kaerlein, 2013: 659). The cybernetic notion of the black box as a basic human condition bears strong resemblance to the ways in which the psychologist Jean Piaget (originally, a zoologist) theorized the cognitive development of children. According to Piaget's notion of playful learning, "children build up a picture of the world through making their own sense of inputs to the black box of the mind, converting experience to personal understanding of concrete objects" (Murray, 2012: 902). Instead of talking about knowledge in a definite sense, the emphasis is put on knowing as a continued and playful process. As biologists Maturana and Varela (1987) later put it, knowledge does not reflect a true world but should, rather, be judged by the construction of meaning from experience.

The focus is on how life takes shape and gains expression through encounters with algorithms. A phenomenological approach also considers the ways in which algorithms are "already embedded in particular circumstances" (Berry, 2011: 121). For Alfred Schütz, a pioneer in bringing phenomenology into sociological analysis, experience and the knowledge people derive from it is situated and contextual. It depends as much on various realms of relevance as it does on various social roles. Not everybody needs to know what algorithms are or how they work, but the "fact that we do not understand the Why and the How of their working and that we do not know anything of their origin does not hinder us from dealing undisturbed with situations, things, and persons" (Schütz, 1946: 463). Using "the most complicated gadgets prepared by a very advanced technology without knowing how the contrivances work" (Schütz, 1946: 463) is just a natural part of human life, but there are distinctions as to how relevant it is for people to know or attempt to know. A phenomenological analysis seeks out those slight transformations of relevance for an understanding of how phenomena change from being taken for granted to becoming a field of further inquiry. For example, Nick Couldry and his colleagues (2016) recently proposed the notion of "social analytics" as the phenomenological study of how social actors use "analytics" to reflect upon and adjust their online presence. As they see it, a "social analytics approach makes a distinctively qualitative contribution to the expansion of sociological methods in a digital age" (Couldry et al., 2016: 120). In a world in which large-scale data analysis takes on a greater hold, it is important to investigate the ways in which actors themselves engage with increased quantification. In Schütz's (1946) terms, we might think of such actors as "well-informed citizens" who seek to "arrive at reasonably founded opinions" about their whereabouts in a fundamentally uncertain world.

A phenomenological approach to algorithms, then, is concerned with excavating the meaning-making capacities that emerge as people have "strange encounters" (Ahmed, 2000) with algorithms. As chapter 5 will show, people make sense of algorithms despite not knowing exactly what they are or how they work. When the outcomes of algorithmic processing do not feel right, surprise, or come across as strangely amusing, people who find themselves affected by these outcomes start to turn their awareness toward algorithmic mechanisms and evaluate it. As with the social analytics described by Couldry et al. (2016), when modes of appearance or senses of identity are at stake, actors may reflect at length on how to influence such operational logics; and, in doing so, they performatively participate in changing the algorithmic models themselves, a key reason it is important to study actors' own experiences of the affective landscape of algorithms.

INTERROGATING THE CONFIGURATIONS OF STRATEGIC UNKNOWNS

The final methodological tactic that I want to address here focuses on examining algorithms as configurations in situated practices. Donna Haraway's notion of figuration is particularly instructive in this regard as it points to the individuation of figures through co-constitutive relationships. Throughout her work, Haraway develops the notion of figures and figuration as a means of talking about the ways in which different elements come together, both materially and discursively, to form the appearance of more or less coherent relations. The cyborg, which is probably Haraway's most well-known figure, is to be understood, above all, as a coalition across boundaries of identity. As a figure, the cyborg is not marked by a stable identity, but by the interaction of different and often conflicting concepts. Figurations, then, hold together "contradictions that do not resolve into larger wholes" because each idea, although conflicting, might be "necessary and true" (Haraway 1991: 149).

By conceptualizing algorithms as particular figurations that comprise and suggest conflicting ideas, we might be able to study the becoming of algorithms and the different ways in which algorithms come to matter in specific situations. As figurations, the identity of algorithms is variously made and unmade, and it is the analyst's task to study when the algorithm becomes particularly pertinent and to challenge the conceptual separation between, for example, the social and the technical. Interrogating the configuration of algorithms begins with tracing out its specific cultural, historical, and political appearances and the practices through which these appearances come into being (Suchman, 2004). In this chapter, I have described this process as one of moving from a question of where the agency of algorithm is located to when it is mobilized, by whom and for what purpose.

What is at stake here, then, is not the black box as a thing but, rather, the process of "blackboxing," of making it appear as if there is a stable box in the first place. If the metaphor of the black box is used too readily as a way of critiquing algorithms, Latour's notion of blackboxing reminds us that we might want to scrutinize critically the ways different actors have a vested interest in figuring the algorithm as a black box in the first place. As discussed in this chapter, the alleged unknowability of algorithms is not always seen as problematic. It can also be strategically used to cultivate an ignorance that is sometimes more advantageous to the actors involved than knowing. By referring to the notion of strategic unknowns as part of this third methodological option, the intention is to point out the deeply political work that goes into the figurations of algorithms as particular epistemic phenomena. In chapter 6, I turn to these questions anew by looking at how algorithms variously become enlisted, imagined and configured as part of journalistic practices and products.

Concluding Remarks

Let this be the general conclusion: For every epistemological challenge the seemingly black-boxed algorithm poses, another productive methodological route may open. The complex and messy nature of social reality is not the problem. Just as algorithms constitute but one specific solution to a computational problem, we cannot expect a single answer to the problem of how to know algorithms. Borrowing from Law, "one thing is sure: if we want to think about the messes of reality at all then we're going to have to teach ourselves to think, to practice, to relate, and to know in new ways" (2004a: 2). In this chapter the black box was used as a heuristic device to deal with this mess—not by making the world less messy, but by redirecting attention to the messiness that the notion of the black box helps to hide.

Not to be taken as a definitive, exhaustive list of well-meant advice, I offered three steps to consider when researching algorithms. First, do not regard the "impossibility of seeing inside the black box" as an epistemological limit that impinges any "futile attempts at knowledge acquisition" (von Hilgers 2011: 43). Ask instead what parts can and cannot be known and how, in each particular case, you may find ways to make the algorithm talk. Second, instead of expecting the truth to come out from behind the curtain or to lay there in the box just waiting for our hands to take the lid off, take those beliefs, values, and imaginings that the algorithm solicits as point of departure. Third, keep in mind that the black box is not as seamless as it may seem. Various actors and stakeholders once composed black boxes in a specific historical context for a specific purpose. Importantly, they evolve, have histories, change, and affect and are affected by what they are articulated to. While we often talk about algorithms as if they were single stable artifacts, they are *boxed* to precisely appear that way.

4

Life at the Top

Engineering Participation

Over a decade ago, a geeky Harvard computer science undergraduate, together with a couple of friends, founded the world's largest social networking site to date. With a claimed 1.4 billion daily active users, 25,105 employees, and a market value of $530 billion as of December 2017, Facebook is not just a site through which users can "stay connected with friends and family."[1] Facebook is also a multibillion dollar business, engineering company, sales operation, news site, computational platform, and infrastructure. As the feature film *The Social Network* (2010) nicely shows, Facebook is also a myth, an entrepreneurial dream, a geeky fairy tale. Far from just a Hollywood story with its founder Mark Zuckerberg in the leading role, Facebook is a carefully crafted brand, which over the past decade has been marketed as a technology company comprising a young, vibrant, and creative class of geeks and hackers. Its mission: to make the world more open and connected.

Indeed, research suggests that, in many parts of the world, "Facebook *is* the Internet." As one recent news article reported, "Millions of Facebook users have no idea they're using the Internet" (Mirani, 2015). When people in countries such as Indonesia, Nigeria, Brazil, and India were surveyed, many reported they did not use the Internet while, at the same time, indicating that they were avid users of Facebook. Despite some media reports about a teenage flight from Facebook to other social media platforms such as Snapchat, the sheer scale and volume of active users and content shared via Facebook remains historically unprecedented. In the American context, Facebook remains the most popular social media site with a large user base that continues to be very active. According to a Pew Research report on social media usage for 2014, fully 70% of Facebook users engage with the site on a daily basis, a significant increase from the 63% who did so in 2013 (Duggan et al., 2015). It is probably no exaggeration to state that, for many, Facebook has transformed the ways in which they live their lives—the way they communicate and coordinate with their friends and family, receive and read news, find jobs and are fired from jobs. Facebook is constitutive of what Deuze calls media life, shaping "the ways in which we experience, makes sense of and act upon the world" (2012: 5). As I argue in this book, our lived experiences are not just permeated by media in general but, increasingly and more specifically, by the principle of the algorithm. *Algorithmic life* is a form of life whose fabric is interwoven by algorithms—of what can and cannot be adapted, translated, or incorporated into algorithmic expressions and logics. Facebook, as we will see, sits right at the center of this algorithmic fabric, making intelligible and valuable that which can be quantified, aggregated, and proceduralized. This fabric is the theme of this chapter, and the question I explore is, what kind of togetherness does software invent? If, as van Dijck (2012) suggests, Facebook is wrapping relationships in code by configuring connections algorithmically, the question is in what ways.

To examine this, I discuss the case of Facebook's news feed, focusing on the ways in which the feed is fundamentally governed and organized by an algorithmic logic. If Facebook is the computational platform that facilitates other things to be built on top of it, an architectural model for communication, then the news feed is the actualization of this model as a communication channel, a designed space in which communicative action can take place. Despite its purported discourse of openness, the Facebook news feed differs in fundamental ways from the ideal public sphere envisioned by Jürgen Habermas and other political theorists based in the idea of mutual deliberation and argumentation. While the intention is not to suggest compatibility between the communicative space of the news feed and the public sphere model, it is not without its warrants. The news feed, I want to suggest, is political insofar as it is exercising a position of governance. Here, I am not referring to politics in the conventional notion of parliamentary politics. Rather, politics is understood in a much broader sense as the encounter and conflict between different ways of being in the world (see also chapter 1). As the French philosopher Jacques Ranciére (2004) has theorized, politics concerns the reconfiguration of the distribution of the sensible. In this sense, politics is productive of "the set of horizons and modalities of what is visible and audible as well as what can be said, thought, made, or done" (Ranciere, 2004: 85). It is a way of informing experience that has no proper place. In this sense, power and politics are not limited to parliamentary governments or ruling bodies. Whereas political theorists such as Habermas considered politics mainly as discursive forms of power produced through arguments in an informal public sphere (Flynn, 2004), I propound a view on politics that is sensitive to its material dimensions as well. In his seminal studies of the Long Island Bridge and the mechanical tomato harvester, Winner (1986) argued that technological arrangements impose a social order prior to their specific use. If taken to the realm of algorithms, we may start to consider them as political devices in the sense that they represent certain design decisions about how the world is to be ordered. After all, as Mackenzie suggests, algorithms "select and reinforce one ordering at the expense of others" (Mackenzie, 2006: 44). It is the work of ordering and distributing the sensible that I am concerned with in this chapter.

Building on a Foucauldian sensibility toward the "microphysics of power" the question is not whom power most obviously belongs or where it is located but how and when power is exercised: those algorithmic techniques and practices that animate it and give it effect.

Before I get to a more detailed examination of the news feed, it is important to acknowledge that "there is an undeniable cultural dimension to computation" (Berry, 2011: 17). Software, code, and algorithms, while mathematical, logical, and mechanical in their materiality, are always made, maintained, and unmade. As computer historian Michael Mahoney says, software is always "constructed with action in mind; the programmer aims to make something happen" (1988: 121). As I discussed in the previous chapter, it can be difficult to study what actions programmers have in mind when the object of study is a commercial social media platform such as Facebook, since the motivations and intentions of software engineers often remain as obscure as the companies they work for. While cultural anthropologist Nick Seaver is right to criticize the tendency among media scholars to focus on figuring out the technical details of popular platforms at the expense of trying to figure out what their engineers think and do, access to the interiors of many of these companies for most researchers remains closed. Whether the scant literature in social media production studies is a result of closed access or merely a disproportionate interest in the study of users and consumption practices is not clear. As Nick Couldry has pointed out with regards to cultural and media studies, "production is often downplayed because it is not regarded as a place where everyday practice can be found" (quoted in Mackenzie, 2006: 14). While this may be true of much previous social media research, a notable exception is Alice Marwick's ethnography of the Silicon Valley social media "technology scene." In her book *Status Update* (2013), Marwick shows how software can embody the values of a group of users or creators—specifically, how software features may reflect the technology scene's cultural beliefs about how the world is ordered and organized.

From a "values in design" perspective (Flanagan and Nissenbaum, 2014), the cultural beliefs and values held by programmers, designers, and creators of software matter. If we want to understand how software and algorithms are imbued in the fabric of everyday life, acknowledging and taking seriously the notion that these artefacts are far from neutral is imperative. By way of introducing the reader to Facebook and situating the object of analysis discussed in this chapter—the news feed—I first turn to the culture of engineering at Facebook. I show how materiality and culture are not separate but inherently entangled. While subscribing to the view that technology and practices need to be seen as co-constitutive, the emphasis in this chapter is on the material side of the sociotechnical framework.[2] This should not be taken as a statement about cause and effect. Rather, it is about acknowledging that, despite purporting a relational view on the social and material, scholarship tends to "lean" toward one side or the other for analytical and empirical purposes. While the next two chapters "lean" toward the social side in terms of looking at social media users and news practitioners' oral histories respectively, this chapter leans toward different aspects of materiality—to spaces and technology. Next, I draw on Michel Foucault's architectural diagram of power introduced in *Discipline and Punish* (1977) to establish an analytical framework through which the news feed can be understood as an example of how sociality is programmed in algorithmic media.

Facebook and the Hacker Way

It is no coincidence that we only see Mark Zuckerberg wearing a washed out gray T-shirt or college sweater when he appears in public. Whatever imagined gap there might have been between users and the mythical founder figure, the T-shirt does its job of letting the world know that he is just a regular guy. He is not in it for the money, for the fancy designer clothes, for the frills. He just wants to do his job, "serving the community" the best way he can, as he himself said when confronted at the company's first in-person public Q&A session with the question of why he always wears a T-shirt.[3] For Mark Zuckerberg, the T-shirt is about eliminating unnecessary decisions. Decisions "make you tired and consume your energy," he claims. Knowing exactly what to wear everyday leaves him more time to "build the best product and services." The T-shirt, Zuckerberg says, helps him dedicate all his time and energy to "reach the company's goal and achieve the mission of helping to connect everyone in the world and giving them the ability to stay connected with the people that they love and care about" (Facebook, 2014). Bolstering his role as the hard-working CEO, the T-shirt comes to solidify Mark Zuckerberg's image as the Samaritan of code and connectedness. Not simply the uniform of the dedicated but the uniform of a particular kind of dedication—the hacker.

Facebook famously cultivates a culture and management approach they call "the hacker way." As described in a letter penned by Mark Zuckerberg and included in Facebook's IPO registration statement, the hacker way is an approach to building that "involves continuous improvement and iteration" (Facebook, 2012: 69). The hacker, Zuckerberg suggests, has typically been portrayed unfairly in the media. In reality, "hacking just means building something quickly or testing the boundaries of what can be done." As Facebook already suggests, there are different versions and meanings of the term "hacker." The Facebook hacker is not like the university hackers of the 1960s described by Steve Levy (2010) in his seminal book called *Hackers*, nor anything like the underground hackers described more recently in Gabriela Coleman's (2014) work on Anonymous. The Facebook hackers specifically "believe that something can always be better, and that nothing is ever complete. They just have to go fix it—often in the face of people who say it's impossible or are content with the status quo". The hacker way is characterized by a number of core values, carefully crafted through slogans and popular sayings that pervade not only the company's discourse but also its physical setting and work place. The word "hack" dominates the facades of one of Facebook's two office buildings in Menlo Park, and the office spaces are "tattooed with slogans that inculcate through repetition the value of speed and iterative improvement: 'Move Fast and Break Things;' 'This Journey Is 1% Finished;' 'Done Is Better than Perfect'" (Fattal, 2012: 940). After moving headquarters in December 2011, Facebook is now even located at "the Hacker Way," and Zuckerberg's office faces onto "Hacker Square." In a fascinating NYT article, journalist Quentin Hardy (2014) details the way in which the interiors of the office spaces at Facebook have been carefully designed to reflect the company's culture of openness and change: Open office plans, of course, where meetings often happen on the fly, where no one has secrets, and common areas that without a warning may have the couches replaced in order to create a space of perpetual change. "Similarly, design changes to Facebook's home page are known as 'moving the furniture around'" (Hardy, 2014). The hacking culture is such an integral part of Facebook that it has become the principal way in which the company now presents itself, internally as well as externally.

However, the hacker identity was not always a part of Facebook's culture. The external hacker brand first had to be created. In 2008, cultural and employment branding manager Molly Graham was hired to create and tell the company's story. Graham describes how the defining moment for Facebook's identity came with a blog post by Paul Buchheit, who joined Facebook from FriendFeed in 2009. The post reframed hacking as "applied philosophy," a way of thinking and acting that "is much bigger and more important than clever bits of code in a computer" (Buchheit, 2009). According to Graham, "When Paul wrote that post, he wrote the story of Facebook's DNA" (Firstround, 2014).

Facebook's DNA is not just externally communicated but internally communicated and "installed" into every new Facebook employee, as one of Facebook's engineers put it in a blog post (Hamilton, 2010). Newly hired Facebook engineers have to go through a six-week boot camp in which they learn almost everything about the software stack and are exposed to the breadth of code base and the core tools for engineering. Moreover, as Andrew Bosworth—the inventor of the Facebook boot camp and a long-time Facebook engineer—puts it, the boot camp is a training ground for the camper to be "indoctrinated culturally."[4] New hires are told from the very beginning to "be bold and fearless," an ethos that is at the heart of Facebook engineering.[5] Just as the company and code base are always changing, so are their engineers expected to change. Whatever they do, Facebook engineers are continuously told to move fast. In terms of the boot camp, moving fast means starting to work on actual code right away, and there are expectations of publishing code to the live site within their first week. Moving fast is also an important part of Facebook hackathons, another cornerstone of Facebook's hacker culture. Hackathons are organized at Facebook every six weeks for engineers to conceive of new products in a short and concentrated timeframe. Some of Facebook's most popular products emerged from a hackathon, including the "like" button, Timeline, and Chat.

Ultimately, culture is embodied. As understood by Raymond Williams (1985), "culture" refers to the meanings and values implicit and explicit in particular ways of life. As a news report on the Facebook boot camp suggests, Facebook counts on its engineers to be as "nimble as ninjas, always ready to change course" (Bloomberg, n.a.). According to Pedram Keyani, engineering director and company culture advocate at Facebook, culture needs to be nourished to evolve, and it needs to be embodied by the management. Being bold, fast, and open, focusing on impact, and building trust constitute the core company values and tenets of the culture at Facebook, allegedly perfectly embodied by its founder Mark Zuckerberg (Keyani, 2014). On the company's 10th anniversary in early 2014, Zuckerberg reflected back on what he called "an amazing story so far," pondering why, of all people, they were the ones to build Facebook. After all, he says, "we were just students." The quick answer: "we just cared more about connecting the world than anyone else. And we still do today" (Zuckerberg, 2014). The ethos and rhetoric of openness is ubiquitous at Facebook, despite or, perhaps precisely because of, continuous allegations to the contrary.[6] Zuckerberg is celebrated for openly answering any questions employees may have at a weekly company Q&A; products are launched "openly" all the time without "secrecy"; and, when Facebook moved from its headquarters, most of the walls inside the building were pulled down to support and reflect Facebook's "open communication environment" (Keyani, 2014).

Mark Zuckerberg's T-shirt, the moving furniture, and the open office space are not simply allegorical accessories. They are not meant to provide a stroke of cultural paint over an otherwise technical canvas. Mark Zuckerberg's contempt for mundane decisions should not simply be dismissed as empty PR talk; nor should the refurbishing of Facebook's headquarters be taken as a token of style. Then, why talk about a T-shirt and hacker culture? From the perspective that culture is a whole way of life, technologies are integral to culture, not separate from it (Slack and Wise, 2002). Culture matters to an understanding of software and algorithms inasmuch as they are inherently intertwined and co-constituted (Pickering, 1995; Slack and Wise, 2002; Williams, 2005). Indeed, as computer historian Nathan Ensmenger suggests, "software is where the technology of computing intersects with social relationships, organizational politics, and personal agendas" (Ensmenger, 2012; Haigh, 2001). Nowhere does Mark Zuckerberg's personal agenda of making the world more open and connected, Facebook's organizational goals of maintaining engaged users to ensure revenue, and users' desire to see stories that interest them and stay connected to the people they care about intersect more with the power of software to frame the world as it does on Facebook's news feed. As a starting point, therefore, we need to acknowledge that what Facebook calls the hacker culture is deeply engrained in the code and products that emerge from the cultural life of its engineers. While Mark Zuckerberg claims the T-shirt keeps his goals and

motivations intact by eliminating one more decision from his life, it also says something about the ways in which the CEO of the world's largest social networking site
thinks about human autonomy and decision-making. Similarly, perpetuating a work
environment in which moving furniture is part of the everyday life of Facebook engineers or tearing down walls for meetings to happen anywhere at any time is much
more that a design decision made by an interior architect. They are the physical
manifestations of the "under construction" ethos that permeates the culture of engineering at Facebook. As John Tenanes, who oversees Facebook's buildings as its
director of real estate, tellingly says about the physical layout Facebook's headquarters: "It's designed to change thinking" (Hardy, 2014).

The engineering of the engineer at which Tenanes hints clearly challenges the
idea that artefacts are socially constructed, as if the social was already a given.
Engineers do not simply engineer artefacts as if their intentions and ideas were the
results of discursive and deliberate processes. These deliberations are always already imbued in materiality, whether it is the architecture of the headquarters,
a piece of clothing, or the infrastructure of the work place. Just as the cultural dimension of computing matters, so does the material dimension of the culture of
computing. It becomes apparent that thinking about the power of software and
algorithms in terms of cause and determination will not do. While STS scholars
have long argued for the necessary entanglement of materiality, practice, and politics (Gillespie, Boczkowski, & Foot, 2014: 4), there is a tendency still among communication scholars to frame technology as an outcome of culture. As Leah
Lievrouw suggests, communication scholars only secondarily, if at all, consider
material artefacts and devices to have anything resembling power (2014: 24).
Indebted to the STS ideal of co-determination and the mutual shaping of technology and cultural practices, while at the same time explicitly opposing the preference for the social/cultural side of this sociotechnical duality, in this chapter I seek
to attend more closely to the physical design and configuration of the (im)material
architecture of the news feed. Echoing the idea of co-production or the dynamic
relationship between the material and social, power is no longer seen as an abstract
"force" or institutional "structure" but, rather, as instantiated and observable in the
physical forms of social practices, relations, and material objects and artefacts
(Lievrouw, 2014: 31).

Toward a Diagrammatics of News Feed Algorithms

My interest in questions of power stems from the view that power is increasingly
materialized in and through software, as software and code have become ubiquitous, slipping into the "technological unconscious" of everyday life (Lash, 2007;
Thrift, 2005). I hold that algorithms have productive capacities not merely by medi-
ating the world but through their delegated capacities to do work in the world and

by making a difference in how social formations and relations are formed and informed. Setting out to explore power through software and algorithms, indeed, seems to be a daunting and, perhaps, even impossible task. However, it is not my intention to investigate power as a totalizing force that can be located and described once and for all. As discussed in previous chapters, algorithms are never powerful in one way only but power always signifies the capacity to produce new realities. What we need, therefore, are *diagrams* or maps of power, tracing how and when power operates and functions in specific settings and through specific means.[7] Following Deleuze in his reading of Foucault and the assertion that "every society has its diagram(s)" (2006: 31), what is at stake here is thus a diagrammatics of algorithms, understood as the cartography of strategies of power. Here, Foucault's analysis of the architectural, technological, and conceptual nature of diagrams provides a useful methodological and analytical framework for examining Facebook's news feed.

Foucault's architectural model of power usefully highlights the ways in which spaces are "designed to make things seeable, and seeable in a specific" way (Rajchman, 1988). It offers a useful avenue to analyze algorithms in terms of architectural structuring in which embedded technically means having the power "to incite, to induce, to seduce, to make easy or difficult, to enlarge or limit, to make more or less probable" (Foucault quoted in Deleuze, 2006:59). For a mapping of power, Foucault's notion of government and governmentality also offers elaborate concepts for the kinds of architectural shaping that he first described in *Discipline and Punish* (1977), as it points to the multiple processes, measurements, calculations, and techniques at play in organizing and arranging sociality. Analytically, this implies a focus on the ways in which algorithms arrange and organize things, its specific techniques and procedures, and the mechanisms used in processes of individual and collective individuation.[8]

I argue in this chapter for the importance of revisiting the idea of the technical and architectural organization of power as proposed in the writings of Foucault, by highlighting an analytics of visibility. Becoming visible, or being granted visibility, is a highly contested game of power in which the media play a crucial role. While Foucault did not connect his theory of visibility specifically to the media, the framework he developed in *Discipline and Punish* helps illuminate the ways in which the media participate in configuring the visible as oscillating between what can and should be seen and what should not and cannot be seen, between who can and cannot see whom. Examining new modalities of visibility, thus, becomes a question of how and when something is made visible rather than what is made visible, through which specific politics of arrangement, architecture, and designs. Although Foucault's writings focused more on the "how of power," I want to suggest that the how is inextricably linked to the when of algorithms as discussed in the previous chapter. If the how of power are "those practices, techniques, and procedures that give it effect" (Townley, 1993: 520), then the when, in this case, refers to the aspects that are rendered important or unimportant to the effectuating of these procedures at different times. In this chapter, I investigate the notion of mediated and constructed visibility through a close reading of the news feed and its underlying algorithmic operational logic. I argue that Foucault's idea of an architecturally-constructed regime of visibility as exemplified in the figure of the Panopticon makes for a useful analytical and conceptual framework for understanding the ways in which the sensible is governed in social networking sites.[9] The intention is not so much to offer a definite account of the role played by Facebook in capturing the world in code but to open avenues for reflection on the new conditions through which visibility is constructed by algorithms online.

The News Feed

Launched in 2006, the news feed is one of Facebook's primary and most successful features. The news feed, placed right in the middle of a users' home page, is a continuous stream of updates, serving users stories of what their friends have been up to. Since its conception, the news feed has changed its design and functionalities so many times that they launched a series of blog posts in August 2013 called *News Feed FYI* so that people could more easily keep track of the most important changes.[10] In its twelve years of existence, the news feed has gone from being a single feed of reverse-chronologically-ordered updates to becoming fully edited and governed by machine learning algorithms. In an older version anno 2009, the news feed was organized as two distinct feeds, separated by easily recognizable tabs, whereby users could choose between viewing the "live feed" or the "top news." When the news feed revamped into a single algorithmically governed feed in the autumn of 2011, Facebook started showing real-time updates in a feed called Ticker, placed on the right-hand column of the Facebook homepage. While nothing stays the same on Facebook, the basic layout of a single filtered news feed at the centre and a ticker on the right has more or less persisted since.

Since much of the empirical material used in this chapter is based on data collected in the time period of April–August 2011, using my own personal Facebook profile, it is important to be clear about the state of the feed and the design at that particular point in time. In this time period, the news feed was divided into two different versions, the default "top news" and the "most recent" feed. According to the Facebook Help Center, the difference between the two is that "top news aggregates the most interesting content that your friends are posting, while the most recent filter shows you all the actions your friends are making in real-time" (Facebook, 2011). Fast forward to 2015 and the Help Center describes the news feed in quite different terms. No longer is there a distinction made between a real-time feed and the "top news" feed. Gone are terms such as aggregation and filter or any other explicit trace of the software doing something. According to Facebook as of January 2018:

Posts that you see in your News Feed are meant to keep you connected to the people and things that you care about, starting with your friends and family. Posts that you see first are influenced by your connections and activity on Facebook. The number of comments, likes, and reactions a post receives and what kind of story it is (example: photo, video, status update) can also make it more likely to appear higher up in your News Feed. (Facebook, 2018)

What we see is the apparent disappearance of the algorithm, seemingly replaced by the agency of the user and the network. Recall just how the logic of the news feed was described by the Help Center in late 2013: "The News Feed algorithm uses several factors to determine top stories, including the number of comments, who posted the story and what type of post it is" (Facebook, 2013). In the midst of what became publicly known as the Facebook emotion experiment during summer 2014, Facebook's Help Center conveniently replaced any mention of the algorithm with human-centered factors. The changes that were made to the Help Center descriptions of the news feed back in 2014 still more or less persist to this day. Now the regime of visibility on the news feed is seemingly determined by "your connections and activity" and "the number of comments and likes a post receives." If users were feeling that they were being experimented on by having their news feeds "manipulated," the change in description may arguably be seen as Facebook's attempt to give back some level of control—but also responsibility—to users, if only rhetorically. But we are getting ahead of ourselves.

Let me quickly revisit some of the important changes and developments to the news feed and its algorithmic logic in order to provide some context to the arguments made. Many of Facebook's most important features and functionalities were implemented in the years 2009–2011, including the "like" button, the open graph protocol, messenger, and timeline. For users, the changing news feed has always been an issue of heated debate and anguish, especially in terms of the many changes in default settings, privacy settings, transparency, and the usability of the platform. In earlier years, the tabs distinguishing between different versions of the feed were visually differentiated to a greater extent and, therefore, easier to control for users. Or so it seems. While one would think that having two feeds called "most recent" and "top news" would imply a clear distinction between an unfiltered and a filtered feed, respectively, a decade of Facebook history has repeatedly shown that nothing can be taken for granted. During February 2011, Facebook changed the settings and options for the "most recent" feed. Two basic settings were implemented, a seemingly unfiltered one, showing stories from "all of your friends and pages" as well as a filtered one displaying only "friends and pages you interact with most." It was not so much the fact that Facebook changed the news feed feature yet again that brought about public outcry on the matter but the fact that Facebook had changed the default setting of the "most recent" feed to "friends and pages you interact with most" so that the feed most users believed to represent every update from every friend in a real-time stream, in fact, became an edited one, much like "top news." What caused the most controversy was the fact that this change in default occurred without Facebook notifying its users about it. The option to change the default was tucked away at the bottom of a drop down menu, barely noticeable. Users who did notice, however, quickly started to warn other users, pointing to the fact that these changes basically meant that people were not seeing everything that they should be seeing (Hull, 2011).

The revelation that the "most recent" feed was filtered is just one of many controversies surrounding the features and functionalities of the Facebook platform that the company has faced throughout the years. Besides representing yet another case of shaky privacy settings, it clearly points toward a certain disconnect between user expectations and reality. As we will discuss in much more detail in the next chapter, user expectations and perceptions about how technology works or ought to work may affect their media practices just as much as the actual working of that technology. As with the example above of users getting a sense of not seeing everything they should be seeing, the aforementioned revelations about the Facebook emotion experiment continue to show how important it is to hold software companies such as Facebook accountable. In late June 2014, the news broke that Facebook had "tinkered" with users' emotions by manipulating the news feeds of over half a million randomly selected users, changing the number of positive and negative posts they saw (Goel, 2014). Facebook researchers had published the findings from the experiment in an academic paper. The experiment itself had been carried out for one week in January 2012, one and a half years prior to the public outcry engendered through the mass media. Notwithstanding the apparently small effects obtained, the experiment unleashed a huge controversy about algorithms, human subject research, and regulation (Meyer, 2014). What was most surprising about the media frenzy following the academic publication was not so much the actual experiments described in the article but the widespread public surprise in the face of this news. Like the public perception of what a "most recent" feed ought to be, the Facebook emotion experiment revealed that there are many persistent beliefs about how technology works and should work. As Gillespie (2014) put it in a blog post:

> There certainly are many, many Facebook users who still don't know they're receiving a curated subset of their friends' posts, despite the fact that this has been true, and "known," for some time. But it's more than that. Many users know that they get some subset of their friends' posts, but don't understand the criteria at work. Many know, but do not think about it much as they use Facebook in any particular moment. Many know, and think they understand the criteria, but are mistaken. Just because we live with Facebook's algorithm doesn't mean we fully understand it.

Indeed, we are only at the beginning of figuring out what it means to live in a society increasingly mediated and governed by algorithms. While it has been "known" for some time that Facebook uses algorithms to select the stories shown at top of the news feed, it is important not to forget how recent this time span really is. Moreover, what exactly this knowledge amounts to varies greatly. While we might never know for sure how the technology—the software and algorithms—of Facebook work in detail, there are enough ways in which we might know its operational principles and logics. As I argued in the previous chapter, algorithms are never so black or so boxed that they do not allow for critical scrutiny of their functions, assumptions, and embedded values. The cybernetic lead does not ask us to reveal the exact content of the box but to experiment with its inputs and outputs. In the following, I will walk you through some of the most important criteria the Facebook algorithm uses to serve people the "most interesting" content on their news feeds. The materials used to present some of the operational logic of Facebook's algorithmic workings I draw from the technical specifications of specific inventions that pertain to the news feed as disclosed and discussed in white papers, computer science conference papers, Facebook patent applications, and recorded talks given by a Facebook engineer. Moreover, I draw on various news reports and blog posts from the technology press, most notably from publications such as *Wired*, *The Atlantic*, Techcrunch, Mashable, the *New York Times*, and the *Guardian*. These documents have been read and coded for the technological mechanisms entailed by the news feed. Technical specifications entailed in patent applications, in particular, contain much important information about how these systems work and are imagined by their inventors. Like any piece of discourse, patent applications also have to be read carefully and within the realms of what they are produced to achieve as rhetorical devices in a particular commercial context. To test some of the operational logics described in these documents, I also report on a technography of my own news feed. What, then, are the principles and logics of Facebook's algorithmic form of editing the news feed?

The News Feed Ranking Algorithm

At Facebook's third f8 developers' conference in April 2010, Facebook for the first time "spilled the beans of some of the magic that is the news feed" as engineer Ruchi Sanghvi put it, introducing developers (and the public) to what was then referred to as the EdgeRank algorithm.[11] Today, the notion of EdgeRank has largely been replaced by the much more generic notion of the Facebook algorithm(s) or the news feed ranking algorithm, respectively. Here, I use these terms somewhat interchangeably, sometimes referring to EdgeRank but, most of the time, simply referring to the ranking algorithm governing the news feed as Facebook algorithm.[12] Let us take it from the start. When introducing the concept of EdgeRank in 2010, engineer Ari

Steinberg explained it as an algorithm "basically looking at the edges in the graph" to decide how to rank the stories in news feed.

For Facebook, every item (i.e., status update, image, video) in the graph is considered an object. Every interaction with the object—for instance, through a "like" or a "comment"—creates an "edge." The formula suggests that the rank of an object in the graph is the sum of the ranks of the individual edges. To paraphrase Ari Steinberg, one may think of each edge as having three main components: a time when it happened, a type of edge (a comment or like), and a user who created that edge. For each user, Facebook computes a score on how much a particular viewer tends to interact with the user—for instance, how often they comment on the user's updates, look at their profile, or send messages. The edge weight component of the formula assigns a weight to each type of edge; for example, a comment may weigh more heavily than a like and so on. Steinberg also suggests that they train models to figure out what the appropriate weights are for different types of edges, hinting at the use of machine learning techniques. The last component is time decay because, as Steinberg suggests, freshness tends to be pretty important (Kincaid, 2010). EdgeRank is calculated by multiplying the affinity, weight, and time decay scores for each edge. Nowadays, however, the Facebook algorithm cannot simply be broken down into three distinct elements (if it ever could). Any time a user visits Facebook, there are on average 1,500 stories for them to see. Needless to say, only a few of these stories can be shown at any given time. The task for Facebook, then, is to decide which stories are the most deserving. By looking at friend relationships, frequency of interactions, number of likes and shares a post receives, how much a user has interacted with particular types of posts in the past etc. Facebook is "capable of assigning any given Facebook post a 'relevancy score' specific to any given Facebook user" (Oremus, 2016).[13] Once the relevancy score for each post has been determined, a sorting algorithm can then put them in the right order for the user to see.

Becoming visible on the news feed—appearing in that semi-public space—depends on a set of inscribed assumptions on what constitutes relevant or newsworthy stories. How many friends comment on a certain piece of content, who posted the content, and what type of content it is (e.g., photo, video, or status update) are just some of the factors at work in determining the rank of an edge. The higher the rank, the more likely it will be that an object appears in the user's feed (Kincaid, 2010). As explained in a Facebook patent application, the system "uses different types of information about users in the process of selectively providing content to users, including user profile objects, an action log, and edge objects" (Luu, 2013). User profile objects refer to all the declarative information that users have explicitly shared with the system. The action log stores different kinds of interactions taking place on the platform—for example, becoming a fan of a musician or adding an event. Edge objects store information about users' connections to other nodes, including the strength of the connections between users, which the system computes into an affinity score (Luu, 2013). In other words, the algorithm is based on the assumption that users are not equally connected to their friends. Some friends "count more" than others. The friends that count more are those with whom a user interacts on a frequent basis or a more "intimate" level—say, by communicating with a friend via "chat" rather than on the "wall." The news feed algorithm is also geared toward highlighting certain types of edges while downgrading others in which the type of interaction becomes a decisive factor. Chatting with someone on "Facebook Chat" presumably counts more than "liking" his or her post. Through tests, Facebook found that, "when people see more text status updates on Facebook they write more status updates themselves"—particularly, when they were written by friends as opposed to pages (Turitzin, 2014). As product manager for news feed ranking Chris Turitzin (2014) says, "Because of this, we showed people more text status updates in their news feed." Clearly, the type of content that is more likely to generate an interaction or prompt users to take action is made more visible and given priority. As Facebook engineers Andrew Bosworth—who is often cited as the inventor of news feed—and Chris Cox wrote in a patent document, the system determines an overall affinity for past, present, and future content based on one or more user activities and relationships:

> Some user interactions may be assigned a higher weight and/or rating than other user interactions, which may affect the overall affinity. For example, if a user emails another user, the weight or the rating for the interaction may be higher than if the user simply looks at the profile page for the other user. (Bosworth and Cox, 2013: 6)

There is a certain circular logic embedded in the algorithm. In order for you to like or comment on a friend's photo or status update, they have to be visible to you in the first place. Any time a user interacts with an edge, it increases his or her affinity toward the edge creator. For instance, we can assume that comments outweigh "likes" as they require more individual effort. The system assigns ratings and weights to the activities performed by the user and the relationships associated with the activities. Many different variables may be used to assign weight to edges, including the time since the information was accessed, the frequency of access, the relationship to the person about which information was accessed, the relationship to a person sharing common interests in the information accessed, the relationship with the actual information accessed (Bosworth and Cox, 2013: 5). In deciding what stories to show users first, Facebook also prioritizes certain types of content over others. For example, content items related to so-called life events such as a weddings, the birth of a child, getting a new job, or moving across the country may be "prioritized in a ranking of news feed stories selectively provided to users to ensure that the most relevant information is consumed first" (Luu, 2013: 2). The weight given to certain types of edges, moreover, is likely to depend on the internal incentives that Facebook may have at any given point in time. If the objective for Facebook is to promote a certain product—for instance, the "questions" or "places" feature, interactions with these features will probably be ranked higher than others. This is understandable. News feed is the best way to increase awareness of new (or neglected) features and functionalities.

Moreover, weights allow the affinity function to be used by various processes and different purposes within the system. Besides "newsfeed algorithms," a measure of affinity may be requested by "ad targeting algorithms and friend suggestion algorithms" to target their content and recommendations (Juan and Hua, 2012). As such, affinity scores may constitute useful social endorsement metrics used to provide a social context for advertisements that are shown to a particular user (Juan and Hua, 2012). For example, "a social networking system may display banner ads for a concert to members who include an affinity for the performing band in their social networking system profile and live near a concert venue where that band might be performing" (Adams and Pai, 2013: 1). Affinity scores are also used by the system to determine which friends automatically to invite for social games or recommend for pokes or other forms of phatic communication.

Facebook acknowledges that the strength of connections may vary as a function of time and context. Because user interests change, weights are continuously adjusted to cater better to specific situations. As the time decay factor emphasized in the original EdgeRank formula indicates, time is of the essence. While there are many excellent accounts of social media as real-time streams (Berry, 2011; Kaun and Stiernstedt, 2014; Weltevrede et al. 2014), the algorithmic logic of Facebook shows how the news feed is not necessarily governed by the logic of real time. Algorithmic media such as Facebook are more about "right time" than they are about "real time." After all, as Facebook repeatedly emphasizes in its News Feed FYI blog series: "Our goal is to show the right content to the right people at the *right time* so they don't miss the stories that are important to them" (Kacholia, 2013; Ge, 2013; Owens and Vickrey, 2014, emphasis added). While the scale of content and activity on Facebook may restrict showing content in real time, the real challenge for Facebook is not showing stories in chronological time but finding the most interesting and relevant pieces of content in an ever-increasing flood of content (Luu, 2013). It is not *chronos* but *kairos* that constitutes the key temporal mode of algorithmic media.[14] *Kairos*, the ancient Greek concept designating the right or opportune moment to say or do something (Smith, 1969), provides a useful way of understanding the kind of temporal work that algorithms perform. As John E. Smith argues, "kairos, or the 'right time', as the term is often translated, involves ordinality or the conception of a special temporal position" (1969: 1). Smith's comparison between ordinal numbers and kairos suggests that the right moment can only be understood in relation to past and future points in time. Under conditions of permanent change, timing becomes critical.

How, then, does the news feed algorithm determine when the time is right? One way for Facebook to show timely content higher-up in the news feed is to factor in trending topics, showing people stories about things that are trending as soon as they occur (Owens and Vickrey, 2014). As is the case with Twitter's trending topics, the notion of what a trend is may not be as straightforward as one might first think. As Gillespie (2011) has argued, "the algorithms that define what is 'trending' or what is 'hot' or what is 'most popular' are not simple measures, they are carefully designed to capture something the site providers want to capture." A trend is not a simple measure but a most specific one, defined as a topic that spikes, as something that exceeds single clusters of interconnected users, new content over retweets, new terms over already trending ones (Gillespie, 2011). Although Facebook generally conceives of a trend as an object, topic, or event that is popular at a specific moment in time, the ways in which a trend is computationally defined is much more complex.[15] Stories posted on Facebook about a topic that is currently trending (for example, about a national sports event or connected to a specific hashtag) are more likely to appear higher up in news feed. In addition, as Owens and Vickrey (2014) point out, deciding what to show on the news feed is not merely a measure of the total amount of previous engagement, as in the total number of likes, but also depends on *when* people choose to like, comment, and share. Moreover, timeliness is not simply a matter of current events. The time may be right to show a story even many days after it was originally posted. Facebook calls this practice story-bumping, meaning that stories people did not scroll down far enough to see are resurfaced, based on measures of engagement and other factors. The ordinality of kairos can be seen in the ways in which the news feed algorithm is clearly geared toward providing stories that are sensitive to a specific time and context. As Zuckerberg et al. explain in a news feed–related patent application:

> For example, a user planning a trip may be very interested in news of other users who have traveled recently, in news of trips identified as events by other users, and in travel information, and then be much less interested in these relationships, events, objects, or categories or subcategories thereof upon his return. Thus, items of media content associated with another user who has traveled recently may receive a large weighting relative to other items of media, and the weighting will decay steeply so that the weighting is low by the time of the user's return. (Zuckerberg et al. 2012: 5)

Affinity, weight, and time are as dynamic as the news feed itself. Constantly changed and fine-tuned, there is no clearcut way in which a certain state of the feed can easily be discerned. Like the prospect of moving furniture at the Facebook headquarters, the news feed offers users a slightly differently designed space to hang out in every time they log in. While it is unlikely that the sofas at the headquarters are really moved that often or to radically different areas of the building, the prospect of continuous change is what is important. The culture of not knowing how the office may look when entering the building each day or the uncertainties Facebook users face when logging in are not that different. The main difference is that users may never really know what they are exposed to, even after entering the digital building that is Facebook. A moving sofa is easily detectable; an A/B test is not. Users will never know exactly what they are witness to or how the world appearing on their screens came into existence. Living in an algorithmically mediated environment means learning to live in the moment and not to expect to step into the same river twice.[16] It also means acknowledging that talking about EdgeRank, the news feed algorithm, or whatever one now wants to call it, means talking about a *general* underlying logic, not its exact mathematic formula.[17]

In general, the system is geared toward maximizing user engagement and will present what it deems to be the most interesting content in the hope that the user will be more likely to "take actions" (Juan and Hua, 2012). The anticipatory logic inherent in the functioning of these algorithms is not primarily geared towards confirming some pre-existing cultural logic but, rather, toward a mode of government that has the capacity to take into account the probability of subjects' actions. After all, "the predictions could then be used to encourage more user interaction" (Juan and Hua, 2012: 2). By looking at the ways in which the specificities of the Facebook platform, exemplified here through the Facebook algorithm, enables and constrains ways of becoming visible online, we can begin to rethink regimes of visibility that hinge on and operate through algorithmic architectures. In doing so, in this chapter I expand on Foucault's idea of "panopticism" as it provides a useful and still highly relevant analytic for understanding the ways in which visibility is technologically structured.

Rethinking Regimes of Visibility

Algorithms establish new conditions through which visibility is constructed online. Social media sites are designed—computational spaces that determine how people socialize and communicate. As we have seen thus far in the book, the sociotechnical assemblage of which algorithms are part produce the conditions though which data are put into forms of meaningfulness, that is, determining what will appear on the screens of our digital devices. To understand how the distribution of the sensible happens and with what possible effects, the question is how visibility comes into being—through what mechanisms, logics, and practices of governance.

PANOPTICISM

Foucault operates with two basic notions of how things are made visible or shown, exemplified in his notion of the spectacle and surveillance. It is not just a matter of what is seen in a given historical context, but what can be seen and how the realm of the seeable and sayable is constructed in order to make a particular regime of visibility appear. As sociologist John Thompson explains, whereas the spectacle designates a regime of visibility in which a small number of subjects are made visible to many, surveillance mechanisms from the 16th century onward are connected to the emergence of disciplinary societies in which the visibility of the many is assured by a small number of subjects (2005: 39). Surveillance as a mode of visibility was famously exemplified in the architectural arrangement of the Panopticon.

Adapting the figure of the Panopticon from Jeremy Bentham, Foucault sought to explain the regulatory force of power inherent in specific architectural compositions. The Panopticon designates an architectural vision of a prison, a circular building with an observation tower in the middle. The principle of this architectural vision is to render the subject, whether "a madman, a patient, a condemned man, a worker or a schoolboy" (Foucault, 1977: 200), to a state of permanent visibility. As Foucault explains: "All that is needed, then, is to place a supervisor in a central tower" in order to create the impression that someone might be watching (1977: 200). More than actually placing a prison guard in the tower, the purpose of the architectural design is to create a space in which one can never be certain whether one is being watched or not. As Foucault elaborates:

> Hence the major effect of the Panopticon: to induce in the inmate a state of conscious and permanent visibility that assures the automatic functioning of power. So to arrange things that the surveillance is permanent in its effects, even if it is discontinuous in its action; that the perfection of power should tend to render its actual exercise unnecessary; that this architectural apparatus should be a machine for creating and sustaining a power relation independent of the person who exercises it; in short, that the inmates should be caught up in a power situation of which they are themselves the bearers. (1977: 201)

The uncertainty associated with the possibility of always being watched inevitably leads the subject to adjust his or her behavior accordingly, to behave as if they are indeed permanently observed. Surveillance, thus, signifies a state of permanent visibility. The novelty of Foucault's notion of visibility, constructed by the specificities of the historically contingent architectural apparatus, lies precisely in highlighting the technical organization of power. As Foucault points out, the Panopticon is not a dream building: "it is the diagram of a mechanism of power reduced to its ideal form […] it is in fact a figure of political technology" (Foucault, 1977: 205). Power "has its principle not so much in a person as in a certain concerted distribution of bodies, surfaces, lights, gazes; in an arrangement whose internal mechanisms produce the relation in which individuals are caught up" (Foucault, 1977: 202). By highlighting the diagrammatic function of panoptic surveillance, Foucault provides a forceful analytical framework for understanding different modalities of visibility and the mechanisms by which it is being arranged.

As Rajchman points out in his discussion of Foucault: "Architecture helps 'visualize' power in other ways than simply manifesting it. It is not simply a matter of what a building shows 'symbolically' or 'semiotically', but also of what it makes visible about us and within us" (1988: 103). Conceiving of visibility as an organization of power in both a negative and a positive sense, Foucault shows that "spaces are designed to make things seeable, and seeable in a specific way" (Rajchman, 1988). Prisons, hospitals, and social networking sites are essentially spaces of "constructed visibility." The realm of visibility created by the panoptic architecture did not work primarily through a certain iconography or a visual semiotic regime but, first and foremost, through the technical structuring of a way of being, implementing an awareness or attentiveness to the constant possibility of inspection. To highlight visibility as a system, a diagram, is to highlight the "distribution of individuals in relation to one another, of hierarchical organization, of dispositions of centres and channels of power" (Foucault, 1977: 205). It is precisely this notion of a material or technical structuring of visibility that seems especially interesting and relevant in terms of new media. The spaces designed by the (im)material conditions of the software are similarly designed to make things visible and, thus, knowable in a specific way.

THREAT OF INVISIBILITY

The mode of visibility at play in Facebook, as exemplified by the news feed algorithm, differs from that of disciplinary societies in one particularly interesting way. The technical architecture of the Panopticon makes sure that the uncertainty felt by the threat of permanent visibility is inscribed in the subject, who subsequently adjusts his/her behavior. While one of the premises of the panoptic diagram pertains to an even distribution of visibility in which each individual is subjected to the same level of possible inspection, the news feed does not treat individuals equally. There is no perceivable centralized inspector who monitors and casts everybody under the same permanent gaze. In Facebook, there is not so much a "threat of visibility" as there is a "threat of invisibility" that seems to govern the actions of its subjects. The problem is not the possibility of constantly being observed but the possibility of constantly disappearing, of not being considered important enough. In order to appear, to become visible, one needs to follow a certain platform logic embedded in the architecture of Facebook.

The threat of invisibility should be understood both literally and symbolically. Whereas the architectural form of the Panopticon installs a regime of visibility whereby "one is totally seen, without ever seeing" (Foucault, 1977: 202), the algorithmic arrangements in Facebook install visibility in a much more unstable fashion: One is never totally seen or particularly deprived of a seeing capacity. As is the case in the Panopticon, the individual Facebook users can be said to occupy equally confined spaces. Like the carefully and equally designed prison cells, user profiles represent templates that "provide fixed positions and permit circulation"

(Foucault, 1977: 148). Just as with the specific machines (i.e., military, prisons, hospitals) described by Foucault, it is not the actual individual that counts in Facebook. This is why spaces are designed in such a way as to make individuals interchangeable. The generic template structure of Facebook's user profiles provide not so much a space for specific individuals but a space that makes the structured organization of individuals' data easier and more manageable. The system, then, does not particularly care for the individual user as much as it thrives on the decomposition and recomposition of the data that users provide. However, whereas the architecture of the Panopticon makes all inmates equally subject to permanent visibility, the Facebook algorithm does not treat subjects equally; it prioritizes some above others. Whereas visibility, as a consequence of the panoptic arrangement, is abundant and experienced more like a threat imposed from outside powers, visibility in the Facebook system arguably works the opposite way. The algorithmic architecture of the news feed algorithm does not automatically impose visibility on all subjects. Visibility is not something ubiquitous but rather something scarce. As content, users, and activities on the Facebook platform grow and expand, visibility becomes even scarcer. According to Brian Boland (2014), who leads the Ads Product Marketing team at Facebook, this means that "competition in news feed is increasing" and that it is "becoming harder for any story to gain exposure in news feed."

In order to see how many posts actually made it to the news feed, I conducted an experiment of what could be considered a process of "reversed engineering."[18] Recall how it was claimed in the previous chapter that the first step in knowing algorithms is not to regard the impossibility of seeing inside the black box as an epistemological limit. Instead, what I termed a "technographic inquiry" starts by asking what algorithms are suggestive of by observing the outcomes of algorithmic procedures as indicative of its "point of view." Over the course of several months (March–September, 2011), I used my own personal Facebook profile to compare the contents of the "top news" to that of the "most recent." The most intensive investigation took place during April 2011 when I did the comparison a couple of times a week, took screen shots of the entire top news feeds, and manually counted the posts in the most recent feeds. I took the oldest story published in the top news and compared it to the number of stories published in the most recent feed up to the same time stamp. On a randomly selected day in April 2011, this amounted to 280 stories/updates published on the most recent feed as opposed to 45 posts appearing in the top news feed within the same timeframe. At first glance, only 16% of the possible stories seem to have made it to the top news. As time decay is one of the major known factors of the Facebook news feed algorithm, it is safe to assume that there is a higher probability of making it into the top news the closer to "real time" the story is published. In fact, my experiment showed that, if a story was published within the last three hours, the chance of getting onto the top news was between 40 and 50%. In addition to selecting from the total number of updates generated by friends from the real-time stream, top news also displays its own tailored news stories that are not displayed in the most-recent feed. I call these stories "communication stories," as they make a story out of two friends' recent communicative interaction.[19] Communication stories in Facebook typically take the form of "X commented on Y's photo" or "X likes Y's link." Taking these tailored stories into the equation, a better estimate for the 45/280 ratio would be a mere 12% chance of getting in the top news. Of all the 45 stories published, 17 were communication stories. What most of these 17 communication stories had in common was a high degree of interaction. For example, a typical story would say: "Anna commented on Claire's photo" along with "11 people like this" and "View all 14 comments." Not only does Facebook tailor specific stories for the top news feed, these stories also receive a significant amount of visibility as opposed to other types of edges. Presumably, the emphasis on quantification is supposed to simulate the impression of high activity in order to lower the threshold for participation on the platform.

A different top news sample from the experiment reveals the following: Of 42 posts displayed, only three of the stories published by my "friends" came without any form of interaction by others (that is, without any likes or comments). My top news was filled with stories that obviously signify engagement and interaction. Although distribution of the specific types of stories published varied over the course of the six months in which I systematically studied the news feed, stories without significant interaction seemed to be filtered out. The fact that there were almost no stories by friends that made it to the top news without any form of engagement by others strengthens the impression of an algorithmic bias toward making those stories that signify engagement more visible than those that do not. No matter how meticulous the counting and comparing between the two feeds may be, the exact percentage of stories making it to the top news remains largely obscure.

However, my initial experiments showed what Facebook only later confirmed— that, on average, Facebook users only see a small percentage of what they could have been seeing. Of the "1,500+ stories a person might see whenever they log onto Facebook, news feed displays approximately 300" (Boland, 2014). Making it onto the news feed has become a competitive advantage, especially for an increasing number of business pages. On Facebook, becoming visible is to be selected by the algorithm. Inscribed in the algorithmic logic of the news feed is the idea that visibility functions as a reward rather than as punishment, as is the case with Foucault's notion of panopticism. This is even truer today than when the data reported on in this chapter were collected. In the first half of 2011, the top news feed primarily showed a mixture of stories from friends and pages, giving prominence to cluster stories or what I have called communication stories to provide the impression of constant activity and engagement. While stories of the type "X commented on Y's photo" are still shown in the news feed, most of these stories are now shown as they happen and displayed as part of the much smaller Ticker feed. Talking about changes to the news feed since its conception in 2006, Chris Cox, vice president for products at Facebook, remarked that the most noticeable changes have come from what he sees as emergent types of activity—specifically, content derived from "groups" (King, 2013). Indeed, when I look at the kind of content shown on the news feed at the time of this writing in early 2015, stories from the different groups of which I am a member figure much more prominently than before. Now, updates from different housing search groups, local buy-and-sell groups, or community groups are competing with updates from friends and "pages" for attention in the news feed.

Algorithms are fundamentally relational in the sense that they depend on some kind of external input (data) in order to function. Algorithms do not just represent a rigid, preprogrammed structure, understood as "recipes or sets of steps expressed in flowcharts, code or pseudocode" (Mackenzie, 2006: 43). They are also fluid, adaptable, and mutable. This means that the Facebook algorithm is not something that merely acts upon users from above. The power of the Facebook algorithm arises instead from its interrelationships with users. For example, as exemplified in the "News Feed FYI" blog series, "People who tend to watch more video in news feed should expect to see more videos near the top of their Feed" (Welch and Zhang, 2014). Not only is there an obvious circularity to this logic of showing more or the same, the agency of algorithms—their capacity for action—is ultimately put into the hands of users. How Facebook's news feed algorithm will process the data that I provide, therefore, also depends fundamentally on me as well as my relationships with my "friends." This is also the principle of machine learning, the ethos of contemporary computational culture. For instance, top news dynamically updates, depending on how many times I visit Facebook, which makes it difficult to make a general claim about the percentage of stories making it to the top news. On a random day in September 2011, I compared the same top news feed before and after checking the most recent feed, which at that time counted over 300 new posts.[20] What I found was a change of about 34% in stories displayed between the two instances of checking top news.[21] After I checked the most-recent feed, 16 of the 47 posts in the top news feed had immediately changed. The quite noticeable change in stories displayed can be explained by referring back to the workings of the Facebook algorithm. In the first round of checking my top news, the algorithm seemed to put more emphasis on the "time decay" mechanism, since I knew that it had been a while since I had last logged onto Facebook. After checking the most recent feed, however, Facebook "knew" I was "up to date" again, replacing 16 of the previous posts with ones that the system had apparently calculated to be of greater "interest" to me. All 16 new stories displayed in the second round of checking had been posted between 12 and 23 hours after the time of checking and were either of the "communication story" type or stories that had generated a good number of likes and comments. In addition to the frequency with which users check their Facebook, time spent also plays a role. This is to say that the dynamically changing feed also takes into account how long users spend engaging with the stories, not merely how often they check them. While the algorithmic architecture works dynamically, thereby making analysis of its workings difficult, we can treat them as a particular way of framing the environments upon which they work (Mackenzie, 2007). We may say that Facebook's news feed algorithm, acting as a gatekeeper of user-generated content, demarcates visibility as something that cannot be taken for granted. The uncertainty connected to the level of visibility and constant possibility of "disappearing" in relation to the "variable ontology" of software frames visibility as something exclusive. Becoming visible on the news feed is, thus, constructed as something to which to aspire rather than to feel threatened by.

PARTICIPATORY SUBJECTIVITY

The threat of invisibility on Facebook, then, is not merely a symbolical phenomenon but is also, quite literally, real. While the regime of visibility created by Facebook may differ from the one Foucault described in terms of surveillance, understood as imposing a state of permanent visibility, discipline is still part of the new diagrammatic mechanisms. While it has become commonplace to argue for the transition of a disciplinary society into a control society after the post-industrial fact described by Deleuze (1992), I do not see a necessary contradiction between the disciplinary diagram and software-mediated spaces. Discipline simply refers to a diagram that operates by making the subject the "principle of (its) own subjection" (Foucault, 1977: 203). Discipline denotes a type of power that economizes its functioning by making subjects responsible for their own behavior. This is still very much the case with the logic of feedback loops perpetuated by contemporary machine learning techniques. Contrary to the notion that we have moved away from a disciplinary society to a control society as the "Deleuzian turn" suggests, I agree with Mark Kelly (2015) in that many of the aspects ascribed to control societies were already covered by Foucault in his notion of discipline. For Foucault, "Discipline 'makes' individuals; it is the specific technique of a power that regards individuals both as objects and as instruments of its exercise" (Foucault, 1977: 170). It imposes a particular conduct on a particular human multiplicity (Deleuze, 2006: 29). It is important here to highlight that Foucault developed the notion of disciplinary power in order to account for the duality of power and subjectivation—effectuated by "training" subjects to think and behave in certain ways and, thus, to become the principle of their own regulation of conduct. Through the means of correct training, subjects are governed so as to reach their full potentiality as useful individuals (Foucault, 1977: 212). Foucault identified three techniques of correct training: hierarchical observation, normalizing judgment, and the examination. In this sense, we could say that the news feed algorithm exercises a form of disciplinary power since discipline, in Foucault's words, "fixes; it arrests or regulates movements; it clears up confusion; it dissipates compact groupings of individuals wandering about the country in unpredictable ways; it establishes calculated distributions" (1977: 219).

For Facebook, a useful individual is the one who participates, communicates, and interacts. The participatory subject evidently produced by the algorithmic mechanisms in Facebook follows a similar logic to those techniques of correct training at work in sustaining disciplinary power. First, the very real possibility of becoming obsolete inscribed in the "threat of invisibility" arguably instigates a desire to participate. Here, we can see the dual logic inherent in Foucault's understanding of power as both constraining and enabling. While visibility is constrained by the failure to conform to the inherent logic of participation, visibility is also produced and enabled by the same logic. As Foucault asserts: "What is specific to the disciplinary penalty is non-observance, that which does not measure up to the rule, that departs from it" (1977: 178). Not conforming to the rules set out by the architectural program is, thus, punishable. That is, not participating on Facebook will get you punished by making you invisible, and not seeing what may be "the most interesting" content to you.

Second, making it appear as if everybody is participating and communicating by emphasizing those stories that generate a lot of comments and likes provides an incentive to like or comment as well. Simulation creates an impression, and it is precisely the power of impressions that Foucault thought was a driving force in the governing of the self. As Hoffman, elaborating on Foucault's notion of disciplinary power, explains: "Disciplinary power judges according to the norm. He depicts the norm as a standard of behaviour that allows for the measurement of forms of behaviour as 'normal' or 'abnormal'" (2011: 32). By creating the impression that everybody participates, Facebook simultaneously suggests that participation is the norm. Normalization, according to Foucault, created a "whole range of degrees of normality indicating membership of a homogeneous social body but also playing a part in classification, hierarchization and the distribution of rank" (1977: 184). The news feed algorithm can be said to function as a disciplinary technique, producing a "desired user" by constructing subjects through sociotechnical arrangements that emphasize and favor participation, sharing, and socialization. Because interaction functions as a measure for interestingness, practices of liking, commenting, and participation become processes through which the subject may approximate this desired normality.

Third, the participatory subject constituted by the algorithm hinges on an underlying idea of popularity. Displaying edges with a high degree of interaction clearly remediates some well-known cultural assumptions and mass media logic—popularity fosters more popularity. There is, thus, a circular logic to the way in which visibility is organized on Facebook. Being popular enhances the probability of becoming visible, thus increasing the probability of generating even more interaction. Being confronted with communication stories that encourage the user to "view all 14 comments," "view all 9 comments," and acknowledge that "Christina and 7 others like this" enhances the impression that visibility is granted to the popular. By emphasizing the perceived popularity of certain connections, the algorithm also reinforces a regime of visibility that runs counter to much of the celebratory Web 2.0 discourse focusing on democratization and empowerment. While Facebook is certainly a space that allows for participation, the software suggests that some forms of participation are more desirable than others, whereby desirability can be mapped in the specific mechanisms of visibility that I have suggested throughout this chapter.

Conclusion

Given the 1.28 billion active daily Facebook users, algorithmic practices, techniques, and procedures play a powerful role in deciding what gets shown, to whom, and in what ways. Algorithms are never neutral but reflect the values and cultural assumptions of the people who write them. This does not mean that we can simply understand algorithms by asking programmers. While ethnographic work exploring how algorithms are created may tell us something about what goes into the ways an algorithm functions, programmers are no more equipped than other people to talk explicitly about their biases, values, or cultural assumptions. Instead, this chapter reveals how an understanding of the power and politics of algorithms can be approached by considering their sociomateriality. Guided by the question of how the news feed works, for what possible purpose, I argued for a critical, architectural reading of algorithms. Through a close reading of publicly available documents describing the workings of the Facebook news feed as well as systematic observations and analysis of my own news feed, several aspects were revealed about the ways in which sociality and subjectivity are imaged by the platform and how it is systematically embedded and engineered into algorithmic arrangements and mechanics. Despite the emphasis on the material politics of algorithms in this chapter, materiality is never decoupled or distinct from the domain of the social. With much recent focus on the algorithm as an object of analysis within the social sciences and humanities, there has been a certain tendency to imbue too much causal power to the algorithm as if it were a single, easily discernible thing. What has become apparent is that there is an urgent need to historicize algorithms, to put algorithms into broader contexts of production and consumption. At the same time, cultural theorists have to grapple with the inevitable ephemerality of social media algorithms. In this chapter, I have tried to engage with this historicity by considering the cultural beliefs and values held by creators of software and by being explicit about the dates and times of data capture. This is to say that we need to acknowledge that the news feed and its algorithm(s) emerge from somewhere; evolve in particular ways; are talked about in certain terms; mystified; reflect certain beliefs and assumptions; work to accomplish certain technical, economic, and cultural goals; stabilize temporarily, then change again; and so on. It also means that tapping into the algorithmic assemblage will only ever be a tapping into a momentary tracing and stabilisation of a series of events.

Indeed, the analysis of the news feed algorithms presented in this chapter reveals the "variable ontology" characteristic of software (Mackenzie, 2006). While it might be a stretch to claim that Mark Zuckerberg's love of gray T-shirts is an algorithmic metaphor, the piece of clothing does reveal something about the values and beliefs he holds. In spite of restricted access to Facebook engineers, we still find plenty of traces of how platforms operate, how their CEOs and managers think and talk, how code is made and work organized, the ways in which culture matters, how culture gets branded, and the values, norms, and cultural assumptions held by the people involved. These traces include but are not exclusive to the principle of moving furniture, the notion that the physical layout of Facebook's headquarters is designed to change the thinking of Facebook employees, the technical specifications described in patent documents, the engineering rhetoric perpetuated at developer conferences, media reports, and user interface. The study shows how algorithms are ontogenetic simply because the problems that require a solution continuously change. While the problem of showing the most "interesting" content remains, what constitutes interestingness or relevance depends on the given context. Facebook is never finished. Whether we are talking about the physical refurbishing of sofas or the news feed ranking algorithm, the object of study is inherently dynamic, changing, and mutable. In an age of machine learning in which the models used to predict user behavior constantly change as a result of increasing user data, it may prove particularly challenging to capture the underlying logic of how the system works. If, as Foucault suggested, disciplinary power is effectuated by means of training subjects to reach their full potentiality as useful individuals, what we see emerging now is a certain disciplining of the algorithm by means of training the machine to learn correctly from a corpus of known data. What we are still only at the beginning of understanding, let alone addressing in the first place, is what "correct training" means and which techniques are put into place to ensure that algorithms reach their full potentiality as useful machines.

Many of the characteristics associated with disciplinary power described by Foucault, such as the function of enclosure, the creation of self-control, and the training of human multiplicity, are apt characterizations of the kind of enclosed architecture of Facebook and its subtle demands for participation and interaction. However, if we follow Foucault in his understanding of surveillance as a form of "permanent visibility," then this notion fails to capture the algorithmic logic of creating modalities of visibility that are not permanent but temporary, that are not equally imposed on everyone and oscillate between appearing and disappearing. While it is true that Foucault described organizations of power within a somewhat fixed technological and architectural form, the idea that architectural plans structurally impose visibility does not seem to come in conflict with the unstable and changing arrangements characteristic of new media. Spaces, both digital and physical, are always delimited in one way or another. That does not mean they cannot also expand or change as new elements come along. As Foucault sees it, discipline is centripetal, security centrifugal. This is to say that discipline functions to isolate a space or determine a segment, whereas the apparatuses of security "have the constant tendency to expand" by having new elements integrated all the time (Foucault, 2007: 67). Security does not supersede discipline, just as discipline does not replace sovereignty but rather complements and adds to it (Foucault, 2007: 22).

With reference to Foucault's concept of panopticism, my aim in this chapter has been to argue for the usefulness of applying an analytics of visibility to (im)material architectures. Following Foucault's assertion that "the Panopticon must be understood as a generalizable model of functioning; a way of defining power in terms of the everyday life of men" (1977: 205), a diagrammatic understanding of the news feed algorithm provides a constructive entry point for investigating how different regimes of visibilities materialize. Taking the material dimensions of social media seriously reveals how politics and power operate in the technical infrastructure of these platforms. In Foucault's terms, the news feed can be understood as a form of government in which the right disposition of things are arranged to lead to a suitable end (2007: 96). Algorithms, it was argued, are key to the disposition of things or what Ranciere would call the distribution the sensible. What the operational logic of the news feed ranking algorithm reveals is a reversal of Foucault's notion of surveillance. Participatory subjectivity is not constituted through the imposed threat of an all-seeing vision machine but, rather, by the constant possibility of disappearing and becoming obsolete.

5

Affective Landscapes

Everyday Encounters with Algorithms

I have been a Twitter user for more than ten years now, but I still do not know how to use it. Tweeting does not come naturally to me, and I would not really be able to explain what the platform is for. However, like most users, I think of Twitter as a real-time micro-blogging platform from which you can tweet small snippets of thoughts, pieces of information, or links to a group of followers. For many, the real-time reverse chronological feed is the most defining aspect of Twitter's user experience. It, therefore, felt somewhat transgressive when Twitter announced in early 2016 they would introduce an "algorithmic timeline" to replace its iconic real-time feed. It did not come as a surprise that the news that Twitter was preparing to change this defining feature completely would cause a massive public outcry. Like any big platform change nowadays, enraged users gathered around a hashtag to protest. For days and weeks, #RIPTwitter demonstrated the dismay people felt at the arrival of the algorithm. "In case you never hear from me again, you can thank Twitter's genius new algorithm system ... #RIPTwitter."[1] "The main thing I love about Twitter is that it does not use an algorithm. Sounds like that's changing. #RIPTwitter."[2] "Every time I hear the word 'algorithm' my heart breaks. #RIPTwitter."[3] I want to start this chapter with the case of #RIPTwitter, not because the user protests surrounding platforms are somehow exceptional, but because of the emerging ordinariness of algorithms that these tweets and many more like them seem to convey. As Christian Sandvig (2015) notes, in the years 2006–2013, "There has been a five-fold increase in the number of times the word 'algorithm' appeared in the major newspapers of the world." This number has likely just exploded since 2013, with the news media now routinely reporting on algorithms. While many people are still not aware of the extent to which algorithms are curating their online experiences (Eslami et al., 2015), we might nevertheless—or precisely because of it—sense the emergence of a new "structure of feeling" (Williams, 1977) surrounding algorithms as evident in various emerging discursive impulses surrounding the algorithm.[4]

The starting premise for this chapter is that algorithms are becoming habitual and part of a felt presence as people inhabit mediated spaces. This is not to say that algorithms are necessarily consciously present to people but that they have the capacity to call forth "something that feels like something" (Stewart, 2007: 74). Sometimes, this something may take the form of an event such as the #RIPTwitter protest, a moment when "collective sensibilities seem to pulse in plain sight" (2007: 74). Most of the time, however, algorithmic impulses become barely noticeable in the mundane moments of everyday life. Recall, for example, the targeted ads for the Lisbon hotel recommendation or the party dress that seemed to creep up on me while I was surfing the Web (as described in chapter 1), or the oddity of having your credit card company put a security ban on you without being able to explain why (as mentioned in chapter 3). In moments like these, algorithms make themselves known even though they often remain more or less elusive. They become strangely tangible in their capacity to create certain affective impulses, statements, protests, sensations and feelings of anger, confusion or joy.

In this chapter, we move away from the disciplinary power of algorithms explored in the previous chapter toward the "micropolitics" of power imbued in the affective and phenomenological dimensions of algorithms. By "micropolitics," I mean something akin to Foucault's (1978) notion of microphysics as a way to pay attention to the generative potential of specific everyday practices and techniques. More specifically, micropolitics "refers to the barely perceived transitions in power that occur in and through situated encounters" and the idea that "different qualities of encounter do different things" (Bissell, 2016: 397). This is not a kind of power and politics that is necessarily repressive, discriminatory, or hierarchical but, rather, productive in the sense that it produces certain capacities to do and sense things. What I am interested in is the question of how algorithms and people meet, and what these encounters make possible or restrict? The notion of affect becomes important in terms of describing what is at stake in thinking about the barely noticeable and more sensible dimensions of algorithms as a key to understanding the power and politics of algorithmic life. Without going much further into the notion of "affect" (many books have been dedicated to this concept alone), suffice it, at this point, to say that "affect" describes the domains of "the more-than or less-than rational" in life, including "mood, passion, emotion, intensity, and feeling" (Anderson, 2006: 734).[5] I specifically focus on the ways in which algorithms have the capacity to affect and be affected (Deleuze & Guattari, 1987) by looking at how users perceive and make sense of algorithms as part of their everyday lives.

The point, however, is not to assess the extent to which people actually feel algorithms as such but to highlight experience and affective encounters as valid forms of knowledge of algorithms (see chapter 3 for a discussion on the phenomenological approach to algorithms). The argument is made that algorithms do not just do things to people, people also do things to algorithms. The word *to* is important as it extends more classic accounts of media use and arguments of audience power. It is not just that people do things *with* the help of algorithms. By using algorithms, they also do things to them—modulate and reconfigure them in both discursive and material ways. As we discussed in chapter 2, the machine-learning algorithms proliferating on social media platforms are never set in stone. These algorithms are continuously molded, shaped, and developed in response to user input. If the previous chapter made a case for analyzing algorithms as governmental techniques directed at the "right disposition of things" through rankings and weights as architectural forms of power, this chapter considers the "productive power" of cultural imaginaries and the significant role users have in reconfiguring the algorithmic spaces that they themselves inhabit.

Encountering Algorithms

Consider the following scene: Michael presses the post button and waits. Normally, it should not take longer than five minutes before the "likes" and "comments" start ticking in. Nothing happens. As an independent musician, Michael has to find his own ways to spread the word about his music and make sure he reaches an audience. Facebook seems like the perfect platform for self-promotion. Michael thinks he has gotten better at playing "Facebook's game," as he calls it. For example: "Statuses do better based on what night you post it, the words you choose to use, and how much buzz it initially builds." He knows from previous experience that, "if the status doesn't build buzz (likes, comments, shares) within the first ten minutes or so, it immediately starts moving down the news feed and eventually gets lost." Michael has just released a new album and needs to get the word out. He picks what seems to him the perfect day of the week, carefully crafts the words of the update, deliberately uses phrases such as "wow!" and "this is amazing!" to make the post more visible. Or so he thinks. But nothing happens, and the post eventually disappears, no downloads, just some scattered "likes."[6]

One more: Rachel is an avid Facebook user, but lately she thinks "the Facebook algorithm is destroying friendships."[7] She's been a Facebook member almost since the very beginning and has over 700 friends. She considers herself a fairly sociable and outgoing person, who likes to post regular status updates and frequently comments on other people's posts. Then, a few weeks back, she saw a post by an old friend from high school. Rachel had totally forgotten they were even Facebook friends. She had not seen this old friend in ages, and, all of a sudden, she "pops up in her news feed." Rachel is curious—how much has she been missing out on? What's been going on in her friend's life that Facebook decided not to broadcast on her own feed? "I'm constantly taken aback by all the info and people Facebook hides from my feed on a daily basis," Rachel says. "So, in that sense, it does feel as if there is only a select group of friends I interact with on the social network, while I've practically forgotten about the hundreds of others I have out there."[8]

More than simply describing the strange feelings of media users, these scenes describe some of the many mundane moments in which people variously encounter the algorithmic realities and principles underlying contemporary media platforms. For 21-year-old Michael, the Facebook algorithm has become an important part of his everyday life. As a musician, he depends on the Facebook platform to promote his music, connect with fans and followers, and engage in a community of like-minded artists in L.A., where he lives. Michael describes his encounters with the algorithm as a game of popularity that hinges on the number of likes and comments his updates are able to attract. In many ways, Michael's story is reminiscent of the "threat of invisibility" described in the previous chapter. To counteract this threat, Michael has developed strategies and tactics that he thinks will guarantee him a better chance at retaining attention and getting noticed. Based on previous experience and videos about the underlying logic of the news feed, Michael has developed theories about how the algorithm works. What is frustrating, he says, is when it turns out not to be true. For Rachel, the Facebook algorithm is not subject to the same kind of frustration as it is for Michael. Rachel, a 24-year-old journalist based in New York City, does not "depend" on the algorithm for her own livelihood in the way that Michael does. As a journalist, however, she has noticed that there seems to be an increasing number of news reports on algorithms lately. An article in the *Washington Post* dealt with the Facebook algorithm; and, ever since, Rachel has been trying to find signs of it in her own news feed. When an old friend from high school appeared in her feed seemingly from nowhere and even "liked" one of Rachel's posts, she finally sensed the algorithm at work. With respect to forgetting people, Rachel says, it feels like the algorithm is trying to make decisions on her behalf, ultimately influencing the way in which she conducts her friendships. The question going forward is how we might want to think about such everyday encounters with algorithms and what, if anything, they might tell about the ways in which algorithms shape our experiences?

Asking about people's encounters with algorithms seems to suggest a conscious meeting of some sort or that people are already aware of and have a grasp of what algorithms are. As existing research has shown this is far from always the case (Eslami et al. 2015; Rader & Gray, 2015). In many ways, the question of how people attend to algorithms is akin to the question of how people start to make sense of that which is not readily available to the senses, which has always been an important area of research in the history of science.[9] Many scientific and technological innovations are not visible as such. Just think of nanotechnology, RFID, or sensor technologies of various kinds. Like algorithms, they are embedded in computers, pieces of clothing, and other more visible interfaces. Dealing with uncertainties and unknowns is part of what it means to be a human; it is part of what it means to live toward a future, what it means to be in love, or what it means to understand things such as physics and climate change. When people are faced with the hidden and uncertain aspects of life, they tend to construct what has variously been described as "mental models" (Schutz, 1970; Kempton, 1986), "interpretive frames" (Bartunek & Moch, 1987), or simply "folk theories" (Hirschfeld, 2001; Johnson-Laird & Oatley, 1992; Johnson, 1993). To interact with technologies, people have to make sense of them, and they do so in a variety of ways—for example, through visualizations, analogies to more familiar domains, or by the use of metaphors. Media discourses, cultural artefacts, stories, anecdotes, and shared cultural beliefs can "provide people with explanatory power and guide behavior surrounding use of a particular technology" (Poole et al., 2008). The increased ubiquity and popularity of depicting unfamiliar phenomena such as artificial intelligence and robotics in films and popular imagery have arguably made these phenomena more available to public reasoning and debate (see Suchman, 2007).[10] This is no different when it comes to the algorithm, which is rarely encountered in its mathematical or technical form. When people encounter or "see" the algorithm, it is typically in the form of simplified images of a formula (e.g., EdgeRank formula) or a newspaper story about a recent controversy as evident, for example, in the recent censorship accusations against Facebook and their "algorithm" removing the iconic "Terror of War" image or through other means of cultural mediation such as films and artworks of various kinds.

Unsurprisingly, perhaps, algorithms are difficult to represent or culturally mediate even for computer scientists.[11] However, as Sandvig (2015) notes, in an attempt to make the algorithm more intelligible to the public we are seeing an epistemic development in which "algorithms now have their own public relations." That is, beyond the technical or educational imagery of algorithms characteristic of earlier times, algorithms materialize in different representational settings. Algorithms have become objects of marketing, represented in commercialized images of mathematical formulas and circulated by various third-party marketing consultants, technology blogs, and other trade press publications. The process of making algorithms a product of public relations is not so different from what Charles Bazerman (2002) calls the production of "representational resting points." In examining the cultural history of Edison's electric light, Bazerman argues that, before the invention "could create its own new world of experience and meaning," it was crucial to develop accepted representations of electric light as stable points of reference (2002: 320).[12] What exactly these representational resting points are with regards to algorithms and machine learning is still up for grabs, but simplified mathematical formulas or cyborg figures are certainly part of it. Though the formula may portray algorithms as objects of science and neutral conduits, this is arguably not what people experience in their day-to-day life. As the stories of Michael and Rachel suggest, what people experience is not the mathematical recipe but, rather, the moods, affects, and sensations of which algorithms are generative. The notion of mental models, then, only brings us so far—not because the theories that people construct about unfamiliar technologies and hidden processes often prove to be inaccurate (Adams & Sasse, 1999; Wash, 2010), but because it does not necessarily matter whether they are correct or not.

From a phenomenological perspective, what is of interest is how the seemingly hidden and unfamiliar technological processes permit or limit people's movements and whereabouts. For people in their everyday lives, what matters is not necessarily the truth (whatever that is) but "practical knowing" (Thrift, 2007: 121); that is, people "know as they go, as they journey through the world along paths of travel" (Ingold, 2011: 154). In other words, people learn what they need to know in order to engage meaningfully with and find their way around an algorithmically mediated world. For Michael, for example, Facebook's news feed algorithm feels like a gatekeeper that stands in the way of his music career. Knowing the algorithm just enough to ensure that his followers receive his updates matters to him—not just personally but also professionally. The kind of knowledge that I am concerned with here, then, treats the beliefs people form about algorithms not as right or wrong but as a point of access for understanding how and when algorithms matter.

Researching Personal Algorithm Stories

Contrary to the notion that "the individual user is incapable of really experiencing the effect that algorithms have in determining one's life as algorithms rarely, if ever, speak to the individual" (Cheney-Lippold, 2011: 176), I suggest in this chapter that people do experience algorithms; and, while algorithms might not speak directly to individuals, they might speak through them. Here, I report on a series of personal algorithm stories, that is, stories about algorithms derived from people's online experiences. Over a two-year period from October 2014 to August 2016, I collected personal algorithm stories from social media users through email and face-to-face interviews with 35 individuals about their perceptions and awareness of algorithms. The data set also contains over 2000 tweets written by social media users that contain popular hashtags such as #RIPTwitter and #InstagramAlgorithm as well as blog posts and archived comment sections of newspaper articles discussing algorithms. Taking my lead from Zizi Papacharissi (2015), who sees the collective discourses organized around hashtags on Twitter as indicative of an emergent structure of feeling, I shall expand this notion to include not just hashtags but also disparate tweets about algorithms as indicative of an affective landscape surrounding the felt presence of algorithms. Going back to Michael and Rachel, their algorithm stories were originally collected using their own tweets as a starting point. Expressing feelings of bewilderment and defeat, their tweets simply read: "This Facebook algorithm is just super frustrating" (Michael) and "Facebook algorithm destroys friendships" (Rachel).[13] Seeing these kinds of utterances as part of my Twitter feed, I could not help wondering where they came from. What had prompted Michael and Rachel to tweet those things?

Methodologically, I engage in what might be called a scenographic inquiry into the affective landscapes generated in and through algorithms by attending to the scenes, situations, episodes, and interruptions that give rise to the felt presence of algorithms in everyday life. By "scenographic," I mean a methodological sensibility akin to writers and scholars such as Lauren Berlant and Kathleen Stewart, both of whom attend to cases or scenes of the ordinary as a way of making affective processes more palpable. For Stewart (2007), scenes are method and genre, a way of writing about ordinary affects as a series of happenings that, taken together, form a story about what it feels like to live in contemporary America. As McCormack writes, the scene or situation "becomes a way of gathering the sense of worlds that matter while also posing the question of how the force of these worlds might become part of their stories" (2015: 93). A situation, as Berlant defines it, "is a state of things in which something that will perhaps matter is unfolding amid the usual activity of life. It is a state of animated and animating suspension," one "that forces itself on consciousness, that produces a sense of the emergence of something in the present" (2011: 5). Algorithms, I suggest, may be productive of such emerging presences and "accessed" via the ways in which they make people feel and the stories that they tell about those encounters. This is closely related to the notion of affect but not exactly the same. As Papacharissi (2015) points out, affect is what permits feelings to be felt, it is the movement that may lead to a particular feeling. Affect, she suggests, can be thought of as the "rhythm of our pace as we walk" (2015: 21). For example, a fast-paced rhythm may lead to and amplify feelings of stress; a slow and light-paced rhythm may make us calm. In the context of this study, the question is how we might think of the force of movement that algorithms create, and how it prompts a "reason to react," as Stewart puts it (2007: 16).

Taking tweets about algorithms written by seemingly ordinary people as my starting point, I was interested in getting a better sense of the kinds of situations and circumstances that had solicited people to react and respond to the ways of the algorithm.[14] During the two years of data collection, I regularly searched Twitter for keywords and combinations of keywords, including: "Facebook algorithm," "algorithm AND Facebook," "Netflix algorithm," "algorithm AND Netflix" and so forth.[15] I queried Twitter every few weeks and manually scrolled down the stream of tweets and took screenshots of the ones that seemed to be more personal rather than marketing-oriented. Using a research profile I had set up on Twitter, I occasionally contacted people who had recently tweeted about algorithms to ask whether they would be willing to answer a few questions related to that tweet. These tweets included statements such as: "I'm offended by the awful taste Twitter's algorithm thinks I have," "Facebook, perhaps there isn't an algorithm that can capture human experience," "It feels like Spotify's algorithm can read my mind—it's both awesome and creepy," "The Netflix algorithm must be drunk," "The algorithm on Facebook confuses me. It seems to think I should lose weight, am broke, pregnant and single." Altogether, I engaged in asynchronous email conversations and synchronous computer mediated chats with 25 individuals, based on questions concerning those tweets.[16] During the spring of 2016, I conducted an additional ten semistructured interviews with long-time social media users in their early twenties about their media use practices and how they viewed the role of algorithms in those interactions.[17]

The answers were first coded for information about the kinds of situations and circumstances that provided the informants a "reason to react." As feminist philosopher Sara Ahmed suggests of strange encounters, "To be affected by something is to evaluate that thing. Evaluations are expressed in how bodies turn towards things. To give value to things is to shape what is near us" (Ahmed, 2010: 31). This became clear in the process of coding the interviews and email transcripts as well. Thus, in a second iteration of coding, all transcripts were analyzed in terms of how they were either explicitly or implicitly evaluating and making sense of the algorithms, the extent to which their awareness of the algorithm affected their use of the platforms in question, what kinds of tactics and strategies they developed in response to the algorithm (if any), and the kinds of issues and concerns they voiced about the algorithms. While these transcripts would not stand up in a court of law, they should be seen as records of happenings that are "diffuse yet palpable gatherings of force becoming sensed in scenes of the ordinary" (McCormack, 2015: 97). What is of importance, then, is not whether the stories that people tell are representative of how algorithms "really are" (if that is even possible). Instead, personal algorithm stories may attest to the ideas and perceptions people have about what algorithms are and how they function and, perhaps more importantly, their imaginings about what algorithms should be and the expectations that people form about them.

Living with Algorithms

People encounter algorithms in all kinds of situations: a recently purchased Christmas gift that appears on the shared family computer as an ad (ruining the surprise), weird recommendations, the almost-forgotten friend who suddenly reappears on the Facebook news feed after years of silence. Although the people I talked to for this chapter claimed to have varying degrees of knowledge about algorithms, a few themes emerged as to when and how algorithms came to matter—here, presented under a few subheadings paraphrased from participants' responses: "People aren't a math problem" describes the different kinds of confounding connections that algorithms seem to be generative of. Whether these connections come across as surprising, uncanny, funny, or bewildering, what unites them is that they do not feel inconsequential to the people affected by them. "Enter the popularity contest" is about the ways in which algorithms become arbiters of difference by "Distributing the sensible" (Ranciere, 2004), demarcating the regimes of visibility in terms of who or what becomes visible. Related to the first theme concerning how algorithms shape the ways in which identity is constituted and experienced, the notion of the popularity contest articulates the ways in which people become aware of and evaluate algorithms based on their capacity to filter content in different ways. Finally,

"Clicking consciously" addresses how algorithms or, more precisely, beliefs about how algorithms work trigger particular responses and ways of being on social media platforms. People develop various strategies and tactics to make themselves "algorithmically recognizable" (Gillespie, 2016) or unrecognizable for that matter. What the data reveal is how being affected by algorithms is not simply a matter of passive observation or subtle awareness but of actionable consequences and movement, of reaction and creativity.

PEOPLE AREN'T A MATH PROBLEM

Meet Jessa. She and her boyfriend, both in their mid-20s, recently moved to New York City for work. The couple has been subletting an apartment for one and a half months, sleeping on an air mattress that gradually seems to be deflating ever faster. They regularly talk about how much they look forward to sleeping on a real mattress. While Jessa trawls Craigslist for new apartments, her boyfriend looks at mattresses on Amazon. Then, one morning, while Jessa scrolls through her Facebook news feed, there it is—an ad for air mattresses. Jessa is so perplexed that she tweets about it: "How on earth did the Facebook algorithm know she was sleeping on an air mattress?"[18] Although the connection may have been coincidental, the effects are not incidental. While Jessa understands that clicks and browser behavior are routinely tracked and used to tailor ads online, there is something almost inexplicably creepy about the ways in which algorithms seem to know you.[19]

Similarly, Kayla, a 23-year-old student from New York, is confounded by the ways in which the Facebook algorithm seems to have her pegged as "pregnant, single, broke and overweight."[20] Sure, she posted a status update a few days ago about being broke and single, she says, so the suggestions for dating sites and loans made sense. But how weird was it when the algorithm for suggested apps showed her dating sites next to apps for expecting mothers? Like Jessa, Kayla had theories about the logic behind the algorithmic profiling of her. As she speculates, "upon further thought, I think the pregnancy ones were because I had been looking at nursery decorations on another website for a baby shower gift."[21] While the inferences that algorithms make on the basis of user behavior might logically make sense to people, there is something socially and culturally "off" about putting dating sites next to advice for expecting mothers. Despite declaring that they do not really know what an algorithm is, many participants, when asked how they would define an algorithm, seem to make a distinction between a technical aspect and its socially perceived outcomes. Take Shannon, a career counselor in her 40s, who happened to blog about Taylor Swift. Now, the Facebook algorithm seems to think she is a "12 year-old with an Amex card."[22] Shannon is not sure "what the Facebook algorithm is—at least, the technical part of it." She understands that "it picks up clues, perhaps using keywords" from her own activities and information she herself has provided "to try to target relevant content." Although it makes technical sense, it may not feel right, Shannon explains. Asking her to provide an example of her experience of being algorithmically profiled, Shannon says:

> I noticed after I published my blog post on Facebook earlier in the week that, suddenly, the ads that Facebook "chose" for me were often about Taylor Swift concert tickets and products she endorses (like American Express), instead of the usual middle-aged woman assumptions like ads for wrinkle cream and fat loss.[23]

While Shannon thinks that the Taylor Swift incident is amusing, she often finds targeted ads to be "slightly offensive as they make assumptions about me, which I don't like to think are true." Such is the work of "profiling machines" (Elmer, 2004) that seek to produce a sense of identity through detailed consumer profiles, which are geared toward anticipating future needs. Based on statistical inferences and inductive reasoning, profiling algorithms do "not necessarily have any rational grounds and can lead to irrational stereotyping and discrimination" (de Vries, 2010: 80). Still, the question of whether "correct" identifications are being constructed may be beside the point. As de Vries (2010) argues, misidentification is not simply a mismatch or something that should be considered inappropriate. Misidentifications may also give some leeway for thinking about how identity construction is experienced.

Experiencing algorithmic landscapes is as much about what the algorithm does in terms of drawing and making certain connections as it is about people's personal engagements. To draw on Ingold (1993), a particular landscape owes its character to the experiences it affords to the ones that spend time there—to their observations and expectations. For Robin, the ways in which Amazon seems constantly to be confused by her gender is not just amusing and confusing but seems to make her transgender subject position simultaneously more real and unreal. As she explains:

> I am transgender and just starting transition. This seems to confuse Amazon like crazy. It tries to make suggestions and gets things wrong quite often. Sometimes, it's obvious but amusing: "I see you just bought some makeup but wouldn't you like some power tools?" (I have never ordered power tools).

Robin has been thinking about "how much a company is willing to go out on a limb on things like this," whether a company like Amazon would actually be willing to try and categorize people according to all possible demographic buckets, not just the ones that do not seem to endanger their profits:

> If I were to examine my purchase history and come up with a narrative, I'd almost certainly read it as one transgender individual, rather than a heterosexual couple who happens to wear the same size clothing and shoes. But

the negative reaction that comes from a false positive might outweigh any potential sales.[24]

What seems to bother Robin is not so much the fact that the apparatus is unable to categorize her but the apparent heteronormative assumptions that seem to be reflected in the ways in which these systems work. As a person in transition, her queer subject position is reflected in the ways in which the profiling machines do not demarcate a clear, obvious space for her. A similar issue came up in my interview with Hayden, who is also transgender and uses social media primarily to read transition blogs on Tumblr and Instagram. He is not particularly impressed by the way in which algorithms seem to only put "two and two together" when "the way things work in society can be quite the opposite." If this is how algorithms work by simplifying human thoughts and identity, Hayden thinks social media platforms are moving in the wrong direction. As he tellingly suggests, "people aren't a math problem."[25]

Algorithmic mismatches may be perceived as problematic when they are no longer perceived as "innocent" but turn into a more permanent confrontation that feels inescapable and more intrusive. For Lena, the Facebook algorithm is at odds with how she identifies in life. She is no longer the person she used to be. Yet, she feels constantly trapped by her past. She no longer hangs out with the same crowd. She does not share their interests. She has moved across the country from a small rural town in Texas to New York City, where she now goes to grad school. She identifies strongly as liberal and, of course, votes for the Democrats, she says. Yet, all the updates Lena sees on her news feed seem to stem from Republican voters and people who are only interested in celebrity gossip. This obvious disconnect between who she identifies as being and how Facebook seems to have her figured out annoys her. She is annoyed that her "own social network is so out of sync" with her interests and beliefs. Although she speculates that her inability to escape her past could be a result of adding most of her FB "friends" when she was attending high school in rural Texas and not adding as many since she moved to New York City, Lena thinks the algorithm "must be incorrectly assessing my social networking desires."[26] While "real" life allows the past to be the past, algorithmic systems make it difficult to "move on." As Beer (2013) notes, the archive records and works to shape memory by defining what is relatable and retrievable. What happens when the world algorithms create is not in sync (to use Lena's own words) with how people experience themselves in the present? To what extent do existing social networking profiles remain forever muddied by past lives and experiences?

Memory is a powerful thing. It lives in the flash of a second and the duration of a lifetime, it emerges in lifelike dreams and the drowsiness of mornings. Memories can be recalled at will or willfully withdrawn. A memory is an event that connects us to the past and makes it possible to project a path for the future. Memory is an encounter, a distraction, an opportunity, a daydream, or a denial. In the digital age, memories can be made, encouraged, and programmed to make people participate more, share more, engage more. For Albert, this is where machines fall short—"just maybe, there isn't an algorithm capable of capturing human experience," he tweets.[27] When asking Albert to provide some context to his tweet, he explains:

> I was tweeting about Facebook's recent "Year in Review" fiasco, where the algorithm they created was generating reviews that included some terrible memories—deaths of children, divorces, etc. My point in the tweet was that, while algorithms might (or might not) be a good tool for effectively serving up the right ad to the right user, they might not be the best way to create emotional content or connect on a human level.[28]

The incident that Albert cites, and which prompted him to speak out about the limits of algorithms, is the story of Eric Meyer and the "cruel algorithm" serving up a picture of his recently deceased daughter as part of Facebook's "year in review" feature. For Eric Meyer and others experiencing these unwanted flashes of painful memories, algorithmically curated and repackaged content does not just materialize in helpful birthday reminders. It also lingers as insensitive reminders of the tragedies of life. Emerging at odd moments, these digitally mediated memories make you "raise your head in surprise or alarm at the uncanny sensation of a half-known influence" (Stewart, 2007: 60). More than anything, however, the incident made explicit for Albert "the most obvious thing about algorithms—they're just machines." What was obviously missing, says Albert, was the "human judgment that says, 'You know, this guy probably doesn't want to be reminded that his daughter died this year, so even though the post got tons of attention, I'll leave it out.'" Indeed, algorithmic systems "judge individuals against a set of contrasting norms, without human discretion intervening or altering decisions" (Beer, 2013: 77).

Similarly, Ryan, a 21-year-old avid YouTube user, thinks that mechanical ways of trying to solve human problems and desires is where the algorithm hits its barrier. The problem with algorithms, Ryan suggests, is "that they are just based on trends and past behavior. It can't predict for you in the future, it just assumes you are going to repeat everything you've done in the past." Algorithms do not take into account that "people are unpredictable and like to try new things all the time," he says.[29] This is why Ryan loves people who put considerable effort into their YouTube channels—particularly, the semifamous YouTube celebrities he follows, who explicitly ask fans to contribute to their next videos. For Ryan, these YouTube celebrities are almost like "human algorithms," making sure they give their audience what they want. Ryan thinks they are "more accurate than an automatic algorithm, because computer algorithms don't really understand human preferences or traits like actual humans do." This is precisely what Hayden seems to touch on when he claims that people are not a math problem: People are more complicated than an equation, more complex and unpredictable than what can be broken down into a few steps of instructions for a computer. In fact, Hayden thinks algorithms are fundamentally not that smart. They were not able, for example, to parse the fact that "views" means beautiful scenery, while it also happens to be the name of the rapper Drake's newest album. So, when Hayden uses the hashtag "views" for all his recent images of sunsets and landscape pictures on Instagram, he is not interested in following a bunch of Drake fans, which an algorithm apparently suggested. What became apparent in many of the participants' responses, then, is not just how algorithms are capable of misjudging humans but how they might not even be able to judge humans at all.

ENTER THE POPULARITY CONTEST

While algorithms might be bad at judging human complexity and emotional valences, they also seem to augment and amplify traditional social norms and hierarchies. For participants, this is most evident in terms of the perceived capacity of algorithms to filter and sort content and people according to their popularity and importance. Algorithms, of course, are not unique in this respect. The media have always operated according to the principle of privileging certain voices and personalities over others. As Altheide and Snow (1979) attested in their influential account of media logic, the mass media fundamentally work by assigning some expressions more weight and importance than others. The logic of popularity is highly evident in the operational logics of social media platforms, which often incorporate some form of personalized ranking mechanism to distinguish popular content from less important items (van Dijck & Poell, 2013). Technically, however, popularity and personalization are not easily squared (Amatriain, 2013). Whereas popularity is generally about recommending items according to a global notion of relevance, personalization is about satisfying members with varying tastes. As Amatriain writes in a paper explicating the models behind Netflix recommendations, the goal "becomes to find a personalized ranking function that is better than item popularity" in order to cater to a variety of tastes (2013: 3). This goal does not just apply to Netflix but to pretty much every platform that seeks to filter and rank its content to retain user attention in some way or another.

Indeed, the balancing act between quantity and quality, between high degrees of links/likes and individual practical engagement, constitutes a core challenge for platforms. When the balancing act fails—as it often does—users notice. Why, for example, did Netflix recommend a horror movie when Katy only ever watches romantic comedies, or why does OKCupid's matching algorithm only seem to suggest outdoorsy types when all Robin wants to do is go to concerts and eat good food? Just because many people like horror movies or because the fit and healthy seem to be a thing on dating apps, this does not mean either is right for everyone. People particularly notice the popularity contest in terms of the ways in which social media platforms such as Facebook have a tendency to make the same people or the same type of content visible time and again. Lucas, a 25-year-old quality assurance engineer, says he spends a lot of his spare time on social media. Lately, he has noticed that there is absolutely no new content popping up on his Facebook feed.

> The same 5-6 stories were showing up at the top of my feed across a 4-hour period. I have a fairly large social graph on Facebook (1,000+ "friends"), so to see absolutely no new content show up agitated me, so I tweeted about my feelings on the algorithm.[30]

Lucas thinks that "Facebook's filtering consistently degrades what he prefer in his online social experience." Like Lena, who seems to be caught in a Republican loop on Facebook, Lucas feels that the platform is holding back important information. The problem for the participants lies not necessarily with filtering in and of itself but with the feeling of *not knowing* what they could have known. This is not simply the fear of missing out but of having "your own content" and relationships controlled or even censored by a platform, as some participants suggest.

Going back to Michael and Rachel's stories, their frustration with Facebook stems in part from the feeling of having someone else decide on their behalf the conditions under which their contributions are either made visible or silenced. Indeed as Amber, another participant tells me, "I am feeling annoyed that the algorithm decides for me [...] it is so unpredictable and strange."[31] Nora, a 21-year-old Canadian public policy student, thinks there is "definitely something strange going on with the Facebook algorithm."[32] In a series of tweets, Nora speculates about the underlying mechanisms of Facebook, noting that some of her posts seem to get far more "likes" and comments than others without any apparent reason. The number of "likes," "shares," and "comments" fuel the popularity game supported by social media platforms in which algorithms feed off on the social disposition towards interaction. Nora worries that the popularity bias of social media algorithms potentially diminishes what people get to see. Specifically, she worries that the algorithmic bias toward "likes" and "shares" makes viral videos such as the "ice bucket challenge" much more prominent, hiding more important but less "liked" current events such as the racial conflicts in Ferguson. As Nora says, "I don't like having an algorithm or editor or curator or whatever controlling too much of what I say—if they're trying to go for more 'trending topics,' will my posts on 'non-trending topics' get shuttered away?"[33]

The notion that algorithms contribute to making the popular even more popular is not just apparent in the participants' understanding of algorithms. It is very much evident in the public discourses surrounding algorithms as well. Let us for a moment return to the #RIPTwitter incident mentioned at the beginning of this chapter and consider some of tweets that contained this hashtag: "Algorithms are a form of censorship. I look to Twitter for unfiltered news in real time."[34] "One of the great rewards of being an adult is deciding ON YOUR OWN who (and what) you should be interested in."[35] "Think about it, with an algorithm you might never see a tweet from specific people ever again. RIP Twitter."[36] "Replacing the chronological time line with an algorithm based feed. Turning Twitter into a popularity contest. No thanks."[37] In my interview with Ryan, he brings up similar issues and worries. He thinks it would be "a big mistake" if Twitter started using algorithms on a large scale, as "it will obviously favor media and links and videos and photos and stuff like that, and it will not favor text posts, which is a majority of what the average user is posting on that platform." Hayden voiced a similar concern about the possibility that Instagram would change into an algorithmically filtered feed. For Hayden, the "Instagram algorithm" would merely make the "Instagram famous" even more famous since they would "automatically pop up on the top, and you won't see your friends who might have fewer followers."[38] Like Hayden, the users who gathered around the hashtag #InstagramAlgorithm only two months after Twitter announced its algorithmically curated feed voiced their worries about the platform turning into a popularity contest—for example: "Meh about the Instagram algorithm change. Popularity contests were never my thing."[39] "Why is everything a popularity contest on social media? Why @snapchat is the healthiest platform for your self esteem. #InstagramAlgorithm."[40] "Why does @instagram think that this is a good idea? It's 'insta'gram not 'popular'gram #RIPInstagram."[41] "The new @instagram algorithm is the end for small timers like me. I'm not winning any popularity contests against big names."[42] These tweets are worth quoting at length not because they are necessarily representative of the general sentiments of the hashtag publics that form around these specific events but because of the ways in which they show how algorithms are variously imagined and the expectations people have of them. What these sentiments show is how algorithms are imagined as control mechanisms and gatekeepers that work to enforce existing power structures.

However, algorithms are not always pictured as "bad" or controlling. The same person may talk about algorithms as problematic in the context of one platform but not seem to have a problem with a similar mechanism on another platform. Some algorithms are regarded as useful, while others are seen as obtrusive. For example, while Nora is worried about the Facebook algorithm controlling too much of what she sees, she says that, "with regards to Google, I think that is an algorithm I would actually place my faith in."[43] When I probe her about her reasons for having faith in Google but not in Facebook, she says she is struggling to find an exact reason. Perhaps, it is because Google *is* search, she speculates, or because Facebook somehow

> feels much more intrusive because the things they are intruding on is really personal things that really could mess someone up [...] Whereas Google, it is just a search engine. When you go to Google you already have an idea of what to find.[44]

The ambiguity surrounding different kinds of algorithms became particularly evident in the semistructured interviews conducted over Skype. Algorithms are not inherently regarded as problematic but, rather, become more or less problematic in terms of how restrictive they feel to users. Several of the interviewees seemed to focus on the degree of agency and control they felt they had in terms of navigating different platforms. Ryan, for example, makes a distinction between helpful algorithms and controlling ones. As with Amber and Nora, Ryan also says "it feels like with Facebook, the algorithm is controlling me." He categorizes Facebook's algorithms as big while Twitter's algorithm, despite the recent news, still feels "small" and "simple." As he explains,

> [T]his simple algorithm that Twitter has is that it shows you briefly that, while you've been away, these are the major things that has happened in the feed [...] I think the Twitter algorithm is very nice, because it is very simple, and it doesn't control that very much, it just helps you a little bit.[45]

When asking Ryan to expand on what he means by the notion of "helpful algorithms," he brings up Netflix, his favorite platform. To him, the Netflix algorithm is like Facebook's algorithm and Twitter's algorithm: Like Facebook because it "shows what is popular right now," and like Twitter in that it focuses on "your own customized feed without any other interference" but still tries to help you find new content "based on what I have watched." Similarly, Melissa, a 22-year-old Canadian college student, thinks that Netflix gives you the "greatest control, because it will pull specifically from what you yourself are doing. They will not pull from what your friends are doing, or what you are looking at."[46] While all of the platforms try to find content that is relevant to users, there is a sense in which it makes a difference whether the user feels in control by setting the parameters themselves and the algorithm is merely helping along, as opposed to a situation in which the algorithm seems to determine relevancy more or less on its own or, at least, without any obvious explicit input from users. In many cases, personalization is seen as an asset if the platforms get it right but an intrusion if the popular seems to get in the way of the personal. Melissa links the demand for personalized content to her generation's desire to feel special. This is how she puts it:

> You are always looking for something that makes you special. And that is one reason why Starbucks' business model was so successful. Because giving the cup with your name on it makes you feel like an individual in the sea of people. And I think the online platforms try to do a similar thing by offering you things they think you want the most. And it makes you feel like it is almost like the media platforms are looking out for you. They try to give you the best experience you can have on that platform. And some succeed and some not so much. But I find the personalization much more

gratifying for the user than having the same standard experience as everybody else.[47]

Just as the platforms themselves struggle to find the right balance between ranking based on a global notion of relevance and/or a more personal model, users also seem to oscillate between a desire for popular content on the one hand and personalized content on the other. More importantly, what these different responses show is that algorithms are not just factual but also normative in the sense that, both explicitly and implicitly, people have an understanding of how things ought to be, that is, how algorithms should perform.

CLICKING CONSCIOUSLY EVERYDAY

Living in an algorithmically mediated environment does not simply mean that algorithms are overruling users. Wanting to collect likes and comments is not just a "narcissistic cry for help" (Agger, 2012: 45). For many users, it has become a necessary strategy to deploy if they want to impact the algorithm's "willingness" to show their posts more prominently. Many of the avid social media users I talked to have in one way or another tried to play or experiment with the operational logics of the platforms they use—to try to be seen or not seen or otherwise to circumvent perceived control mechanisms. Several of the participants, for example, mention the experience of being caught in a temporary feedback loop. Ryan says of the YouTube recommendation algorithm's tendency to reinforce a viewing pattern, no matter whether it is correct or not:

> Sometimes, I click on a video and think it is something and it is actually about something else, but now that I watched it, YouTube will show me a bunch of videos connected to that in the recommended section, and I don't really care about any of it.

In order to "correct" the algorithm, Ryan says he either stops clicking on anything for a while or just starts clicking on as many other more-related videos as he can. Similarly, Rachel, the woman who tweeted about Facebook destroying friendships, says that:

> I find myself "clicking consciously" every day. This is going to sound crazy, but I remember the one time I accidentally clicked on a former high school classmate's profile and cursed under my breath: "damn it, now I'm gonna see her stuff 24/7."

"Clicking consciously" emerged as a key theme in people's responses to how algorithms affect their use of platforms. Moreover, the notion of being trapped in a temporary bubble because of the way one clicks and likes seemed to constitute a rather common experience of being in algorithmic spaces. As the comments of Rachel and Ryan suggest, either you take charge of the clicks or the clicks will catch you up in a perpetual feedback loop.

Clicking consciously, however, is not just a defense strategy of sorts. It emerges quite prominently in a much more proactive sense as well. Take Kate, a former school teacher who now runs a Facebook page for parents in her neighborhood. For Kate, it is vital that her posts are seen and circulated as widely as possible. In order to secure "maximum reach" as she puts it, Kate takes great care to post "consciously," which, in her case, means using multiple pictures instead of one, always trying to choose the right words, and the right time of the day. As a page owner, Kate says, "I have completely changed how I share information to make it work best for the algorithm."[48] In a similar vein, Nora tailors her updates in specific ways to fit the Facebook algorithm. Like Michael, Nora has been observing the working of the news feed for a while, taking notes of what seems to work and what does not. As she puts it, "If I post things and they receive no likes within the first 5 minutes, or very sparse likes (1–2 in the first minute), then they'll drop off and not get many comments or likes at all." Over the years, Nora has developed different strategies for making her "posts more frequently recognized" by the algorithm.[49] These strategies include posting at a certain time ("usually around late evening on a weekday that's not Friday"), structuring the post in specific ways, making sure that other people are *not* shown in her profile pictures (otherwise, they are "likely to get fewer likes") and making sure to avoid or include certain keywords in her updates.

As Gillespie (2016) has usefully pointed out, adapting online behavior to social media platforms and their operational logics can be seen as a form of optimization, whereby content producers make their posts "algorithmically recognizable." When users wait until a certain day of the week and for a particular time of day, use multiple pictures instead of one, carefully choose their words, and deliberately use positive sounding phrasing, they are not just strategically updating their social media profiles or hoping to be seen by others. Reminiscent of Gillespie's (2014) argument about using hashtags for optimizing the algorithm, the personal algorithm stories shared as part of this study suggest that many of the participants are redesigning their expressions in order to be better recognized and distributed by the algorithm. Like Kate, Ryan thinks the underlying logic of social media matters a lot. As he says, "how social media works really, really impacts what I post and how I post it." For example, posting "life events" on Facebook or using certain hashtags on Twitter and Instagram was seen by some of the participants as a particularly effective means of increasing the probability the algorithm will make them visible.

Of course, people have always developed strategic efforts to be seen and recognized by information intermediaries. As Gillespie writes, "sending press releases to news organizations, staging events with the visual impact that television craves, or making spokespeople and soundbites available in ways convenient to journalists" have long been media strategies for visibility (2016: 2). Users have in a sense always tried to reverse engineer or playfully engage with the seemingly impenetrable logics of media institutions and powerbrokers. However, in this day and age, the logic that people are trying to crack is not about human psychology but machine processing.

Part of this task involves figuring out how these platforms function. For example, posting "life events" on Facebook or using certain hashtags on Twitter and Instagram were seen by some of the participants as particularly effective means for increasing the probability of being made visible by the algorithm. According to Zoe, a 23-year-old self-employed Canadian designer, it is not just about knowing which hashtags to use in order to get noticed but also about knowing how different platforms treat and value them in the first place.[50] For an up-and-coming designer like Zoe, who depends on reaching an audience (much like Michael), being unable to navigate certain platform conventions could be detrimental to business. The blogging platforms Tumblr and Instagram, for instance, have different hashtag conventions that are not just about knowing which are the most popular. Take a seemingly small technical detail such as whether or not a platform allows typing spaces in hashtags. Zoe says it took her a while to figure out that cross-posting images between the blogging platform Tumblr and Instagram failed to attract new followers or interest simply because the hashtags would not synchronize in the right way. While the hashtags worked on Tumblr, they turned into gibberish on Instagram. Zoe speculates that this may have cost her valuable opportunities to be noticed due to the algorithm's unwillingness to feature her profile on other users' "explore" section of Instagram. Using the right hashtags in the right way will increase your chances of becoming one of those suggested profiles, Zoe says.

Unlike a traditional public relations person or strategic communicator, the majority of people in this study did not tailor their messages for business reasons but often did so for what they thought their friends and family would like to see. Particularly striking was the notion of not wanting to burden people with unnecessary postings, that is, of not wanting to add to their friends' information overload; and the social norms around accepted sharing behavior were frequently mentioned in this regard. For Ryan, catering to what he thinks his network is interested in seeing goes hand-in-hand with knowing how platforms work. Because he knows that a photo album on Facebook "is much more likely to appear on someone's feed than a text status update," he makes sure that the photos he posts are worthy of other people's attention. He will only share a photo album with "thoughtful, funny captions" because he knows people are probably going to see it, given the algorithm's perceived preference for photo albums. In a similar vein, Ryan only rarely "likes" things on social media platforms because as he says "people notice." If you "like" too many things, the "likes" become meaningless. So, Ryan tries to "save those for actual important times." This way, when people see he liked something, it actually means he really enjoyed it. "I save my likes for interesting articles or funny videos that are posted by major commercial pages that already have a million followers or likes,"

Ryan explains, because as he speculates, accumulated likes on big, important pages are more likely to show up on other people's news feeds.

Taking care of personal online communication in this optimized and strategic manner takes a lot of time and energy. Indeed, algorithms act as attention gatekeepers of sorts that users need to "crack" or play along with in order to increase their chance to get their message across. As the public discourse around the Twitter and Instagram algorithmic timeline suggests, algorithms are seen as powerbrokers that you either play with or play against. Part of the reason Ryan thinks it is a big mistake that Twitter and Instagram are "using algorithms" on a large scale is that it "will change what people post and change how people use the platform, and they won't use it the same way as they used to." For Ryan, the difference between a service such as Snapchat and Facebook is that the former "takes less thinking time." As he elaborates:

> But, with Facebook, there are so many things going on there, so I have to plan out strategically what I am saying, how I am posting it, when I post it, all that stuff. Just to make sure that everyone I want to see it actually sees that.[51]

The notion of strategically planning what to say is just another side of "clicking consciously," a way of being oriented toward the operational logics of platforms. For Ryan, the problem with Twitter rolling out an algorithmic logic on a much greater scale than before is not so much about the algorithm in and of itself but the consequences it entails for practical engagement with the platform. So, if Twitter were to "start with an algorithm, you really have to start thinking about what you're posting," Ryan suggests.

While users often need play along with the algorithm if they want to get noticed, there are also the inverse efforts of *not* making oneself "algorithmically recognizable." Indeed, as the personal algorithm stories attest, avoiding or undermining the algorithm requires people to pay attention to the workings of the platform. Louis, a respondent from the Philippines, says he is deeply fascinated by the Facebook algorithm; yet, he thinks of it as a trap. For Louis, users have various options to counteract the logic of algorithms. Indeed, as Hill argues, "resistance cannot merely be about opting out, but about participating in unpredictable ways" (2012: 121). As Louis sees it, "privacy online does not really exist. So, why not just confuse those who are actually looking at your intimate information? That way, it misleads them."[52] Others, too, reported engaging in activities of data obfuscation, whether explicitly or implicitly. Lena has been trying to "manipulate content" with which she interacts in order to "control the suggestions" Facebook gives her, while Jessa attempted to confuse the algorithm by liking contradictory things.

Whether or not people try to make themselves algorithmically recognizable or not, the responses suggest that playful learning on the part of users should be thought of as a mode of knowing that is geared toward an active exploration of unknown objects.[53] In many ways, the various ways in which users orient themselves toward the platform's operational logic is not that different from the ways in which I tried to "reverse engineer" Facebook's news feed algorithm in the previous chapter. While we might not know the exact workings of algorithms, their consequences are often both observable and felt. According to Eleanor Gibson, "the active exploration of objects, leading to observable consequences and more specialized exploratory activities, has important results for learning about what an object affords, what can be done with it, its functional possibilities and uses" (1988: 24). Not only does the playful exploration of algorithms that some (albeit quite reflexive and knowledgeable) users engage in result in users learning more about what systems afford and what can be done with them, these activities also have the power to shape the very algorithms that perpetuate these responses in the first place.

THE ALGORITHMIC IMAGINARY

Algorithms seize the social imaginary through the various affective encounters of which they are part. As the many different personal algorithm stories analyzed in this chapter attest, algorithms are generative of different experiences, moods, and sensations. The different scenes and situations can be understood as forming part of what might be called an algorithmic imaginary—ways of thinking about what algorithms are, what they should be, how they function, and what these imaginations, in turn, make possible. While there is no way of knowing for sure how algorithms work, the personal algorithm stories illuminate how knowing algorithms might involve other kinds of registers than code. Indeed, "stories help to make sense of events, set forth truth claims, define problems, and, establish solutions and strategies" (Ainsworth & Hardy, 2012: 1696). Stories account for events and experiences in ways that help actors make sense of what is going on in specific, situated encounters. Personal algorithm stories illuminate what Charles Taylor (2004) has termed "the social imaginary," understood as the way in which people imagine their social reality. The imaginary, then, is to be understood in a generative and productive sense as something that enables the identification and engagement with one's lived presence and socio-material surroundings.

However, my use of the imaginary is not about the *social* imaginary per se. The algorithmic imaginary is not necessarily a form of "common understanding that makes possible common practices" (Taylor, 2004: 23), nor is it necessarily about the ways in which algorithms, for instance, can be generative of an "imagined community" (Anderson, 1983) or a "calculated public" (Gillespie, 2014). While these notions could certainly be part of an "algorithmic imaginary," I want to use the term here to suggest something slightly different but no less related. I have no reason or desire to claim, for example, that people's personal algorithm stories are part of a more commonly held cultural belief about algorithms in general. While they might be shared or overlap in important ways and be part of larger debates and discourses about algorithms in society, they are also imaginaries that emerge out of individual and habitual practices of being in algorithmically mediated spaces. In other parts of the book, I have discussed the notion of programmed sociality as the ways in which software and algorithms support and shape sociality and lived experience that are specific to the architecture and material substrate of the platforms in question. In this sense, algorithms may, indeed, have the power to generate forms of being together that are reminiscent of Benedict Anderson's notion of imagined communities. As Anderson famously declared, a nation "is an imagined political community—and imagined as both inherently limited and sovereign" (Anderson, 1983: 15). Importantly, as Strauss points out, Anderson emphasized the role of media, particularly newspapers and books, in "creating a reader's sense of being part of a larger community of other assumed readers" (Strauss, 2006: 329). The algorithmic imaginary that I want to address in this chapter, however, is not a public assembled by the algorithm but the algorithm assembled, in part, by the public. In other words, the algorithmic imaginary emerges in the public's beliefs, experiences, and expectations of what an algorithm is and should be.[54]

Using the notion of the imaginary to describe what the encounters between people and algorithms generate is not to suggest that people's experiences of algorithms are somehow illusionary. Quite the opposite, they are "real."[55] Algorithms are not just abstract computational processes; they also have the power to enact material realities by shaping social life to various degrees (Beer, 2013; Kitchin & Dodge, 2011). When Rachel finds herself "clicking consciously everyday" to influence what will subsequently show up in her news feed, the algorithm is not merely an abstract "unreal" thing that she thinks about but something that influences the ways in which she uses Facebook. Similarly, Lucas says his awareness of the Facebook algorithm has affected not just how he posts but also how he responds to others. As Lucas explains:

> I know that, if a friend of mine posts something they are passionate about,
> I will go out of my way to "like" and "comment" because I know that will
> programmatically "support" them and hopefully put them into more people's
> feeds because EdgeRank will give them more points for my participation.[56]

Lucas' willingness to go out of his way to like his friends' posts and enhance their visibility echoes some of the findings in recent work on social media surveillance. As Trottier and Lyon (2012) have shown, Facebook users engage in "collaborative identity construction," augmenting each other's visibility through practices of tagging, commenting and liking.

Users' perceptions of what the algorithm is and how it works shape their orientation toward it. Several of the participants reported having changed their information-sharing behavior "to make it work best for the algorithm," as Kate put it. The practical engagement with social media platforms as lived-environments implies developing tacit knowledge about the underlying logic of the system. While most technologies are designed in such a way that people do not have to know exactly how it works (Hardin, 2003), people tend to construct "mental models" and theories about its workings as a way of navigating and interacting with the world (Orlikowski & Gash, 1994). Despite explicitly pointing out that they did not know what an algorithm is, most participants had more or less elaborate theories about what algorithms are and ought to be. In the case of Facebook, for example, Kayla says she has "no idea what the algorithm is" but suspects it works in response to all the data tracked by the platform. Similarly, Michael has "no clue what the actual algorithm is" but still had a clear idea about how best to construct a status update in order to increase the likelihood of getting his posts widely distributed.

Far from naming an illusory relation, the algorithmic imaginary is a powerful identification that needs to be understood as productive. The sites and situations through which people encounter and experience algorithms arguably shape ways of thinking, talking, and feeling about them. While seeing an ad for wrinkle cream may not be surprising when you are 45 or an ad for a dating site when you have declared yourself as "single" on Facebook, these connections may not *feel* incidental. Algorithms create a "cybernetic relationship to identification" by constructing "categories of identity" (Cheney-Lippold, 2011: 168, 172). These statistically derived patterns of cybernetic categorization, however, may be in conflict with how users feel about and see themselves. Some participants, such as Shannon and Kayla, feel uncomfortable with the ways in which they are apparently being categorized, while others, such as Lena and Larry, feel distanced and even angry at the algorithm for "thinking" they would be the kinds of persons who would actually be interested in the content they are served. While it might be difficult to escape the digitally constructed categories of identity, Papacharissi suggests that affect may extend beyond "just emotions and feelings to describe driving forces that are suggestive of tendencies to act in a variety of ways" (2015: 12). Whether or not the algorithm makes a correct inference does not necessarily matter. For example, a child who is mistakenly addressed as an adult may like the fact he or she is being taken "seriously" and start to behave in a more adult-like manner (De Vries, 2010: 78). Similarly, it seemed that Lena's anger at being "wrongfully" identified and associated with her former classmates provoked her to update even more on the Democrats to counter the algorithm's insistence on showing "Republican" updates.

The algorithmic imaginary does not merely describe the mental models that people construct about algorithms but also the productive and affective power that these imaginings have. Driven by machine learning, the algorithms that drive social media platforms evolve and change as a result of being exposed to an ever-increasing set of data. As Emilee Rader and Rebecca Gray (2015) point out, the feedback-loop characteristics of these systems make user beliefs an important component in shaping overall system behavior. When users "click consciously," disrupt their "liking" practices, comment more frequently on some of their friends' posts to support their visibility, only post on weekday nights, or emphasize positively charged words, these movements or reactions are not just affected by the algorithm (or, rather, by people's perceptions of the algorithm); the practices also have the ability to affect the very algorithms that helped generate these responses in the first place. The social power of algorithms—particularly, in the context of machine learning—stems from the recursive relations between people and algorithms.

Conclusion

Everyday encounters with algorithms constitute an important site for analyzing the power and politics of algorithms in a way that does not necessarily assume a top-down or macroscopic view of power. Instead, in this chapter I have focused on the micropolitics of powers that emerge in the lived affects of people as they encounter algorithmic forces in their online surroundings. Micropolitics becomes a useful concept for thinking about what these encounters generate. As events, these situated encounters "might have powerful consequences through the way that [they transform] relations of enablement and constraint" (Bissell, 2016: 397). It is not just that algorithms may constrain or enable people's capacities to do things—for example, to be seen and heard online, to permit feelings to be felt or to prompt reactions and evaluations about one's lived environments. The barely perceived transitions that occur in situated encounters are by no means unidirectional; people certainly constrain or enable the algorithm's capacity to do things as well.

The algorithmic body—particularly, the one driven by machine learning—is characterized by its capacity to change as a result of an encounter. Just as people learn to navigate their whereabouts, algorithms learn and adapt to their surroundings as well. While we might not be able to ask the algorithm about its capacity to affect and be affected, its outcomes can certainly be read as traces of how it evaluates its encounters with the social world. It is important to understand the affective encounters that people have with algorithms not as isolated events that are somehow outside the algorithm but as part of the same mode of existence. When people experience the Facebook algorithm as controlling, it is not that the actual news feed algorithm *is* powerful in the restrictive sense. In its perceived restrictive functionality, the algorithm also becomes generative of various evaluations, sensations and moods.

If power is to be understood relationally, then we must think about the encounters between algorithms and people as both adversarial and supportive. Power, Foucault reminds us, "traverses and produces things, it induces pleasure, forms of knowledge, produces discourse. It needs to be considered as a productive network, which runs through the whole social body, much more than as a negative instance whose function is repression" (1980: 119). More than anything, then, power is a transformative capacity that always already implies forms of resistance (Foucault, 1978: 95). Resistance is not so much about the refusal to be governed by algorithms or to use a particular platform but about the practical engagement with an ascending force. The personal algorithm stories examined as part of this chapter are precisely indicative of such engagement. As Williams argued, people's affective encounters with algorithms should not be read as "formally held or systematic beliefs" about algorithms but, rather, as generative of "meanings and values as they are actively lived and felt" (Williams, 1977: 23). Still at the cusp of semantic availability, these meanings, perceptions, and expectations cannot be adequately described as a social imaginary if we take that to mean a culture's ethos or shared sense of understanding. As individual and idiosyncratic, these stories point to the more subtle conditions, ways of being and imaginaries that surround algorithms.

In this chapter, I have suggested viewing these "ordinary affects," to use Stewart's term, as forming part of an algorithmic imaginary, understood as ways of thinking about what algorithms are and, perhaps more importantly, what they should be. While encounters between algorithms and people are generative of stories and certain beliefs about algorithms, these imaginations have a transformative capacity, too. In an important sense, then, it is not the algorithm, understood as coded instructions that enables or constrains actions but, rather, the perceptions and imaginations that emerge in situated encounters between people and algorithms—indeed, the algorithmic imaginary. If we want to understand the social power of algorithms, then, critiquing their workings is not enough. While algorithms certainly do things to people, people also do things to algorithms.

6

Programming the News

When Algorithms Come to Matter

"People are beginning to believe what they want." Such was the explanation for Macquarie Dictionary to name "fake news" the word of the year for 2016. Similarly, the Oxford English Dictionary named "post-truth" word of the year 2016, suggesting: "Objective facts are less influential in shaping public opinion than appeals to emotion and personal belief." Questions about the status of truth, news, and facts have acquired renewed prominence in the wake of the complex political developments of 2016, particularly with regard to the possible consequences of a misinformed public in the aftermath of the US presidential election. But the arrival of "fake news" and "post-truth" into the popular vocabulary do not merely describe the notion that beliefs and emotions *trump* facts and truth.[1] These concepts are symptomatic of a time when algorithms have emerged as a particularly prominent matter of concern in public discourse. When debates about fake news and whether we live in a post-truth era emerged, they were already part of a much longer and ongoing discussion about the powerful role that social media platforms have in circulating news and information.

In 2016 alone, Facebook was involved in at least three major public controversies surrounding its alleged editorial responsibility. I briefly discussed the first controversy, which centered on the human role of editing what was believed to be a fully automated process for determining trending news, in chapter 3. When the news about Facebook employing human editors to curate its "Trending Topic" section first broke in May 2016, the public response was one of outrage. After all, the algorithm was believed to be neutral, free from human intervention and subjective bias. Through these controversies, among other things, the world learned that algorithms do not function apart from humans. Part of the controversy centered around a belief that humans were interfering with the supposed neutrality of the algorithm. But the matter was made worse by the way it turned out that the humans involved held left-leaning political inclinations. The story became one where politically biased humans deliberately edited out and thereby prevented conservative news from making it into the trending topic section.

After much public pressure, Facebook's responded in August 2016 by diminishing the role of human editors, making "the product more automated," in that it no longer required people to write descriptions for trending topics (Facebook, 2016). In an interview, Facebook's manager in charge of news feed, Adam Mosseri, claimed the trending topics section "is a 'better' product without human curators" (Chaykowski, 2016). However, mere days after removing the human curators, so-called fake news started to appear in the trending section. This included a factually incorrect headline involving Fox News personality Megyn Kelly (Ohlheiser, 2016). Laying off 26 employees (19 curators and 7 copyeditors) and putting the robots in charge apparently did not make the trending topic section more accurate or better. Why Facebook would make any such promise in the first place, given that it repeatedly denies being a media company, is, of course, another question to raise.

At nearly the same time that Facebook fired the journalism graduates editing the trending topic feature and the first accusation of fake news emerged, Facebook became embroiled in another major controversy surrounding its algorithms. In early September 2016, the social media platform came under much public scrutiny for having deleted the famous Pulitzer Prize–winning photograph "The Terror of War." Nick Ut's photograph of a naked 9-year-old girl running away in agony after a napalm attack during the Vietnam War was deleted from Facebook for violating the company's terms of service. Although the image had been deleted from the platform many times before, this time it did not go unnoticed. On September 8, the editor-in-chief of Norway's largest newspaper *Aftenposten*, Espen Egil Hansen, used the front page to publish an open letter to Mark Zuckerberg, where he expressed a worry about Facebook's inability to "distinguish between child pornography and a famous war photograph." "Dear Mark Zuckerberg" the letter began, "[editorial responsibility] should not be undermined by algorithms encoded in your office in California." Like most reporting on the topic of algorithms, Hansen's letter was quick to construct a dichotomy where the automatic and mechanical contrasted with human decision making. In addition to highlighting a strong concern over Facebook's growing power as an information intermediary, the incident also says something about the ways in which the algorithm is strategically called out and framed as a potential threat for a democratic society. In what is becoming an all too familiar tale, the algorithm is the villain, and the human—in this case, the press—is portrayed as the hero.

The above controversies call our attention to a particular messy and complex part of the current algorithmic media age. It is not simply that the Facebook algorithm does or does not do certain things—say, censor a famous picture or favor click-bait journalism and the spreading of fake news. What the trending topics controversy, censorship allegations, and fake news story suggest is the extent to which various actors are always differently involved in setting the stakes for when the algorithm is called out as particularly powerful in specific situations. In chapter 3 the argument was made that algorithms only matter sometimes, and that their power and politics have to do with the circumstances of making them matter in specific ways and for specific purposes. In this chapter I continue this discussion by examining how algorithms are "problematized" in the current media landscape. In writing about the history of sexuality, Foucault described how sexual behavior was "problematized, becoming an object of concern, an element for reflection, and a material for stylization" (2012: 23–24). Similarly, this chapter takes the news industry as a case in point to address the circumstances under which algorithms are rendered more or less problematic, and how their power and politics can be understood by examining the conditions under which algorithms become objects of concern.

As we will see, the news industry constitutes a place in which the emergence of computation, machine learning, and data science have wide-reaching and persistent consequences. Although computerization has long been part of the news industry, the use of algorithms as an integral part of news work is a relatively recent phenomenon in this context. As I claimed in chapter 2, algorithms do not exist in a vacuum. Nor can their power and politics simply be framed in a top-down manner, for example, as something exercising power over another actor or object. Algorithms are always built and embedded into the lived world, at the level of institutional practice, individual behavior, and human experience. In chapters 2 and 3 I referred to the notion of ontological politics to denote how reality is never a given, but rather shaped and emerging through particular interactions. The purpose of this chapter is to provide more empirical evidence for the claim that algorithms are imbued with such ontological politics.

So far in this book, I have shown that algorithms matter in a variety of ways: in their capacity to govern participation on platforms, distribute information flow, embed values in design, reflect existing societal biases and help reinforce them by means of automation and feedback loops, and in their powers to make people feel and act in specific ways. As I have argued throughout, understanding the ontological politics of algorithms cannot simply be done by looking at the materiality of code, as if formulas have a deterministic force or causal relationship to what they are supposed to compute. Regarding the notion that we need to take materiality of technology seriously, I already take this for granted.[2] While algorithms can be said to possess what Jane Bennett calls "thing-power" (2004: 348), a capacity to assert themselves that cannot be reduced to human subjectivity, here I want to focus on the specific circumstances of their material-discursive enactment—or *mattering*—in the context of the news industry.

How exactly are algorithms enacted to shape the realities of contemporary journalism, and when do algorithms come to matter in the first place? To speak of matter, "mattering" (Law, 2004b) and "material-discursive practices" (Barad, 2003; Orlikowski & Scott, 2015) is to be interested in the ways in which algorithms are materialized in different manners, made out and carved into existence at the intersection of technology, institutional practice, and discourse. Drawing on the process-relational framework that was introduced in chapter 3, what I am interested in here are the processes through which algorithms are demarcated as an entity and made separate from other things. What an algorithm does and the impact it may have is not tied to its materiality alone, but also to the ways in which it enters discursively into accounts, and makes things happen as part of situated practices. This *eventfulness* of algorithms is thus inextricably linked to the question of *when* algorithms matter, understood as the ways in which the algorithm emerges as objects of knowledge and concern, defining and being defined by those who are touched by it. Matter and mattering are key terms in this regard, describing an ongoing process of becoming, whereby different actors and elements are brought together and aligned in ways that shape certain realities (Barad, 2003; Mol, 2002). To understand the realities that have allowed controversies surrounding "fake news," Facebook's trending topic, and its censorship of an iconic photograph to flourish, we need to first understand how algorithms come to matter at the intersection of journalism, social media platforms, and institutional practice. When, then, do algorithms matter and whom do they matter for?

Algorithms in the News

Espen Egil Hansen, the editor-in-chief of *Aftenposten*, did not call out what he called Mark Zuckerberg's "Californian code" because of an opposition to algorithms as part of the news dissemination process, but because he disagrees with the ways in which Facebook uses them. In an interview about the newspaper's role in tackling Facebook on censorship, Hansen described his growing frustration with the platform's "unprecedented power as an editor," contrasted with an unwillingness to admit its status as a media company: "I think that one of the core tasks of the independent press... is to expose people to different views.... What we see now is that the press is becoming weaker." Social media platforms, the interview suggested, have a tendency to trap users in bubbles that prevent them from reading "the other side" of stories. Hansen furthermore claims:

> By far, [Facebook] is the most important carrier of news today, and it is editing at least in two ways. Every post you see on your feed is there for a reason; it's not neutral at all, it's an algorithm that decides. (Sullivan, 2016)

Hansen's worry is that the world's most powerful editor, the algorithm, and the people controlling it—Mark Zuckerberg and his associates—do not operate according to the same principles and professional ethics as the "independent press." This worry concerns the power struggle over editorial responsibility, and the question of who should have a right to claim it. On the one side, we have the independent press, whose task it is to inform the public and expose people to different views. On the other side, we find the curated filter bubbles created by social media algorithms that relentlessly "trap users in a world of news that only affirms their beliefs" (Sullivan 2016). However, this reduces a complex issue to a false dichotomy of being either for or against the algorithm. Facebook does not connect users and provide them a platform due to an altruistic, benevolent motivation. Nor does *Aftenposten* and the news industry rally against Facebook because of mere anger over the removal of a photograph. And even though he partly construes such a black-and-white narrative himself, Hansen says in the interview that the problem is not the algorithm per se: "I of course use algorithms myself, and my ambitions are to use them on a much higher level than we do today."

While algorithms in many ways have become an entrenched part of the logic and functioning of today's news media, their status and purpose are still very much up for debate and contestation. In this chapter I look more closely at the content and circumstance of these debates by considering how key actors in the news media, such as Hansen, make sense of and negotiate algorithms in the institutional context of journalism. To understand the power and politics of algorithms in the contemporary media landscape, the argument is made that it is vital to see algorithms as neither given nor stable objects, but rather made and unmade in material-discursive practices. Sometimes algorithms are rendered important, while at other times deemed insignificant. Knowing more about processes of mattering, I suggest, enables us to understand the multiple realities of algorithms, and how these relate and coexist.

Although the many recent controversies surrounding algorithms certainly call into question what algorithms do to the current informational landscape, what news is and ought to be, and what it means to have editorial responsibility, algorithms are already an integral part of journalism and journalistic practices. As is evident from much of the current literature on the intersection of technology and journalism (e.g., Anderson, 2013; Coddington, 2015; Diakopoulos, 2015; Dörr, 2016; Lewis, 2015), algorithms, robots, and data analytics are now contained in the standard repertoire of the way in which news outlets organize, produce and disseminate new content.[3] However, to posit these changes and developments as new forces changing journalism is to miss the point. From the telegraph and the typewriter to databases, spreadsheets, and the personal computer, various forms of technology have for centuries been used to support and augment news work (Boczkowski, 2004; Pavlik, 2000; Weiss & Domingo, 2010). Indeed, computers have been part of journalistic practice at least since the mainframe computers of the 1960s, which also gave rise to the tradition of computer-assisted reporting (CAR). In his seminal book *Precision Journalism*, Philip Meyer ([1973] 2002) describes how computers and statistics would be the most effective tools by which journalists could strengthen journalistic objectivity and transform journalism more broadly.[4] In order to fulfil the "real" goal of journalism, which in Meyer's view was to reveal social injustices, journalists would have to work with statistical software packages, database programs, and spreadsheets to find stories *in* the data (Meyer, 2002: 86; Parasie & Dagiral, 2013).

Today, these ideas are no longer mere predictions of a distant future. The computerization and algorithmization of news and news work have increasingly become the norm. While many of the core tools identified by Meyers remain the same, the scale and extent to which computational tools and processes are incorporated into news work are what's novel.

If the digitization of news once meant making analogue content digitally available, it now signifies a series of processes that go far beyond simple online newspaper distribution. The digitization and computerization of news can be seen at every stage of the production cycle: how journalists use computational tools to collect and produce news stories, the way in which systematized tagging and metadata practices are used to archive content, through the implementation of digital paywalls to ensure revenue and access to valuable user data, and in the algorithmic presentation and curation of news.

Let's at this point recall the common understanding of an algorithm as a set of instructions for solving a problem. What are the problems that algorithms are supposed to help solve in this context? One obvious problem for journalism is the "challenge to the economic viability of newspapers triggered by the digital revolution in publishing and news distribution" (Alexander, 2015: 10). Sociologist Jeffrey Alexander observes how many "leading journalistic institutions in the West have experienced great economic upheaval, cutting staff, and undergoing deep, often radical reorganization—in efforts to meet the digital challenge" (2015: 10). These cuts and reorganizations have also been felt acutely in the Nordic context, where many newspapers, including *Aftenposten*, are currently experiencing a dramatic reduction in staff—primarily those working with the print edition. As Alexander notes, the cultural mantra "information wants to be free" that came along with the Internet has become an economic headache for journalism today.[5] Declining advertising and the rise of blogs and social media platforms as fierce market competitors have contributed significantly to the economic crisis in journalism in recent years. Rasmus Kleis Nielsen notes how over "half of all digital advertising revenues globally go to Google, Facebook" (2016: 86), and the stigma that was once attached to paywalls continues to be an obstacle for their economic and cultural feasibility (Alexander et al., 2016).

The rise of computational journalism, here broadly understood as news entangled with algorithmic practices, comes at a time of crisis not only for the newspaper industry and journalism in general, but also in terms of broader social and economic unrest. Not unlike the rhetoric surrounding the rise of CAR in the 1960s, the discourses of computational and algorithmic journalism are characterized by a continuum of utopian and dystopian visions. Algorithms, data science, and everything that comes with them are distinguished by a great degree of techno-optimism and promise, but also marked by a notable skepticism and worries about machines taking over jobs. On the optimistic side, computational journalism is talked about as a way of upgrading and equipping journalism for the demands of the 21st century

(Hamilton & Turner, 2009; Cohen et al., 2011). As Lewis and Usher note, "many argue that computational journalism will both lead to better investigative journalism and create new forms of engagement with audiences" (2013: 606). The sentiment here is that journalism needs "to adapt to technological and economic changes in order to survive" (Peters & Broersma, 2013: 2). More than just as a celebration of technical possibilities, many see these digital transformations as a changing condition of news to which one simply needs to adapt in order to stay in the game.

But as with all technical change and innovation, discussions surrounding the computerization of newsrooms and the digitization of news have typically been accompanied by worries about the changing status quo. The emergence of social media, for example, fostered discussions around the potential replacement of journalists and other news workers by bloggers (Lowrey, 2006; Matheson, 2004; Rosen, 2005) or non-professionals engaging in citizen journalism (Goode, 2009; Rosenberry & St. John, 2010). These debates and worries have been replaced by similar discussions and worries about the rise of the so-called robot journalism (Clerwall, 2014). Companies such as Narrative Science or Automated Insights, which train computers to write news stories using automated algorithmic processes, have spurred much discussion about the sustainability of journalist as an enduring profession and the vulnerability of the human work force in the age of the purportedly "smart machine" (Carlson, 2015; van Dalen, 2012). Without committing to news robots being either a threat or a salvation, it is clear from the now burgeoning literature on what Anderson calls the "shaggy, emerging beast" of computational journalism (2013: 1017; see also Rodgers, 2015: 13) that algorithms are here to stay. The question, then, is not whether algorithms play an important part in journalism and news work, but in what way this role is playing out in practice, how it is accounted for and made relevant, and when it, indeed, comes to matter to specific actors in a given setting.

Making Algorithms Matter

A SCANDINAVIAN CASE STUDY

What is at stake in this chapter is an exploration of algorithms as enacted in practice—in other words, how news organizations are dealing with algorithms, both in terms of the algorithmic logics of digital intermediaries such as Facebook, and the journalistic algorithms developed internally within the organizations in question. Drawing mostly on qualitative expert interviews with news editors and digital product managers from ten different Scandinavian newspapers and media outlets, the aim is to explore how algorithms come to matter in the specific setting of news work.[6] The data sources on which I rely are 20 interviews I conducted personally among key actors in news organizations in Norway, Denmark, and Sweden from 2014 to 2016.[7] The interviewees were digital project managers, editors-in-chief, technology directors, social media editors, developers, and journalists at leading news organizations. These organizations include the Scandinavia-based publishing house Schibsted, the Norwegian media group *Polaris Media*, Norway's national newspapers *Aftenposten* and *Verdens Gang* (*VG*) and the Norwegian local newspapers *Adresseavisen* and *iTromsø*, Denmark's national newspapers *Jyllandsposten* and *Politiken*, Sweden's national newspaper *Svenska Dagbladet*, the public broadcasting service *Sveriges Radio* and the digital-only news service *Omni*.[8] The news organizations reported on in this chapter all use algorithms in some way or another to select, create, edit, and publish the news. While there are many similarities among the different news organizations and their attempts to make sense of algorithms in journalism, the aim here is not to tell one master story of algorithmic journalism in Scandinavia. What is of interest are the politics entailed in trying to establish the meaning of algorithms. As such, it is a story of the ontological constitution of algorithms, of what happens when its status is up for grabs.

While the interviews certainly ascribe meaning to algorithms, meaning should not be seen as a "property of individual words or groups of words but an ongoing performance of the world in its differential intelligibility" (Barad, 2003: 821). There are at least two sides to this that we need to acknowledge before moving on. First, materiality and discourse do not stand in opposition to each other; they are mutually constitutive (Barad, 2007; Orlikowski & Scott, 2015). The notion of a constitutive relation between the material and discursive implies that relations enact entities as part of situated practices. Like discourse and meaning, then, materiality or matter should not be understood in fixed terms. As Barad puts it, "matter does not refer to a fixed substance; rather, matter is substance in its intra-active becoming—not a thing, but a doing" (2003: 822). For Barad, "materiality is discursive […] just as discursive practices are always already material" (2003: 822). Matter and materiality, in other words, are not substances but accomplishments made pertinent in a given situation (Cooren et al., 2012). This also means that "any distinction of humans and technologies is analytical only, and done with the recognition that these entities necessarily entail each other in practice" (Orlikowski & Scott, 2008: 456). In other words, studying how algorithms come to matter implies an understanding of how algorithms are made relevant and pertinent in a given situation—for example, by examining how and when different aspects of the algorithm are variously enacted in people's accounts of them.

This brings me to the second point that we need to take into consideration when examining the meanings that news professionals ascribe to algorithms. Echoing ethnomethodological sentiments, we need to reflect on speech itself. News professionals necessarily speak as editors, managers, executives, and so on, which means that there are specific preoccupations and concerns that animate the person who occupies these positions. Consider the "Terror of War" incident again. As the editor-in-chief of one of Norway's leading newspapers, Hansen does not merely speak up against the power of social media platforms, but also as a spokesperson for the independent press more broadly. The perceived wrongdoing of Facebook's algorithms is here used as a justification and legitimation of the news media. As Cooren et al. (2012) note, speaking *as* also implies a speaking *for*, not just in terms of being a spokesperson for a specific company or brand but also in terms of speaking *to* the particular interests and issues that such a position is supposed to entail. The preoccupations and concerns that news professionals speak to, then, are not mere reflections of a material referent but must, rather, be understood as marking the agency of what appears to them. In this sense, I follow Lucy Suchman's call for "the need to attend to the boundary work through which entities are defined" (Orlikowski & Scott, 2008: 464):

> Beginning with the premise that discrete units of analysis are not given but made, we need to ask how any object of analysis—human or nonhuman or combination of the two—is called out as separate from the more extended networks of which it is a part. (Suchman, 2007: 283)

Finally, there are two things to note with regard to this being a Scandinavian case study, as opposed to an investigation with a more global focus. In the way in which leading staff from select Nordic news organizations describe the coming together of journalism and algorithms, I believe that these interviewees' strategic roles and, in many cases, their position as experts beyond the Scandinavian context, provide a valuable and convincing account of how, where and when algorithms have come to matter.

Also, in emphasizing the notion of enactment, I reject the notion of context as an explanatory factor. This may seem somewhat counterintuitive at first, given that I have been talking about "the particular context" of news media as my starting point. However, as Steve Woolgar and Javier Lezaun point out, there is a crucial difference between what ethnomethodologists call "context of action" and "context in action"—"between context as an explanatory resource available exclusively to the analyst, and the context as an emergent property of interaction available to its participants" (2013: 324). Although algorithms need to be understood in context (in this case journalism) the meaning of algorithms cannot be reduced to context either. Just as news media professionals' talk about algorithms cannot be understood separately from the context of journalism, journalism itself needs to be understood as the contingent upshot of material-discursive practices.[9] The interviews provide rich and important data about journalism's current condition, especially as it relates to the Scandinavian countries and to algorithms. Yet, this chapter is not about journalism or specific news organizations per se. To invoke the way I put it at the end of chapter 2: "Yes, journalism. Yes, Scandinavia. Yes, technology. Yes, economic challenges. Yes, social media platforms. Yes, algorithms. Yes, to all of the above, and no one in particular." The story is more about the relationship between the elements and the new realities that emanate from that, rather than any one of these in isolation.

THE ALGORITHMIC LANDSCAPE OF NORDIC NEWSROOM

On the basis of interviews with news media professionals in senior positions, in this chapter I provide an in-depth case study on the ways in which algorithms matter and how organizational actors are handling, making sense of, and differently orienting themselves toward the algorithmic logics of the current media landscape. In the previous two chapters I considered how algorithms are productive of certain subjectivities and orientations. Here I extend these conversations, by looking in more detail at the ways in which algorithms affect core understandings of institutional practice and professional values. Within the news media organizations studied, algorithms are put to work in two main ways. On the one hand, algorithms are enlisted as part of the production of news—primarily, in terms of automating certain processes or otherwise making the workflow more efficient by helping journalists find, produce, and disseminate the news. On the other hand, algorithms are applied to find new and better ways to connect audiences and readers to revenue—primarily, by means of personalization and recommendations. In the following sections, I go beyond considering algorithms to be problem-solving devices (as the standard definitions would have us), and analyze them as problem-creating devices, and point to the social and ethical dilemmas that emerge when news media use algorithms. Beyond simply solving or creating problems, algorithms also "problematize." There are at least two aspects to this: On the one hand, algorithms are rendered problematic, that is, judgements are passed, moral domains carved out, and certain concerns allowed to circulate (Arribas-Ayllon & Walkerdine, 2008). On the other hand, algorithms can also be seen as problematization devices, working to question the accepted boundaries and definitions of journalism itself.

The Algorithmic Potential

When people think of algorithms in journalism, it very often has to do with how they influence the final presentation of the news. Although it is important, this is only one of many ways in which algorithms are entrenched in journalism. For example, to list but a few of the ways in which algorithms are currently being used as part of the news media, algorithms are applied to find and research stories, verify sources, write and produce a story, and track the performance of articles after they have been published. They can also serve in A/B-testing headlines and the automatic production of news items by robots (Diakopoulos & Koliska, 2017; Lewis & Westlund, 2015; Linden, 2017). While it's still early days with respect to algorithmic journalism, there seems to be a growing sense among news media professionals that algorithms have great potential and many areas of application. The interviews suggest that algorithms are deemed particularly useful in the production of news, both in the ways in in which they transform editorial workflows and the dissemination of news, by way of making sure the right content reaches the right persons. When algorithms are articulated as having potential, what is generally emphasized are the various possibilities and promises that they seem to entail. For many of the interviewees, algorithms promise to reduce the cost of production, make it more efficient, automate tedious and repetitive tasks, provide valuable insights into users and readers, help predict future preferences, help find links and correlations in the data, and present the news in new, personalized ways.

Interestingly, there seems to have been progress over time. When first contacting people in the news media to talk about algorithms and their role in journalism, people seemed less articulate about their potential than they seem today. While the early days of new technologies are always accompanied by a certain level of skepticism, particularly in fields engrained with strong professional values and cultures such as journalism, the interviews conducted in 2016 suggest a degree of normalization with regard to algorithms in news. This gradual normalization of algorithms is also reflected in the rate at which journalism conferences, industry seminars, panel discussions, and interest organizations put algorithms on the critical agenda. At the same time, news media professionals seem less apprehensive about algorithms than they were only a few years ago. As Hans Martin Cramer, former product developer at *Aftenposten* and now product manager at Schibsted Media Platform noted when I interviewed him for the second time in August 2016, the algorithms themselves are not a sufficient explanation for this change in attitude. What changed since we first spoke in early 2014 was not so much the actual implementation of algorithms in the news (although things had certainly been happening) but, rather, the gradual normalization of discourses surrounding algorithms.[10] "In addition," he pointed out, "we are faced with a much more challenging economic situation, compared to just two years ago" (Interview 1, August 2016). As Cramer sees it, the media industry needs to move beyond the question of whether algorithms or robots will diminish or save the news. What is at stake is whether the new, emerging forms of journalism can be made sustainable from an economic point of view. Despite a great deal of talk about algorithms, the last few years, Cramer suggested, have shown that there are no easy solutions for developing algorithmic news production and dissemination: "it is either too complicated or too challenging."

Yet, Scandinavian news outlets have long been at the forefront of digital innovation. Many of the managers and key staffers I talked to work for some of Scandinavia's largest news organizations and publishing houses, including Schibsted, Polaris Media, and JP/Politikens Hus. As described by the *Reuters Institute for the Study of Journalism* in their annual digital news report 2016, these news outlets have a reputation for digital innovation in content and business models. Or, as *The Columbia Review of Journalism* recently wrote: "Leave it to the Scandinavians to be open to change and innovation, even in the ever-traditional world of newspaper journalism" (Garcia, 2017). For Espen Sundve, vice president of product management at Schibsted, news organizations essentially find themselves at an important crossroads:

Either they make themselves even more dependent on platforms like Facebook "that dictate the editorial and business rules without claiming any editorial and financial accountability for independent journalism," or, they need to reinvent themselves by dictating the terms of what and whom algorithms are being used to serve (Sundve, 2017).

For Sundve, the algorithmic potential lies in making journalism more personal, which is not to be mistaken for what we usually think of in terms of personalization. In my interview with him, he worries that, by using a concept such as personalization, which primarily belongs to the world of technology, one may too easily lose sight of what is important from a journalistic point of view. Though "journalism can be a lot of things [...] algorithms are primarily there to complement the human understanding of it," Sundve says (Interview 7, May 2016). A central theme in Sundve's discussion of journalism and the role of algorithms is the fundamental difference between news organizations and technology companies such as Facebook and Google. He likes to compare journalism and algorithms by talking about both of them as optimization tasks. It helps, he says, when talking to programmers in the newsrooms to speak about journalism in these terms. Essentially, journalism is about "closing the gap between what people know and should know but also want to know," he adds. In principle, this is an optimization task that can be solved both technically and editorially, but "What distinguishes us from a technology company is that we include that which we think you *should* know" (Interview 7, May 2016, emphasis added). As with Hansen and his critique of Zuckerberg's "Californian code," Sundve's description of the difference between journalism and technology companies is essentially about legitimizing and sustaining the role of news media as powerful channels of information and communication. Where social media platforms fail, journalism succeeds.

Faced with the algorithm's arrival, news media professionals have a choice: either develop a proactive stance, or reactively adapt to the new technological landscape. As is evident in most of the interviews, simply dismissing algorithms is no longer an option. As we will see later in this chapter, one of the most pervasive storylines when it comes to algorithms in news, concerns their potential threat to the informed democratic public. Yet, there are limits to how sustainable these arguments about so-called filter bubbles and echo chambers are (a topic to which we will return shortly), as the news organizations themselves are increasingly using algorithms to present the news. The challenge, therefore, is to balance critique with actual practice, to *make* algorithms good as it were, and to engage in practices of making them matter in *the right way*. In talking to different news media professionals, it became clear how the algorithm in part derives its value from what is already valued. That is, algorithms are judged, made sense of and explained with reference to existing journalistic values and professional ethics: Algorithms and objectivity, algorithms and newsworthiness, algorithms and informed citizens, and the list goes on.

METRIC POWER

As with any commercial business, what is of course greatly valued is profit. The algorithmic potential is less about the specific code than it is about the economic promise that algorithms provide, and their perceived capacity to act on the data in new ways. If algorithms promise to reduce production and circulation costs, there might not be much to argue against. As Stig Jakobsen, editor-in-chief at the local Norwegian newspaper *iTromsø*, told me when I interviewed him in May 2016, the choice of implementing an algorithm to personalize the "mobile-front" of the newspaper was rather easy: "If you find something that gives you 28% more traffic, as we have done, all you can do is say thank you" (Interview 2, May 2016).[11] We may call this the pragmatic route. Here quantification and the measurement of traffic is the new language of success, readily supported by algorithms that allow for seemingly objective decision making. Increased access to user data implies new insights and new possibilities for action. Jakobsen, who came to the local newspaper in mid-2015 after having spent much of his career in the magazine business as founder and editor-in-chief of some of the biggest Scandinavian lifestyle magazines, says real-time analytics and algorithms promise to support more informed journalistic decisions. In the magazine business as in journalism more generally, decisions were often taken purely on the basis of a "gut feeling." In times of economic hardship, however, a "gut feeling" is too risky, while metrics and numbers can potentially save you many unnecessary missteps. Though Jakobsen is enthusiastic about the seemingly objective promise of algorithms to deliver more relevant news to the right readers, he is careful not ascribe too much power to algorithms as such. The algorithm is merely a tool that can be used to make sure the right news reaches the right person, Jakobsen suggests, "If you are not interested in Justin Bieber, the algorithm will not recommend that article for you" (Interview 2, May 2016).

The power of metrics to influence editorial decisions, however, is not new (Anderson, 2011; Domingo, 2008; Vu, 2014). As journalism scholar Chris W. Anderson (2011) describes, based on his ethnographic research in Philadelphia newsrooms, new measurement and web traffic tools have contributed to the emergence of a "generative, creative audience." Anderson found that "Editors were clearly adjusting their understanding of 'what counted' as a good news story based on the quantified behavior of website readership" (2011: 562). For digital director at the Danish newspaper *Jyllandsposten*, Jens Nicolaisen, the extent to which big data and new computational tools provide actionable insights is one of the most promising avenues for the news business. As Nicolaisen sees it, the widespread use of analytics and metrics inside newsrooms has resulted in something of a power shift in journalism more broadly. Previously, the news was largely produced from the inside out, he says, without too much thought dedicated to what readers actually wanted to read. This lack of journalistic responsiveness to audience desires was most famously observed by Herbert Gans in his seminal work *Deciding What's News* (1979). Gans notes that he was surprised to find how little knowledge about the actual audience existed within newsrooms: "Although they had a vague image of the audience, they paid little attention to it" (Gans 1979: 229). Today, however, Nicolaisen observes, value creation increasingly starts from the outside—with what users actually click on, what they say they are interested in, what they share and talk about in social media (Interview 3, February 2015).

Ingeborg Volan, then director of innovation and newsroom development at Norway's oldest newspaper *Adresseavisen,* shares this sentiment, suggesting that the landscape of journalism has changed profoundly with regards to digital media. Traditional newspapers were constrained by their technological affordances: "You simply could not print personalized newspapers for every subscriber," says Volan. These technological constraints are now largely gone, and with it, an obvious rationale for producing the same paper for everyone. After all, Volan says, "Not all of our readers are alike. People's interests vary a lot, and they read different things" (Interview 4, August 2016). This does not mean, however, that Volan thinks journalism should simply cater to people's tastes and likes. "I don't think anyone would want that," she says when I ask her to elaborate on the power of users and readers to shape the news. It is not that power has shifted from editors to users— or to algorithms and data analytics for that matter. Although algorithms and social media platforms certainly challenge the privileged position news media organizations have historically occupied, they also provide a renewed opportunity for reaching people. As Volan sees it, it's not an either or, but rather a question of careful realignment.

BETTER WORKFLOWS

The interviews also suggest that the potential of algorithms is strongly linked to their role in organizing news work, particularly with regard to being perceived as strategic change agents. From a managerial point of view, algorithms offer an opportunity for speeding up the production cycle, making journalistic practices more efficient and news more consumer-oriented. It has, for example, become a fairly common practice for journalists to track their performance by monitoring how well their articles are doing in terms of readership and distribution. At the Danish newspaper *Politiken,* journalists and front desk editors are equipped with dashboards that help monitor and analyze how well specific articles and stories are doing. There are a few staple software systems that most organizations tend to use, including Chartbeat for tracking user behavior on site in real time, and Comscore or Google analytics for analyzing those data. Often elements from these "off-the-shelf" products are combined and adapted to the specific needs and interests of the organization in custom-made software solutions. As Anders Emil Møller, then director of digital development at *Politiken,* explains, dashboards and analytics software are important working tools that provide journalists with a better understanding of their work processes. It may even give them a sense of success and agency, given that they are able to better understand when an article is doing particularly well or what they may have to change to increase performance. A system like Chartbeat is used to monitor how much time a reader spends on a particular article and where he/she might move next. In this sense, software systems and dashboards become an epistemic tool, enabling an understanding of journalists' own performance, or the behavior and interests of readers. In addition, they are used to realize the expectations that exist at the managerial level about what constitutes good news work. When asked whether the many different metrics and tracking mechanisms might possibly drain journalists in their work, Møller says these systems are merely there to help and support journalists to do the best they can (Interview 5, March 2014). Møller suggests that these systems may even support journalists in promoting their own work. For example, tracking systems are able to give journalists leverage to argue for a more prominent position on the front page, based on the metrics provided. In this sense, the dashboards and the metrics supplied by different analytic tools become imbued with discursive power used to negotiate with the front desk.

Yet, algorithms are primarily directed at the consumer, not so much at practitioners, Aske Johan Koppel StrFor Strde, new director of digital development at *Politiken* says, when I interview him in September 2016. This is where Strde locates the algorithmic potential, in helping journalists find, contextualize and frame the news in innovative ways. Rather than setting the agenda, algorithms can be used to provide journalists with new tools to "make it easier to set the agenda," Strde suggests. Whether these tools mine Twitter for important topics or track what people are talking about on Facebook, algorithms can be used productively to support journalistic practices, many of the informants suggest. During the interviews, I was struck by the way it appeared easier to talk about algorithms in a positive spin when they were invoked as human helpers, rather than as automated gatekeepers of sorts. Understood as less confronting, invoking algorithms as tools for making the editorial workflow more efficient can be a way of saying yes to algorithms without compromising on the democratic function of journalism. As we will see in the next section, the conversations around algorithms tend to shift when they are more directly linked to the values and institutional role of journalism. Journalists often see themselves as using algorithms to serve publics with better news, and the managers tend to defend this public function of journalism as well.

While algorithms are variously regarded as helpful tools that support news workers in accomplishing their tasks and make the production cycle more efficient, they are not merely supporting journalists but also slowly changing the very condition of news work itself. Algorithms help to *make* journalism in new ways, by creating new genres, practices, and understandings of what news and news work is, and what they ought to be. As described in the burgeoning literature on digital and algorithmic journalism, algorithms are now used to find relevant stories on social media platforms (Thurman et al., 2016), create catchy headlines (van Dalen, 2012), use data sets to generate stories (Karlsen and Stavelin, 2014), and aggregate and recommend news stories (Just & Latzer, 2017). In many of the news organizations studied large investments go into experimenting with new computational tools to make news work more effective. At Schibsted, Cramer explains, one problem is that journalists often write in a form that is too long, too complicated, and too intricate without really taking the user's perspective into consideration (Interview 1, August 2016). There's potential, as Cramer sees it, in the way algorithms can be used to "atomize" the news. Such an approach, which is also known as "structured journalism," works by treating every bit of content as a separate block of data that can be reassembled into a new form, depending on what a specific reader already knows.[12] As Cramer points out, by simply treating every sentence, word, or paragraph as a separate "atom," newsrooms may use the power of algorithms and databases to produce news stories "on the go" and avoid unnecessary overlaps. Perhaps it is time to rethink the genre of the traditional news article itself, Cramer speculates, referring to a study conducted by Norway's leading tabloid and most read newspaper *VG*, which showed an overwhelming overlap in content produced between their journalists on a daily basis. More than simply writing articles like journalists have always done, atomizing the news essentially implies a personalization of the storytelling process itself, a process that is fundamentally powered by algorithms and structured data. For Sundve, whose rhetorical mission at Schibsted seems in part to be about establishing "the true purpose of journalism" vis-à-vis technology companies, atomization, however, represents much more than a new computational technique. In the ongoing battle for attention, revenue, and control over informational flows, content is king. If what social media platforms do is merely to distribute content, creating original and personal content may just be the news media industry's "greatest weapon in the fight for relevance" (Sundve, 2017). More important, perhaps, is the editorial accountability that comes with creating journalistic content. In order to succeed in keeping a distinct and accountable editorial voice, Sundve thinks it is crucial to develop new ways in which algorithms and people work together (Interview 7, May 2016).

To this end, it might be instructive to turn our attention to the Schibsted-owned Swedish mobile news app *Omni* as an example of the algorithmic potential found in organizing the editorial workflow in new ways. Relying on a combination of developers, editors, and a news-ranking algorithm, *Omni* seeks to provide users with what editor-in-chief Markus Gustafsson describes as a "totally new way of experiencing news" (Interview 8, April 2014). Gustafsson, who came from the position as managing editor at Sweden's leading tabloid newspaper *Aftonbladet* before co-founding *Omni* with Ian Vännman, says it all started with a mission to create something like the Swedish version of *Huffington Post*. But instead of copying an existing news service, *Omni* developed into a unique service of its own. Rather than creating original content, *Omni* aggregates news from other sites and provides manually written summaries of the news while linking to the original sources. Readers may also follow certain topics and personalize the mix of news. At the time of my visit to the *Omni* headquarters in Stockholm in March 2015, about ten editors worked in shifts to handpick the news. I spent a week on site, observing the editors day-to-day work, conducting informal interviews with some of them, and also conducting more formal interviews with designers, developers, and editors connected to *Omni* and the Schibsted media house (Interviews 9–16). The editors, who all come from a background as reporters and journalists before starting at *Omni*, do not write their own stories or work like reporters in a traditional sense. Instead, the work involves picking interesting news items from a content delivery system in order to make it "algorithm-ready." That is, editors summarize existing stories using a custom-built content management system—for example, by giving the story a new headline, providing a short written summary, linking it up to the original sources, and finding a suitable image to go with it.

A key part of making a story algorithm-ready (which, in this case, refers to preparing the news items in such a way that they can be processed and, subsequently, ranked by an algorithm) is setting news and lifetime values for each story. Before editors can publish the edited stories, they have to assign each and every one a unique news value on a 5-point scale and a lifetime value on a 3-point scale. As Gustafsson explains, these values act as tokens of relevance and newsworthiness, and are subsequently fed into an algorithm that, ultimately, "decides exactly where and how to show the news" (Interview 8, April 2014). The algorithm ranks every story based on a combination of news and lifetime value, the reader's personalized settings, time decay, and the relative weights predefined for each major news category (i.e., foreign news is weighted slightly higher than sports). The news and lifetime values that editors assign, Gustafsson suggests, are "subjective values" based on journalistic know-how and gut feeling (Interview 9, March 2015). The algorithm's job, then, is to process the subjective values in an objective and predictable way. While the news-ranking algorithm is rather "banal and simple," and the human efforts involved are "crucial and decisive," Gustafsson is clear when he suggests that they "couldn't have done it without the algorithm," as "it does, in fact, influence quite a lot" (Interview 9, March 2015, and notes from field observations). There's algorithmic potential in providing a better user experience but, perhaps, "first and foremost in making the work flow more efficient and time-saving" (Interview 9, March 2015).

The (Un)Problematic Algorithm

While the notion of *potentiality* is an important aspect of how algorithms are talked about in journalism, algorithms are simultaneously conceptualized as more or less problematic. I say more or less because, when the algorithm appears as unproblematic it is largely due to its role being downplayed as trivial or insignificant. As with the notion of potentiality, algorithms become problematic in specific situations.

The interviews reveal how algorithms are deemed particularly problematic when they threaten to diminish the journalistic mission of ensuring an informed public. Moreover, algorithms become problematic when they threaten to automate *too much*—especially when they compromise people's jobs, or when they become unruly and can no longer easily be controlled, starting to challenge the fundamental touchstones of editorial responsibility. Algorithms are not just problematic in terms of the various concerns and challenges to which they point: They are also conceived of as problematic at different times and circumstances. The notion of the problematic algorithm appears, for example, during moments of negotiation and breakdown, or when it becomes permeated with people's worries and concerns.

Incorporating algorithms as agents in the newsroom is not without its challenges. Most news executives I talked to describe a variety of obstacles and trials encountered in the process of adding an algorithm to the mix. When algorithms are incorporated into the editorial workflow, the process is often characterized by much debate and tweaking in the beginning, before the algorithm gradually slips into the background and becomes, at least temporarily, stabilized. Many news outlets have dedicated teams of programmers and data journalists who experiment with new tools and techniques on an ongoing basis; however, when organizations instigate more pivotal and far-reaching technological changes, the process is often more top-down. A few dedicated people, often digital project managers and editors, make decisions that are subsequently rolled out into different sections and parts of the newsroom. First, you need to figure out what you want the algorithm to do. While some news organizations spend considerable time on concept development, others such as *iTromsø*, release the code to see what happens. Even in cases where algorithms are released more quickly, the process of implementation implies subjecting the algorithm to a series of trials and questions. As Jakobsen says of the process at *iTromsø*, "first, we had to ask ourselves, should we ask our readers for permission" and to what degree should the algorithm be opt-in or opt-out? (Interview 2, May 2016). When implementing an algorithmically generated newsfeed for the first time, they decided not to ask their readers for permission explicitly but rather to "just go ahead and ask for forgiveness later." When I asked Jakobsen how often they think about or tweak the algorithm now, he replied, "not so much anymore." In the beginning, "we tweaked it every day" until it became more stable and less problematic he says. While nobody seemed to complain about the opt-in solution, there were other issues that had to be dealt with, Jakobsen adds. It proved increasingly difficult to find the same article twice because the algorithm was constantly showing new items and personalizing content. To combat the disappearing archive that comes with personalization, *iTromsø* implemented a section called "my reading history," where you could easily find old articles again. They also implemented an opt-out button at the bottom of the mobile interface to make it easier for readers to go back to a non-personalized feed. One of the things that is far more difficult to handle algorithmically, however, is knowing when to show certain content. In setting the parameters for personalization, having a sense of "right time" seems crucial (see also chapter 4). Like the annoyingly reap-pearing Lisbon hotel ads that plagued my Facebook news feed in the introductory chapter, Jakobsen uses a similar example to explain how an algorithm can provide stupid output. In order to prevent the algorithm from "showing you hotels in Ljublana 14 years after you've been there," you need to make sure to give your algo-rithm a sensible lifetime, Jakobsen says (Interview 2, May 2016).

The decision to start using an algorithm in the first place is not always as clear-cut as one might think. Christian Gillinger, who works as head of social media at *Sveriges Radio*, says of the process of developing the concept for a socially generated top list to be shown on the front-page of the public service broadcaster's website that "all of a sudden we discovered that what we were doing was creating an algo-rithm" (Interview 17, May 2016). The social media team had been given the task of finding new ways of promoting socially engaging content. They started down the obvious route, looking at how well certain programs did in terms of likes, shares, and comments. However, they quickly realized that the list would merely reflect and be skewed toward the most popular programs. As Gillinger says, there is nothing particularly social about merely looking at the number of likes and shares for a par-ticular program. If you are a small program, say a Kurdish program with 2000 listen-ers in total, and you still manage to mobilize 1900 people to share or like you posts, then you are really doing a good job in terms of being social, he adds. Initially, "we didn't know that what we were developing was an algorithm, but we knew we could not leave it up to the different news sections" to define the social; "it had to be done with the help of mathematics." Because "an algorithm is *just* a mathematical for-mula," the critical task is to decide what the algorithm is supposed to reflect (Interview 17, May 2016, emphasis added). For Gillinger, making decisions about what the algorithm is supposed to reflect is critically dependent on the people involved in actually developing the algorithmic logic. While algorithms are often accused of foreclosing diversity in terms of access to content, the diversity of people designing the algorithms is much less discussed. The more people who think about algorithms and help develop them inside news organizations, the better, Gillinger argues, suggesting that algorithms require diversity in the teams that create and are responsible for them.

While the algorithm reveals itself as problematic in the initial phases of develop-ment and implementation, it may not always solve problems, and it may also create news ones. Sometimes, algorithms simply personalize too much, or they turn out not to automate things as much as anticipated. The news-ranking algorithm at the center of *Omni*'s editorial infrastructure does not merely support the editors' work-flow; the editors also have to support the algorithm in various ways. As the field of infrastructure studies has taught us, infrastructures require ongoing human com-mitment and maintenance work (Bowker et al., 2010; Star & Ruhleder, 1996). Infrastructures can be understood as enabling resources; yet, in order to function properly, they are dependent on "human elements, such as work practices, individual habits, and organizational culture" (Plantin et al., 2016: 4). Initially, the idea of assigning the function of curating the front page at *Omni* to an algorithm was to reduce the need for manual labor. As "Frank," one of the editors working at *Omni*, explained to me while I sat next to him observing him at work, the idea is that editors only have to set the news and lifetime value *once* based on their journalistic know-how; and, then, the algorithm would take care of the rest (Interview 12, March 2015).[13] Despite the relative simplicity of the algorithm at work, it turned out that not only did the algorithm not eliminate the need for humans in the workplace, it also, somewhat paradoxically, seemed to put new tasks on the table. As was described earlier, part of the work that editors do at *Omni* is to assign news and lifetime values to each news story, so that the news-ranking algorithm is able to process it accordingly. Based on these values and a few other signals (i.e., user's explicit news settings and different weights assigned to different news sections), the algorithm works to compute the right order on the front page and the right length of time a news story is allowed to remain in that position.

Although the algorithm is programmed to curate the front page, the editors need to check on the algorithm's performance continuously. As "Emma" (another editor) explained, they need to keep track of how the stories actually appear on the front page and the extent to which the front page reflects the front pages of other major newspapers (Interview 13, March 2015). In other words, editors cannot simply assign their news and lifetime values and trust that the algorithm will do its part of the job correctly. It needs to be checked constantly. It is not just that editors need to check the actual front page to see how their stories are displayed. They also need to make sure that the collective product—*Omni*'s front page—comes together nicely. In order for the front page to be displayed in the desired way, editors sometimes have to change the initial values given to a news item after it has already been published. This practice, more commonly referred to as "sedating the algorithm," is by no means uncontroversial among the news professionals at *Omni*. Having to "correct" the algorithm by manually refurbishing the front page seems to go against the purpose of employing an algorithm in the first place. As Gustafsson and several of the editors told me, the whole idea of assigning values is premised on the notion that the values represent more or less objective and stable journalistic criteria of newsworthiness. For example, changing a story that would, in reality, only merit a news value of 3 into a 5, which normally indicates breaking news of major importance, may not just feel counterproductive. It can also complicate the workflow itself. There is a certain sense in which the initial values cannot be taken as a given, and that you as an editor have to be prepared to change and adjust your own valuation practice to accommodate the practices of your colleagues and whatever story they are working on, in order to achieve the final product that is the front page.

While everyone at *Omni* seems to agree that "sedating the algorithm" may not be ideal, there is also the sense in which these unintended consequences become an opportunity to engage in an ongoing conversation about what news should be and how the editorial news flow should ideally be organized. At *Omni* the meaning as-cribed to algorithms had less to do with the algorithm in the technical sense and more to do with the algorithm as an infrastructural element. Despite describing the algorithm as "labor-saving device," for "Frank," the algorithm seems to be merely one among many other elements that allow him to work in the way that he does—"without anyone telling you what to do" and with a great deal of responsibility and freedom (Interview 12, March 2015). The unintended consequences of algorithms notwithstanding, the same consequences may on a different occasion be turned into a welcome argument in favor of using algorithms. The need to check up on the algorithm's performance as evident from the editorial workflow at *Omni* becomes at the same time an argument in support of human labor and know-how.

Humans Have Heart, Computers Do Not

Algorithms, it seems, have their obvious limits, especially when people position al-gorithms in opposition to human capacities. Humans have heart and instinct, while computers do not. The ability to judge newsworthiness is seen as a distinctly human quality and a central factor of what journalism is about: craft. It is contingent on journalistic instincts and professional know-how. While some of the interviewees, as we have seen, think there has been too much emphasis on "human instincts" in jour-nalism, "gut feeling" is still an important part of the professional self-understanding of journalists and editors (Schultz, 2007). The journalistic "gut feeling" constitutes a tacit form of knowledge about the newsworthiness of a story. To most practitio-ners, it is so self-evident that explaining what this gut feeling actually amounts to can be difficult. Even textbook authors charged with articulating the nuances of news practice for newcomers, describe the end-product of journalistic socialization as "instinct" (Cotter, 2010: 77). Indeed, many of the interviewees rely on well-known journalistic discourses of professionalism when talking about the role of algorithms in journalism.

As the role of information gatekeeping increasingly lies in the hands of engineers and computer programmers, journalists and news professionals are faced with the difficult task of revisiting professional codes of conduct, and defining what the role of journalism should be. Major concerns in these discussions are whether robots will supersede human labor and what increased automation means for job security. When prompted to think about this, many of the informants talked instead about the limitations of algorithms. While algorithms promise to make the editorial work-flow more efficient, this is also where the relationship between algorithms and auto-mation hits its boundary. Algorithms, most interviewees contend, are basically just math, formulas, and calculations. Geir Larsen, then head of analysis at Norway's most read newspaper *VG*, notes how the growing amount of data is just a fact, something news organizations have to deal with sooner rather than later. Yet, the influence of data and algorithms should not be exaggerated. "An algorithm is just a form of programmed logic," Larsen replies when I ask what kind of algorithms *VG* is using. "Big data or not," Larsen continues, "we do a lot of interesting things with small data, too. Whether the data set is big or not is not that important." At the end of the day, "the most important working tool you have is your journalistic instinct" (Interview 20, March 2014). Even at a news organization such as *Omni*, which fundamentally relies on algorithmic intermediaries, the computer's inability to infer contextual information or understand irony means that "there is no chance that algorithms will ever be able to replace the human heart and brain in knowing what is best for the readers" (Interview 8, April 2014). This juxtaposition of human judgment and computational mechanisms does not just reveal a way of thinking about algorithms as mechanical and inferior; it also speaks to the desire of maintaining journalists' professional environment. As Larsen suggests when I ask about the prospects for automating the curation and presentation of the front page at *VG*, "We have thought about it, but the answer is no."

As do many of the other informants, Larsen emphasizes the "democratic" function of news and the journalistic values. While he is open to the possibility of using algorithms to automate some limited and carefully controlled parts of the newspaper, he insists on the fundamental role of human editors in deciding what readers should know. The newspaper's role, in Larsen's view, is not to serve content based on individuals' past clicking behavior. If something important just happened in the world, "it is our role to inform people about it and say 'this is important, this is what you need to understand'" (Interview 20, March 2014). Key to this public information function is maintaining people's trust in the newspaper as a credible source. The editors and managers talk about their brand name and the importance of having a distinct editorial line that people recognize. For some, the advent of an algorithmic logic in journalism seems to threaten the unique and recognizable editorial line that people have come to know. As Møller says when I ask about the prospect of using algorithms to personalize *Politiken*'s front page: "We want *Politiken* to remain a credible media outlet. The best way to accomplish that is through our own prioritizations, not through something automatic." People come to *Politiken* because they know what "we stand for," Møller adds. He explains, "One of our greatest values as a newspaper is that it is created by people with a specific worldview" (Interview 5, March 2014).

The informants' concerns about the damaging effects of algorithms are familiar ones. Over the past decade, concerns about the algorithmic creation of so-called filter bubbles and echo chambers—the idea that users only get served more of the same content based on their own clicks—have regularly been voiced (Pariser, 2011). These discourses constitute an important backdrop against which the informants express their own concerns. There was a sense in which the linking of journalism and the computational almost *required* informants to reflect upon the perceived dangers of algorithmic personalization. While Jens Nicolaisen, digital director at

Jyllandsposten, says it has been "absolutely fantastic to discover the strength in having something 100% algorithmically controlled," he was quick to point out the danger of compromising the public ideal of journalism by creating filter bubbles. Similarly, Møller says that filter bubbles are exactly what they want to avoid. The question for many of the news organizations is how to solve this conundrum. On one hand, there is an increasing need to cater to the specific interests of individual readers. On the other hand, as Møller contends, "If everything were based on algorithms, we would be worried that you were missing some of the other things we would like to tell you about" (Interview 5, March 2014).

There is a general wariness among editors and managers of granting too much agency to algorithms. What really matters is how algorithms can be used to augment and support journalists in accomplishing their work. Jørgen Frøland, project manager for personalization at *Polaris Media* and developer of the algorithm at *iTromsø* thinks that much of the fear and concern surrounding algorithms stems from the fact that many people still do not understand what they really are. In most instances, Frøland points out, "algorithms are just plain stupid" (Interview 19, August 2016). It is not an either/or but a matter of using technology for the things that technology does well and people for what they know best. For example, Frøland adds, algorithms cannot make decisions based on common sense. For Ingeborg Volan (who works in the Polaris Media–owned regional newspaper *Adresseavisen*) the relative dumbness of algorithms means that their role in journalism should not be considered too problematic. She draws on a familiar argument voiced in debates about robot journalism: the algorithm is not as a threat to the job security of journalists but something that has the potential to make the job more exciting by "relieving journalists of some of their most tedious tasks" (Interview 4, August 2016). Because "good journalism is about asking critical questions, being able to judge the trustworthiness of sources, and to go out into the world and talk to people," Volan does not think that algorithms pose a very serious threat to the journalistic profession.

The words people choose to talk about algorithms matter. Ola Henriksson, web editor and project manager at Sweden's national newspaper *Svenska Dagbladet*, thinks that the word "algorithm" is too confusing and abstract. When I ask what the word "algorithm" means to him, he says "mathematics" and "calculations" (Interview 18, June 2016). However, this is not what journalism is really about, he says, suggesting that the term itself may do more harm than good. The Schibsted-owned *Svenska Dagbladet* became the first newspaper to implement the algorithmic infrastructure and valuation practices developed by *Omni*. Rather than talking about an algorithm, the *Omni*-inspired approach became more widely known as an "editor-controlled algorithm." I asked Henriksson whether he thinks calling it editor-controlled makes a difference. "Yes, for some, it actually seemed to make a difference," he replied. The notion of "editor-control" helped ease people's minds, and ensure them that they would still play an important role, despite the emergence of an algorithmic media landscape.

It is not difficult to see the appeal of the notion of an "editor-controlled algorithm" as described by several of the news professionals. It conveniently limits the power of code, while allowing for human agency at the same time. The result is something less threatening, yet modern and innovative. Since its implementation at *Svenska Dagbladet*, the algorithm and new publishing platform has widely been heralded as a success. Partially guided by editors and partially by reader preferences the algorithm delivers a personalized homepage for each website visitor based on timeliness, news values, and interest. Since launching the algorithm the newspaper claims to have seen a boost in traffic by up 15% in page views and 9% in unique visitor. This is the story of an algorithmic hero, not a villain. While the Swedish newspaper was practically pronounced dead, the algorithm made the future look bright again, or so at least the story went (Garcia, 2017). What makes *this* algorithm applaudable are its owners. That is, what sets the journalistic and "editor-controlled algorithm" apart from Facebook's "Californian code" lies in the former's moral salience. Fredric Karén, editor-in-chief at *Svenska Dagbladet*, puts it in this way in an interview with *Storybench*:

> I believe that you need to control and own your own technology. Google and Facebook would be thrilled for us to join their ad platforms. But to be a publisher is also about integrity: To own the way you publish, when you publish and where you publish is really important moving forward. (Rodrigues, 2017)

Let's pause for a moment and consider what the word "integrity" is doing in the above account and how it works to make the algorithm matter *in the right way*. In light of the many recent controversies surrounding the Facebook algorithm, especially regarding the discussions about the extent to which Facebook should assume editorial responsibility, the news media find themselves in the welcome position of highlighting and strengthening their institutional legitimacy. For Espen Sundve at Schibsted, the prospect of becoming too absorbed with Facebook's news feed algorithms is one of his biggest concerns about the future of news. Although Sundve has Facebook's publishing platform "Instant Articles" in mind when he talks about the risk of being engulfed by the Facebook algorithm, these concerns have ramifications far beyond its financial accountability. For news professionals, the problematic algorithm does not merely manifest itself inside news organizations but, perhaps more importantly, in terms of the external algorithms governed by Facebook and Google. Sundve says of the Facebook news feed that, "from a democratic perspective," it is very problematic to "give away your editorial position to someone who clearly does not take any editorial responsibility" (Interview 7, May 2016).

Becoming too dependent upon algorithms that do not reflect the right values is risky. As Sundve says, technology companies may attempt to give people what they want, but journalism is primarily about providing people with information they *should* know and taking responsibility for that. Giving people information about what they should know, Sundve adds, also implies giving people the opposite view of an issue. "If you are a vaccination opponent, you should also be exposed to facts on the other side of the spectrum and not just find 50 other people supporting your views on your Facebook news feed," Sundve says (Interview 7, May 2016). One way to avoid filter bubbles, many informants suggest, is to think more carefully about the design of algorithms. It is not that algorithms always create bubbles and echo chambers. The question is what a specific algorithm is actually optimized for. As Gillinger sees it, there is no necessary opposition between algorithms and diversity—"it all depends on what it is that you want your algorithm to reflect." It is entirely possible to optimize for clicks if that is what you want; "but, in my world, that is a badly written algorithm," Gillinger says (Interview 17, May 2016). While critics worry about Facebook's alleged power to create filter bubbles and misinformed publics, there is also the sense in which the democratic crisis can be resolved by writing better and journalistically sound algorithms.

Algorithms as Problematization

Algorithms do not merely solve or create new problems, as the interviews make perfectly clear. They also need to be understood as "problematization" devices that work to question the accepted boundaries and definitions of journalism itself. It is here that we see most clearly the eventfulness of algorithms at play. As I argued in chapter 3, the notion of event allows for an analytical position that is not so much interested in establishing the "empirical accuracy" (Michael, 2004) of what the algorithm is or what it means, but which instead looks at how algorithms have the capacity to produce new orderings or disorderings.[14] As Mackenzie points out, "event thinking" has helped scholars "think about the contingency of new formations or assemblages without 'front-loading' a particular ontological commitment" (2005: 388). In talking to news media professionals and observing the ways in which algorithms have emerged as an object of concern within journalism, it seems to me that the power and politics of algorithms are manifested in the way they problematize accepted boundaries. Paul Rabinow says of an event that it makes "things work in a different manner and produces and instantiates new capacities. A form/event makes many other things more or less suddenly conceivable" (1999: 180). Just as "events problematize classifications, practices, things" (Rabinow, 2009: 67), an algorithm, I suggest, "puts into question or problematises an existing set of boundaries or limits within" journalism (Mackenzie, 2005: 388). In going forward, the question is not just what happens to particular domains when they introduce an algorithm, but how algorithms as events make it "possible to feel, perceive, act or know differently" (2005: 388).

In the previous sections, I identified at least two distinct ways in which the understanding of algorithms is realized in Scandinavian newsrooms: as forms of potentiality and as something that is articulated as more or less problematic. In this final part of the chapter, I suggest that the notions of potentiality and the problematic do not necessarily stand in opposition to one another, but rather should be thought of as a "relational play of truth and falsehood" (Rabinow, 2009: 19). That is, when algorithms become contested, when they fluctuate between discourses of promise and closure, achieve recognition outside of accepted boundaries, and become imbued with certain capacities for action, they emerge as forms of "problematization." A problematization, Foucault writes:

> Does not mean the representation of a pre-existent object nor the creation through discourse of an object that did not exist. It is the ensemble of discursive and nondiscursive practices that make something enter into the play of true and false and constitute it as an object of thought (whether in the form of moral reflection, scientific knowledge, political analysis, etc.). (1988: 257)

The term "problematization" suggests a particular way of analyzing an event or situation—not as a given but, rather, as a question. As Rabinow suggests, the analyst's task is to understand how, in a given situation, there are "multiple constraints at work but multiple responses as well" (2009: 19). For something to be problematized, a number of things must first be made uncertain or unfamiliar or "have provoked a number of difficulties around it" (Foucault, 1994: 117). As we have seen, the ways in which actors respond to algorithms in the news industry need to be understood against several constraining and enabling factors—most evidently, the dire economic circumstances in which most news organizations find themselves. Moreover, the responses of news professionals need to be understood against the broader landscape of the algorithmic media of which news organizations are a part. This applies in particular to their relationship to powerful competitive players such as Facebook and Google.

One aspect of this has to do with the way the figure of the algorithm problematizes existing boundaries of what journalism is and ought to be, an issue to which I will soon return. Another aspect has to do with the way news media are increasingly caught up in powerful "algorithmic configurations" (Callon & Muniesa, 2005) that involve other calculative agencies such as Facebook that help to organize their business. Of course, social media platforms have long been important to established news media. As Jens Nicolaisen at *Jyllandsposten* points out that, from a business perspective, their biggest competitors are not the other major Danish newspapers but social media platforms. "Facebook has had a tremendously greater impact on our business than *Berlingske* and *Politiken*," he says (Interview 3, February 2015). However, research on the rise of social media platforms and their impact on the existing mass media environment show how social media do not replace but, rather, supplement and challenge more established forms of media and media use (Chadwick, 2013; Hermida et al., 2012; Kleis Nielsen & Schrøder, 2014). As Nicolaisen puts it, news media and social media seem to have entered into a marriage of convenience of sorts. In the "hybrid media system," the news information cycle is no longer defined by the mass media alone but needs to be understood, instead, as an assemblage composed of many different media forms, actors, and interests in mutual relations of co-dependence (Chadwick, 2013). While we know that many news media sites attract a fair share of web traffic from social media—in particular, from Facebook (Kleis Nielsen & Schrøder, 2014), the notion of hybridization would also suggest that Facebook is dependent on the news media. Indeed, news is crucial for Facebook. People seem to share less of their personal lives on platforms like Facebook and Twitter than they used to (Griffith, 2016) and interact more with news shared by professional content producers. According to Will Cathcart (2016), who is vice-president of product at Facebook, 600 million people see news stories on Facebook on a weekly basis. Moreover, the company claims that a big part of why people come to Facebook in the first place is to catch up on the news and talk with their friends about it. As personal updates seems to be in decline, Facebook clearly counts on the news media and external content producers to help attract those much-needed clicks, likes, and engagement metrics that fuel its advertising business.

The hybrid media system extends well beyond web traffic and "likes," encompassing the operational logics of platforms and the players involved. Similar to how users reorient their social media behavior to accommodate the algorithmic logics of platforms, as was discussed in the previous chapter, the news professionals in this chapter note how algorithmic logics increasingly also inform journalistic practices. Ingeborg Volan at *Adresseavisen* observes how journalists in many ways have to orient themselves toward the algorithmic logic of external players like Facebook. Volan emphasizes how vital it has become to be good at playing Facebook's game. Becoming more attuned to the algorithmic logic of Facebook is now a necessary ingredient in reaching as many existing and new readers as possible. This does not mean, however, that you simply "dismiss all your journalistic principles and just follow Facebook blindly," says Volan. The question is whether you can find ways of "gaming Facebook's algorithms to serve your own journalistic purpose." The tricky part, Volan adds, is finding good ways of adhering to the "things we know Facebook will reward but without compromising journalistic principles." If you want your audience to come to your own site to watch a particular video, you do not put the whole video up on Facebook. What you do, instead, is share a "teaser" on Facebook, which directs people to your own site, according to Volan. However, producing videos also makes sense from the perspective of the operational logics of platforms. Given that Facebook's algorithms privilege videos over text, Volan suggests, they make sure to publish more videos on Facebook in order to be prioritized by the algorithm (Interview 4, August 2016).

The case of *Omni* further underscores the fact that the journalistic practice in the social media age cannot be reduced to making the news "algorithm ready," blindly following the dictations of Facebook. Here, it becomes apparent that algorithms also problematize the practice and meaning of *doing* journalism. In contrast to previous research on journalists' responses to new technologies in the newsroom, which is "nearly unanimous in concluding that journalists react defensively in the face of such boundary intrusions on their professional turf" (Lewis & Usher, 2016: 15), many of the editors working at *Omni* see new technologies as part of the attraction of working there in the first place. Although, of all the organizations studied, *Omni* has, perhaps, gone furthest in making the algorithm an essential component of the editorial workflow itself, we can conclude that the algorithm by no means deskills the workforce, as critics often worry. Instead, the inclusion of an algorithm into the workflow repositions and displaces the work in new ways. As the notion of problematization is meant to highlight, one cannot look at algorithms as something new and detachable that has been added to a preexisting journalistic domain. Such a notion falsely presupposes that algorithms and journalism are discrete and free-standing domains that suddenly have been forced to interact. Conceived instead as "eventful," algorithms are defined by their capacity to produce new environments. This alternative view is much more nuanced analytically, providing greater explanatory force to the cases I have been considering in this chapter. As a consequence, it renders the question of whether algorithms are responsible for deskilling the workforce superfluous. Instead, it urges us to ask how forms of algorithmic interventions are productive of new journalistic realities, and to what effect. Simply claiming that algorithms make people redundant will not do. While it seems safe to say that algorithms do something that, in some cases, may imply reducing the need for human labor, we should be wary of claims that simply end there.

What, then, do algorithms problematize? In the remainder of this chapter, I will focus on two possible answers, aware of there being no exhaustive explanation for a question like this. First, algorithms contest and transform how journalism is performed. As the interviews suggest, algorithms do not eliminate the need for human judgment and know-how in news work; they displace, redistribute, and shape new ways of being a news worker. Similarly, seeing machines as lacking instincts and, therefore, ill-suited to replace journalists and their "gut feelings" is a too simple a view. What journalists may have a "gut feeling" about expands and transforms as well. The field observations and conversations I had with staff at *Omni* revealed how editors in particular have developed an instinct for how the machine works. As "Clare" tellingly suggests, it is not just a matter of having an instinct for news at *Omni*, it is also about "developing a feeling for the algorithm" (Interview 11, March 2015). In contrast to much recent discourse on computational journalism, which hinges on the notion of "computational thinking," the case of *Omni* suggests that not all "computational thinking" requires journalists to learn to think more like computer scientists. Whereas the notion of "computational thinking," as originally

conceived, refers to an approach to problem solving that draws on concepts fundamental to computer science such as abstraction, automation, and recursivity
(Wing, 2006), editors at *Omni* do not necessarily think of their work in computational terms. Rather, they think like journalists who have learned to optimize their
product and practice not just for an outside reader but also with an algorithm in
mind. In contesting existing professional boundaries, the algorithm contributes
to the emergence of different readers, different journalists, and, ultimately, different
news.[15]

Second, as I have already alluded to, algorithms problematize existing boundaries of what journalism is and ought to be. The interviews reveal how the inclusion of
algorithms in journalistic practices and products fuel important discussions about
the nature of news. A central theme in Gillinger's discussion of developing an algorithm to curate and rank socially engaging content at *Sveriges Radio* is the way in
which the process itself brought about important reflections and discussions on the
significance of journalism today. As he says, "In my 20 years of working in various
editorial teams, I have witnessed a lot of implicit ideas about what constitutes news
values." Talking about what an algorithm is supposed to reflect and how it ought to
work has forced people to reflect on these implicit and often unspoken believes and
ideas about news, Gillinger says (Interview 17, May 2016).

Moreover, algorithms problematize journalism through "boundary-drawing
practices—specific material (re)configurings of the world—which come to matter"
(Barad, 2007: 206). As a contested matter, algorithms have become the focus of
much public discussion surrounding journalism, making important marks upon the
journalistic institution itself. As "pharmacological" objects of sorts, algorithms
make themselves known as both remedy and harm.[16] The question, however, is not
so much whether algorithms *are* poison or cure but *what* is at stake in their differential configuration as one or the other. As Suchman writes, "Objects achieve recognition within a matrix of historically and culturally constituted familiar, intelligible
possibilities [in which] we might understand 'things' or objects as materializations
of more and less contested, normative identifications of matter" (2007: 10). As the
interviews and various controversies surrounding algorithms suggest, the news
media are by no means a neutral component in the differential mobilization of algorithms. In line with the broader argument of the book, this chapter reveals how algorithms do not always matter (as much), but are rather made to matter in certain
ways. We can think of this form of differential mattering as a form of ontological
politics, insofar as algorithms are carved out as entities with specific features and
"normative variability" (Marres, 2013). That is, algorithms do not always carry the
same moral or normative capacities. Sometimes they are rendered bad or inferior,
do the wrong things, as indicated in the discussions over filter bubbles. At other
times, algorithms do the right thing, for example, by helping journalists do a better
and more effective job. What the algorithm does and how it is made meaningful is
not set in stone. This variability suggests that the power and politics of algorithms

cannot necessarily be found *in* the algorithm, but rather, as it was also suggested in chapter 3, is more a question of when the agency of algorithms is mobilized and on whose behalf.

Concluding Remarks

Algorithms are not simply algorithms, as it were. Their ontology is up for grabs. Let's briefly return to the notion of fake news introduced at the beginning of the chapter. While Facebook should not be blamed for creating a misinformed public, or for determining the outcome of elections, the debate over fake news and post-truth underscores the general point I make in this chapter about the power and politics of the algorithmic media landscape. If we want to understand the ways in which algorithms matter, we need to pay attention to the ways in which they are made to matter, as well as the ways in which they are made to matter differently in different situations and for different purposes. Going beyond viewing algorithms as problems solvers, as the standard computer science definition would have it, or creating new problems and concerns, a trope on which the social science perspective on algorithms tends to focus, I have made a case for attending to the eventfulness of algorithms that constitutes them as particular forms of problematization. Investigating the ways in which algorithms become relevant, I discussed how relations of sameness or difference are enacted on given occasions, with given discursive and material consequences.

As I showed, the "truth" of algorithms is "played" out in material-discursive practices. Constitutive of what Foucault called "games of truth," the narratives of news media professionals show how the mattering of algorithms is predicted on establishing certain norms and values of what is desirable/problematic, good/bad, true/false. Similar to how truth games were set up in the organization of medical knowledge and the designation of madness in Foucault's writings (1988; 1997), the truth games surrounding algorithms have to be connected to a whole series of socioeconomic processes and professional practice. As Foucault makes sure to highlight, a game "is not a game in the sense of an amusement," but rather, "a set of rules by which truth is produced" so that something can be "considered valid or invalid, winning or losing" (Foucault & Rabinow, 1997: 297). These rules, however, are never static. While implicit and explicit "rules," such as journalistic objectivity and professional ethics endure, the meaning of these "rules" change. In an algorithmic age, news media are not merely adapting to the presence of algorithms or simply using algorithmic systems as part of journalistic practices. What it means to be a journalist and publisher changes, as do definitions of what news and newsworthiness is and should be. News selection only moderately falls to a "gut feeling." The "hard facts" of metrics, traffic data and new media logics help transform feeling from gut to byte. The way news professionals talk about developing "a feeling for the algorithm," or "gaming the

Facebook algorithm" to their advantage, is indicative of the operation of politics. Whether we are speaking of the "internal" algorithm developed inside a specific newsroom or the "external" ones of Facebook, they seem to have the capacity to disturb and to compose new feelings, instincts, and sensibilities. In the hybrid media system where traditional publishers increasingly rely on traffic from social media platforms, people's engagement with the news is configured by the algorithmic systems of increasingly interdependent, yet professionally and ideologically distinct, information providers. News happens on different platforms, it migrates from publishers to social media and back again, and in the process gets caught up in complex sociomaterial dynamics of ranking, sharing, linking, and clicking. It reconfigures how journalism is apprehended, and what counts as news at all. Such is the ontological politics of algorithms, shaped in the encounters and conflicts that make them matter.

The overarching themes that emerged from the interviews with Scandinavian news media professionals revealed how algorithms are entangled in and emerge as contested matters in various processes of drawing boundaries. That is, algorithms are materialized as they become invested with certain social, political and ethical capacities. A "good algorithm," for example, is one that reflects the right kind of values—in this case, journalistic values. By the same token, the "bad algorithm" is one that takes no editorial responsibility. But the good and the bad vary too. The "bad" or inferior algorithms of social media become the condition of possibility for the "good" journalistic algorithm. Facebook's problematic algorithm simultaneously represents an opportunity for news sites. As *Aftenposten*'s censorship allegations against Facebook in the "Terror of War" case usefully suggests, algorithms are not inherently bad or good, but can be used more or less strategically to make such claims. While the "bad algorithm" of Facebook may instigate worries about declining conditions for democracy, it may also be mobilized as a productive tool insofar as it allows the news media to strengthen their authority as public watchdogs. As media scholar Charlie Beckett (2017) provokingly suggests, "fake news" may be the best thing that has happened to journalism in recent years, as it "gives mainstream quality journalism the opportunity to show that it has value based on expertise, ethics, engagement and experience." Conversely, the journalistic algorithm is manifested as the solution to a problem that social media made more or less conceivable. According to such a view, there is no such thing as a problematic algorithm in and of itself, only algorithms that become problematic as an effect of differentially attributed forms of agency. With regard to the allegations of the algorithmic propagation of fake news on Facebook and its alleged effects of a misinformed public, it is my claim that any fruitful explanation needs to move beyond the algorithm per se. Although it certainly matters that Facebook's news feed algorithms are optimized for shares and engagements, how and when it matters may matter even more.

7

Conclusion

Algorithmic Life

I began this book by asking readers to consider the following scenario: Copenhagen on a rainy November day, where a semester is about to finish. The festive season is around the corner, but it's otherwise a normal day like any other, filled with the habits of everyday life. Many of these involve media, such as checking Facebook, reading online news, searching Goggle for information, writing emails, tweeting a link, buying a Christmas present from Amazon, watching an episode of "House of Cards" on Netflix. While there is nothing particularly eye-opening about these moments, that was exactly the point. It describes life lived with, in and through the media. Or more precisely, a life fundamentally intertwined and entangled with algorithmic media of all sorts. As I am writing this concluding chapter it so happens to be a remarkably similar day in November, albeit two years later.

Of course, nothing ever stays exactly the same. This time around it is sunny, not raining, and I have much less time to check Facebook or watch Netflix, as I am trying to finish this book. The platforms and algorithms have changed too. While we might not always notice, the calculative devices of contemporary media constantly work to give us more of what we seemingly want. Attuned to users' clicks, shares, and likes, algorithms are constantly updated, revised, and tweaked to make the flow of information seem more relevant and timely. As Wendy Chun suggests, "New media live and die by the update: the end of the update, the end of the object" (2016: 2).[1] This condition of *the perpetual update* means that I am never guaranteed to see the same content on Facebook or Twitter as my neighbor or friend, due to network logics and algorithmic processes of personalization. Every day, or even several times a day, users are implicitly confronted with the question of "what will I see this time"?

It used to be that one could expect a certain sense of chronological order to the ways in which information was presented online. Today, *chronos* seems increasingly to have been replaced by *kairos*, the right or opportune time to say and do something. As evident in news feeds of all kinds, time is no longer about the linear, continuous flow, but rather about the very punctuation of linear time itself. As it was argued in chapter 4, kairos is what constitutes the temporal regime of algorithmic media. After all, as Facebook tellingly suggests, the goal of the news feed "is to deliver the right content to the right people at the right time so they don't miss the stories that are important to them" (Backstrom, 2013). In the past few years, many more media platforms have followed suit. Instagram and Twitter are only some of the more prominent platforms that have started to punctuate the flow of the "real-time" feed by highlighting "right time" content instead. The previous chapter shows how the logic of "the right content, to the right people, at the right time" is increasingly becoming part of traditional news media as well. Faced with economic hardship, news media are reorienting themselves to the new digital realities. One consequence is the way news organizations adapt to the algorithmic media landscape by deploying algorithms to produce, distribute and present news in ways that readers are already familiar with from being in social media spaces. But even more significance is carried by the fact that traditional news media are becoming *algorithmically attuned*.

This brings me to a third difference between November two years ago and today. Socially and culturally speaking, algorithms have emerged as a social and cultural imaginary of sorts. Algorithms are seemingly "everywhere." They have become sites for cultural and social production. As objects of news stories, academic papers, and conferences, as well as the focal point of public controversies, popular discourse, cultural production, and affective encounters, algorithms are producing calculative results. And while algorithms are oriented toward us, we, too, are increasingly becoming oriented toward the algorithm. In chapter 5, I showed how the algorithmic output of social media becomes culturally meaningful, as seen in the ways that people form opinions about specific systems and act strategically around them.[2] Algorithms are not just making their mark on culture and society; to a certain extent they have become culture. As Roberge and Melançon suggest "algorithms *do* cultural things, and they are increasingly active in producing meaning and interpreting culture" (2017: 318).

However, algorithms are not simply means of interpreting culture, they are also productive of culture, understood in terms of the practices they engender. Hallinan and Striphas claim "engineers now speak with unprecedented authority on the subject, suffusing *culture* with assumptions, agendas, and understandings consistent with their disciplines" (2016: 119). Although engineers and computer scientists are perceived to be in a privileged position to hold opinions about the term "algorithm," we are at the same time seeing an emerging trend where "ordinary" people and institutions are speaking and thinking about algorithms. They do so by permeating algorithms with assumptions, agendas, and understandings that are consistent with their specific backgrounds and life worlds. For someone who encounters the Facebook algorithm as a suppressor and regulator of content, the algorithm gets suffused with agendas and assumptions that may not be shared by someone else who encounters similar types of posts but in a different situation.

What, then, are we to make of the algorithm amid the condition of perpetual change? How can we know algorithms and the systems they are part of, if they are constantly changing? This book has suggested that neither the changing nature of the object nor the way it is engulfed in trade secrets and proprietary systems should be seen as a necessary deterrence. I have argued that our understanding of how algorithms shape everyday life is not inhibited by not knowing the thing, simply because the thing is always already "many quite different things" (Law, 2002: 15). In chapter 3 I offered three methodological tactics one could apply in the analysis of algorithms. Each of these maps to how algorithms were examined in chapters 4, 5, and 6, respectively. One approach serves as an aid in delineating how technologies materialize cultural imaginaries. Here, the notion of technography was presented as a way of interrogating algorithms as spatial and material arrangements that help to configure users in certain ways (chapter 4). Second, I proposed a phenomenological understanding of the productive force that people's imaginaries of algorithms have for the practical engagement with their lived-in environment (chapter 5). The third (but by no means final) option was to think the material and the discursive together, by looking at the ways in which algorithms are differently configured and made to matter in specific settings (chapter 6).

Developing an understanding of the power and politics of algorithmic media depends on acknowledging their "variable ontology." As Introna and Wood contend, "we cannot with any degree of certainty separate the purely social from the purely technical, cause from effect, designer from user, winners from losers, and so on" (2004: 180). To counter the assumption that algorithms are essentially technological things or coded objects that can be easily delineated as separate entities, in this book I sought to examine what I have called the ontological politics of algorithms. Based on the manner in which notions of the machine, software, and artificial intelligence are bound up in and entangled with sociality, subjectivity, and social issues, the ontological politics of algorithms refers to the ways in which these categories are made differentially relevant and available as part of specific configurations. The manyfoldedness of algorithms, moreover, raises the question of whether a distinction between knowing subjects and objects known is misguided to begin with. Perhaps, as Mol suggests, we are better served by "spreading the activity of knowing widely" (2002: 50). In chapter 3 I therefore suggested a particular way of attending to the variable ontology of algorithms by shifting attention away from questions of ontology—of where agency is located and whom it most obviously belongs to—to questions of politics, of *when* agency is mobilized and to what end. In order to understand the power and politics of algorithms, there is a need to attend to the question of "*when* the algorithm is"?

The "when" of algorithms becomes particularly evident if we look at some of the recent public discussions concerning algorithmic systems that are perceived to have gone astray. Such public controversies reveal how algorithms are often materialized differently depending on the setting. In the case of Facebook's "trending topic controversy," which hit the news in May 2016, human editors were accused of censoring conservative topics on the platform's trending topic feature. The story was largely framed in terms of "biased" and "subjective" humans distorting the "neutral" and "objective" algorithms responsible for ranking and sorting Facebook's trending topic feature. Interestingly, only a couple of months later, in early September 2016, Facebook became the target of another "algorithm controversy." Yet this time, the algorithm was accused of doing the censoring. Several prominent members of the public, the then Norwegian prime minister, Erna Solberg, among them, expressed worries about the fact that Facebook's news feed algorithms had deleted a famous Pulitzer Prize winning war photograph from people's news feeds. As described in the previous chapter, the story culminated when the editor-in-chief of Norway's national newspaper *Aftenposten* challenged (with great pathos) Mark Zuckerberg to take editorial responsibility for the algorithm's actions. These controversies show how algorithms can be mobilized and materialized in different manners, depending on the specific constellations they are part of. Also, they demonstrate that we cannot with any degree of certainty separate the purely social from the purely technical—nor should we necessarily want to. In both of these cases there was an algorithmic system at play, including both humans and machines. If we want to understand questions of power and politics, then, it is not enough to look at one element only. Precisely because we are not dealing with two situations of radical difference but, rather, with situations were these differences were made, an understanding of algorithmic power and politics must necessarily entail an examination of such boundary-making practices.

When algorithmic systems "do wrong," or are otherwise perceived as erroneous, questions frequently arise as to "who is to blame," "who or what is responsible," and "whose fault it was, the algorithm or the human." While it might not be the most satisfactory of answers, at least not from a tabloid standpoint, this book has made clear how the answer must always remain partial. Even more important is the claim that, by framing questions as an opposition of terms, as it often done in the public discourse surrounding algorithms, the risk is to simply think of algorithms *as* purely technical, or mechanical entities devoid of any human agency. When the Microsoft bot Tay started to tweet obscene and misogynist statements, or when Google image search suggested "ape" as an appropriate tag for a person of darker skin color, "the algorithm did it" is only an acceptable response if by algorithm we mean the "socio-technical assemblage that includes algorithm, model, target goal, data, training data, application, hardware—and connect it all to a broader social endeavor" (Gillespie, 2014). A core tenet of this book is therefore to think of algorithms *not* merely as "coded instructions telling the machine what to do," but rather as emergent accomplishments or socio-material practices. How algorithms come to matter in contemporary society is not about trying to define what they are or at what points they act, but rather about questioning the ways in which they are enacted, and come together to make different versions of reality.

Technicity

How are we to think of the capacity that algorithms have to bring new realities into being? At the start of the book, I suggested a specific approach to the question of "how algorithms shape life in the contemporary media landscape," by looking at how platforms like Facebook condition and support specific forms of sociality in ways that are specific to the architecture and material substrate of the medium in question. I described how Facebook encodes friendship in ways that essentially support the circuit of profit, and introduced the notion of *programmed sociality*. At the same time, in chapter 1 I warned against taking this notion of programmed sociality to credit for technological determinism. Software and algorithms do not simply operate in isolation or exercise power in any unidirectional way. Rather, their capacity to produce sociality always already occurs in relation to other elements, and as part of an assemblage through which these elements take on their meaning in the first place.

This is the technicity of algorithms, understood as the capacity they have to make things happen as part of a co-constitutive milieu of relations. For the French philosopher Gilbert Simondon, who introduced the concepts of transduction and technicity as useful frames to account for the productive power of technical objects, humans and machines are mutually related, where the technical object always already appears as a "theatre of a number of relationships of reciprocal causality" (1980: 22). Technicity, then, pertains not so much to what the technical objects are, but rather to the "forces that it exercises on other beings as well as in and through the new virtualities, and hence realities, it brings into being" (Hoel & van der Tuin, 2013: 190). This understanding comes close to the Foucauldian manner in which power was perceived in chapter 2. For Foucault, power pertains precisely to its exercise and force, to the "way in which certain actions modify others" (1982: 788). For an understanding of algorithms, this implies resisting reading algorithms as either technology or culture. Rather one is prompted to think of algorithms as "dramas"—or "theatre" of relationships in Simondon's terms—that algorithmic mediations bring about. The concept of technicity, then, offers a way of thinking about the productive power of algorithms that doesn't rely on the attribution of power to some fixed characteristics or stable artefact devoid of human agency. To speak of the technicity of algorithms is to emphasize how algorithms do not possess power in and of themselves, but how power unfolds as an "ontological force" (Hoel & van der Tuin, 2013).

Let's briefly consider the examples of Amazon book recommendations and Twitter's "While you were away" feature. The technicity here should be understood as the co-evolving conditions that emerge from the algorithm's dynamic functioning. An analysis of an event such as the recommendation of a book, or having one's fear of missing out catered to by a promise of a peek into what happened "when you were away," should be grounded in an "understanding of the nature of machines, of their mutual relationships and their relationships with man, and of the values involved in these relationships" (Simondon, 1980: 6). Though I have not made any claims about "*the nature*" of algorithms, I propose that algorithmic modes of existence are grounded in the relational drama of diverse environments. In the process of recommending books, Amazon's "collaborative filtering" algorithms *create conditions* through which certain books are brought to user attention while others remain elusive. Collaborative filtering is based on the assumption that customers who share some preferences would also share others. Rather than matching users with similar customers, Amazon uses "item-to-item" collaborative filtering to recommend similar books or other items, and this calculated chain of similarity relies heavily on user input. Thinking of the power of algorithms in terms of their technicity leaves no one off the agential hook, so to speak. The nature of the machine always needs to be understood in relation to other machines and "man," in Simondon's terms. On Amazon, we buy books (often several at the same time), put them into wish lists, search for items, browse the platform, write reviews, and provide ratings. On Twitter, we tweet, browse, spend time, build non-reciprocal networks of relationships, reply, and retweet. We are already implicated. According to Barad, "we are responsible for the world in which we live not because it is an arbitrary construction of our choosing, but because it is sedimented out of particular practices that we have a role in shaping" (2007: 203). This means that we cannot treat the power of algorithms as a one-way street. If power refers to the way in which certain actions modify others, our actions count too. The tweets we post, items we purchase, and likes we hand out all factor in to the sum total. As we saw in chapter 4, actions such as these modify what becomes visible to us and to our networks.

This also means that the roles of designers, developers, and other decision-makers are crucial. Just because algorithms learn and amplify existing societal biases, inequalities or stereotypes, it does not mean that they cannot be corrected for. On the contrary, algorithm developers *can* compensate for the bias in datasets, and companies *do* make choices about when to intervene in correcting certain algorithmic outcomes.[3] When algorithms end up as biased toward certain groups, these instances can be identified and handled computationally. As was discussed in chapter 6, using algorithms in journalism does not automatically entail the creation of filter bubbles, contrary to what is often claimed. As one of the interviewees suggested, "If you want your algorithm to reflect diversity that's what you have to design for." What's important is how designers, developers and decision makers think about what algorithms should be optimized for, and what possible consequences this may have for different social groups.

Orientations

Agency is not all or nothing. To say "the algorithm did it" will not do. Nor is it an option to assign responsibility to others, just because there are always other entities involved. As with the controversies surrounding algorithms discussed in the book, it is not a question whether algorithms conceived of as non-human objects *or* humans did this or that, but *how* the attribution of agency is realized in particular settings. Yet, the question of "how *exactly* to be responsible, how to hold or to be held accountable if agency is distributed?" (Simon, 2015: 153) remains. As crucial as this question is, distributed agency does not make accountability impossible. On the contrary, the agential messiness entailed by such a relational view makes accountability mandatory (Barad, 1998). There are at least two aspects to this. First, agency is not necessarily equally or symmetrically distributed. Secondly, the process of making certain elements more or less available or unavailable to specific actors is not something that occurs naturally, but rather enacted through boundary-making practices. What does this entail for an understanding algorithmic power and politics?

First, it needs to be pointed out that while agency, in theory, is symmetrically distributed, in practice this is not necessarily the case. Different entities do not hold agency or exercise power in the same way.[4] When Foucault stated that "power is everywhere," he did not suggest that everybody has equal access or opportunity to exercise power (1990: 93). Rather, power is "the moving substrate of force relations which, by virtue of their inequality, constantly engenders states of power, but the latter are always local and unstable" (1990: 93). Because power is not something that one group, person, or thing holds, the analyst's task is not about identifying who holds power or where the proper source of action is, but to understand "the effects of particular assemblages, and assessing the distributions, for better and worse, that they engender" (Suchman, 2007: 11). In order to understand how algorithms exercise power and what it would mean to hold them accountable, we need to assess the distributions that algorithmic forms of operations help to engender. In chapter 4, the operative functioning of algorithms was examined with regard to the forms that "categorize the individual, marks him by his own individuality, attach him to his own identity [...] a form of power which makes individuals subjects" (Foucault, 1982: 212).

It matters how algorithmic systems position subjects. In going forward it is therefore crucial that we develop a better understanding of how we are addressed and positioned as objects of algorithmic attention. What sorts of subjects become possible in the algorithmic landscape? The research presented in chapter 4 on the Facebook news feed suggests that the algorithms work to enact and support a form of participatory subjectivity that hinges on continued and ongoing engagement with the platform. Tellingly, a recent patent document filed by Facebook expresses this very sentiment: "Stories are frequently selected for inclusion in a newsfeed because they are likely to be of interest to the user viewing the newsfeed. This encourages the user viewing the newsfeed to continue using the social networking system" (Rubinstein et al., 2016). While the particular configurations of the Facebook algorithms have certainly changed since chapter 4 was written, the basic factors guiding the ranking of the news feed remain. These are affinity (i.e., the strength and nature of interactions between friends), weight assigned to types of objects (i.e., status updates, videos, comments), and time. In general terms, algorithms do not control *what* users say or how they behave. Rather, algorithms shape how users *come to* speak and what actions are made possible to begin with.[5] In the terms of Foucault, algorithms can be seen as instantiating a particular form of "government," in terms of "the way in which the conduct of individuals or of groups might be directed [...] To govern, in this sense, is to structure the possible field of action of others" (Foucault, 1982: 790).

While algorithms do not determine how people behave, they shape an environment in which certain subject positions are made more real and available to us. As Sara Ahmed suggests in her book *Queer Phenomenology*, we are "directed in some ways more than others" (2006: 15). Her book takes up the question of what it means to be oriented, that is, to become attuned in certain ways. Ahmed instructively asks: "What difference does it make 'what' we are oriented toward?" (2006: 1). While Ahmed talks about human orientations mainly in terms of how social relations are arranged spatially, algorithms are certainly also oriented toward users. Algorithms, particularly in the age of machine learning, *need* us, depend on us, and thrive on us. In the midst of ongoing, fervent arguments about Facebook disseminating "fake news," Facebook worries about "data-dirtying" practices, whereby users willingly provide misinformation (Ctrl-Shift, 2015). As chapter 5 shows, these worries are far from unwarranted. People do not necessarily post what is on their mind (to paraphrase Facebook's status update prompt) or what is actually happening (to use Twitter's expression). Instead, people may post much more strategically, in attempts to make themselves more or less "algorithmically recognizable" (Gillespie, 2017).

Ahmed suggests that "orientations matter," because they shape how the world coheres around us. That is, orientations matter because this is "how certain things come to be significant" as part of situated encounters (Ahmed, 2010: 235). Moreover, Ahmed writes, orientations matter in that it "affects how subjects and objects materialize and come to take shape in the way that they do" (ibid.). As I have suggested, algorithms are not just oriented toward us, we are increasingly becoming oriented toward algorithms and algorithmic systems as well. In chapter 5 I show how we are developing our own sense of sociality and sense of self in, through, and around algorithms. There is an interesting relational drama at play when a single person gets served an ad for engagement rings or a middle-aged woman gets suggested recommendations for wrinkle cream. Was it an algorithm or merely the person's clicking behavior that was responsible for these recommendations popping up, and to what degree does it matter? Can one simply attribute agency to the machine, and laugh off the stereotypical ways of depicting personal relations inscribed into the design of algorithms? What would it mean to take responsibility in this case?

I suggest in chapter 5 that the attribution of agency is realized in the encounters that people have with what they perceive as algorithmic phenomena. Depending on specific situated encounters, algorithms are perceived as creepy, helpful, disturbing, intrusive, and so on. The notion of the "algorithmic imaginary" was introduced to denote ways of thinking about what algorithms are, what they should be, how they function, and what these imaginations, in turn, make possible. While algorithms may produce certain conditions for action, these conditions are not necessarily attributable to algorithms in a purely technical sense. Rather, *how* and *when* people perceive algorithms may sometimes matter even more. Thus, when looking at what people do online, there is no way of telling what made them act in certain ways. The notion of the algorithmic imaginary suggests that what the algorithm is may not always be about the specific instructions telling the computer what to do, but about the imaginations and perceptions that people form. It follows from the logic of machine learning, that what people "do in anticipation of algorithms," as Gillespie suggests, "tells us a great deal about what algorithms do in return" (2017: 75). In terms of accountability and responsibility, then, we are all implicated, machines and humans alike.

Boundary-making Practices

From a strictly technical perspective, an algorithm can be defined as a step-by-step procedure for solving a problem in a finite number of steps. Throughout this book, I have argued that algorithms are much more besides this narrow, technical concept. Algorithms do not only instruct, they *mean* something, and often they mean different and conflicting things. Algorithms manifest as objects of social concern, as they become inscribed into the fabric of everyday life. Algorithms, moreover, help to shape the ways in which we come to know others and ourselves.

If the textbook definition of algorithm is but one version implicated in the many-foldedness of the term, then where and when besides code do algorithms manifest? As I attest in this book, algorithms exist in the conversations of academics, in media portrayals, public controversies (i.e., debates over "fake news" on Facebook), in people's perceptions and imaginations, in representational resting points (i.e., simplified images of formulas), in metaphors (i.e., the notion of algorithm as recipe), as part of films and popular imagery, stories, and professional practices. In an expanded understanding of the term, algorithms are seen as events. Without front-loading an ontological commitment with regard to algorithms, the notion of the event helps directing attention to the ways in which algorithms make other things suddenly conceivable.

Who or what is made accountable and responsible for algorithmic outcomes depends on how and where the boundaries are drawn. Disentangling the ontological politics of algorithms requires "remembering that boundaries between humans and machines are not naturally given but constructed, in particular historical ways and with particular social and material consequences" (Suchman, 2007: 11). Again, there are at least two sides to this. What counts as an algorithm, as well as *when* it counts, are not given. Following Suchman, we need to pay attention to the "boundary work through which a given entity is delineated as such" (2007: 283). As we have seen, what counts as an algorithm may vary greatly. Yet, most people would probably have little problem acknowledging that the computer science textbook definition of an algorithm, at least partly, constitutes the phenomenon in question. With this book, I hope to have made people more susceptible to the idea that algorithms exist and manifest on scales and levels that go far beyond the narrow, traditional definition.

Clearly, the question of what counts as an algorithm is highly site-specific, and even when algorithms are assumed they may count differently. In terms of professional practice the interviews presented in chapter 6 reveal the extent to which algorithms perpetuate designer's values, beliefs, and assumptions. I also showed that they reflect the different institutional and organizational settings in which algorithms linger. News media professionals frequently contrast the "good" journalistic algorithm to the "inferior" algorithms of social media platforms. News editors and managers speak of the importance of coding the "right" journalistic values into systems, equating the "bad" algorithm with systems that merely give people more of what they already had. While it might be tempting to take sides, to say that one algorithmic system is better than the other, we must also be wary not just of the politics embedded in design but the politics of making boundaries. As was suggested in chapter 6, what constitutes a "problematic algorithm" in one setting (i.e., the Facebook algorithm challenging the livelihood of journalism), may simply be rendered unproblematic and desirable in another (i.e., Facebook itself touting the algorithms as merely helping people get closer to their friends). Problematic values in design aside, it is also important to point out that there are no "innocent" ways of knowing or talking about algorithms.

Returning to what was the starting point of the book, we are now in a better position to think through some of the more general claims that were made at the outset. The question was raised as to how algorithms are shaping the conditions of everyday life. One answer is that the materiality of algorithms, the values and assumptions designed into the technological properties of algorithmic systems, govern sociality in specific ways. A claim was made to the effect that algorithms "program" ways of being together, producing the conditions through which people come to speak and connect online. Now we are hopefully in a better position to see how questioning the ways in which algorithms shape life also requires us to question how life shapes algorithms. Through the continuous collection of user data, algorithmic systems reach a higher level of flexibility and responsiveness: The relations between self and others change continuously. What I want to suggest, then, is that the notion of programmed sociality at play in the algorithmic media landscape is one where what's at stake are the ongoing actualization of "becoming together" in ways that temporarily stabilize, rather than a result of pre-programmed forms of being. The way we are together can only be thought of in terms of becoming, where the "we" implied by sociality is never confined to any specifies or essence, but to the "we" as relation.

Programmed sociality, then, implies a mutual reciprocity between machine and human, and the recognition that however life is shaped, responsibility is shared.[6]

The "if…then" conditional statements of algorithmic rules imply that certain conditions must be met in order to have particular consequences. But in order for algorithms to solve problems and have consequences, they are contingent on a wide variety of people, technologies, investments, and resources (Neyland & Möllers, 2017). Just as algorithms and platforms are perpetually changing, so are the worlds created in and around them. In other words, as the "if" changes, so does the "then." The way in which one can solve the problem of showing the "right content, to the right people, at the right time" is never set in stone. As the content changes, whom the content is right for might change as well. The right time for one person may be utterly wrong for someone else. When algorithms draw boundaries by deciding which of the 1,500 potential Facebook stories to make visible on a particular user's news feed, such decisions are never made in isolation of people. When people make boundaries by attributing algorithmic outcomes to inferences made by a piece of computer code, these attributions rely on the material arrangements that let people make such claims to begin with.

If the machine is involved, then people are too. The notion of algorithmic power and politics is not about the ways in which algorithms determine the social world. Nor is it about what algorithms do in and of themselves. Rather, we have to ask *how* and *when* different aspects of the algorithmic are made available or unavailable to actors in a given setting. In looking at what constitutes an algorithmic life, the central question therefore becomes: who or what gets to be part of whatever is being articulated as the algorithm.

Notes

Chapter 1

1. Facebook's tagline as of June 2017.
2. Netflix's tagline as of June 2017.

Chapter 2

1. http://cs-exhibitions.uni-klu.ac.at/index.php?id=193
2. According to Hromkovič, Leibniz was the first philosopher who conceptualized mathematics as an "instrument to automatize the intellectual work of humans. One expresses a part of reality as a mathematical model, and model, and then one calculates using arithmetic" (2015: 274).
3. Not all algorithms depend on "if…then" statements. Other control structures include "while" or "for" loops.
4. Elegance, as first proposed by Donald Knuth in *Literate Programming* (1984), can be measured by four criteria: the leanness of the code, the clarity with which the problem is defined, the sparseness of the use of resources such as time and processor cycles, and implementation in the most suitable language on the most suitable system for its execution.
5. Some of the most basic data structures include the *array*, the *record*, the *set*, and the *sequence*, of which array is probably the most widely used. More complicated structures include: lists, rings, trees, and graphs (Wirth, 1985: 13).
6. For more on the history, cultures, and technical aspects of databases, see Bucher (2016), Codd (1970), Driscoll (2012), Dourish (2014), Manovich (1999), and Wade & Chamberlin (2012).
7. In a program written in the programming language C, the different steps can usefully be illustrated by the program's file-naming convention. The source code file ends in ".c," the object code ends in ".obj," and the executable files end in ".exe."
8. While it is beyond the scope of this chapter to lay out how the extremely complex fields of cognitive science or children's cognitive development understand human learning, it may suffice to say that "many machine-learning researchers take inspiration from these fields" (Domingos, 2015: 204).
9. A fourth category of machine learning that is usually listed is reinforcement learning, which is about learning in situ as the system interacts with a dynamic environment, for example, in the case of self-driving cars.
10. For a good overview of the technical details on how data mining and machine learning work, see Barocas & Selbst (2016). They provide an excellent description of the different processes

and steps in data mining, including defining the target variable, labeling and collecting the training data, selecting features, and making decisions on the basis of the resulting model.

11. Probabilistic models or classifiers called Naive Bayes usually power spam filters. For more on the history and working of Naive Bayes classifiers, see Domingos (2015: 151–153) or Rieder (2017). According to Domingos, it is supposedly the most used learner at Google.

12. See Barocas & Selbst (2016: 9) on the creditworthiness.

13. Rules of thumb and systematic searching through the performance of different parameter values on subsets of the data (cross-validation) which are also often used.

14. Numbers based on consulting Facebook's newsroom on December 31, 2014: http://news-room.fb.com/products.

15. Neural networks in machine learning do not work exactly like the brain but are simply inspired by the ways in which the brain is thought to learn. The first formal model of a neuron was proposed by Warren McCulloch and Walter Pitts in 1943. It was not until 1957, when Frank Rosenblatt pioneered neural nets with his conception of the perceptron, that neurons were thought to be able to learn to recognize simple patterns in images. For more on the early history of neural nets, see Minsky & Papert (1969) and M. Olazaran (1996). For a literature overview of the field of neural networks and deep learning, see, for example, J. Schmidhuber (2015).

16. For more on how Google image recognition works using deep learning and neural networks, see http://googleresearch.blogspot.dk/2015/06/inceptionism-going-deeper-into-neural.html.

17. Bayes' theorem sits at the heart of statistics and machine learning, though what a Bayesian means by probabilities may differ from the ways in which statisticians use the concept. As Domingos (2015) explains, statisticians usually follow a much stricter "frequentist" interpretation of probability.

18. For the most comprehensive bibliography on critical algorithm studies, put together by Tarleton Gillespie and Nick Seaver, see: https://socialmediacollective.org/reading-lists/critical-algorithm-studies (last accessed, May 2, 2016).

19. The need for coding skills is one of the most discussed topics in software studies. While it certainly helps to know the principles of writing code, some syntax of a programming language, and how the computer works, a sociologist of algorithms needs to know how to code no more than a television scholar needs to know mechanical engineering.

20. On the notion of "algorithmic culture," see also Galloway (2006b); Kushner (2013).

21. For an overview of Foucault's concepts of power, see Lemke, 2012; Faubion, 1994; Rabinow, 1994. Foucault's public lectures (held at the *Collége de France* as part of his appointment as chair of the "history of systems of thought" between 1970 and his death in 1984) provide a comprehensive survey of his various conceptualizations of power, including the notions of disciplinary power (Foucault, 2015), biopower (Foucault, 2007, 2008), and pastoral power (Foucault, 2007). Foucault's text on *The Subject and Power* (1982) provides a classic statement of how he understood the notion of power and how it can be studied.

22. Foucault's ideas of omnipresent power, however, have a much longer historical philosophical tradition going back, at least, to the philosopher Baruch Spinoza (1632–1677) who is known for his metaphysics of substance monism, the view that everything is a "mode" of one ontological substance (God or Nature). Monism is typically contrasted with Cartesian dualism or the view that the world is made of two fundamental categories of things or principles. For Spinoza, modes (or subsets of the substance) are always in the process of entering into relations with other modes (i.e., humans, animals, things, etc.). As Jane Bennett puts it, Spinozan nature is "a place wherein bodies strive to enhance their power of activity by forging alliances with other bodies in their vicinity" (2004: 353). Foucault's way of understanding power as omnipresent and relational bears resemblance to Spinoza's monism and his concept of immanent causality, see Juniper & Jose, 2008; Deleuze, 1988.

23. Gatekeeping is the idea that information flows from senders to receivers through various "gates." Originally conceived by the social psychologist Kurt Lewin in 1947, the idea of gatekeeping became crucial to journalism studies and information science as a way to explain the

process of editing information. In the domain of communication, the gatekeeping concept is usually attributed to Lewin's research assistant David Manning White, who in 1950 studied how "Mr. Gates," a wire editor in a small US newspaper, based his selection of news on some highly subjective criteria (Thurman, 2015). Ever since, the notion of gatekeeping has been used to designate the editorial decision-making process in journalism and media.

24. Within scholarship on computational systems, previous research emphasizing a "values in design" perspective includes discussions about the politics of search engines (Introna & Nissenbaum, 2000; Zimmer, 2008), cookies (Elmer, 2004), knowledge infrastructures (Knobel & Bowker, 2011; Bowker & Star, 2000), and game design (Flanagan & Nissenbaum, 2014). "Values in design" approaches typically hold that technology raises political concerns not just in the way it functions but also because the ways in which it works often seem to be at odds with people's expectations (Introna & Nissenbaum, 2000: 178).

25. For a good discussion of the concept of government and governmentality, see Michel Senellart's overview in Foucault, 2007: 499–507.

26. For his conceptualization of government in his *College de France* lectures, Foucault draws heavily on the anti-Machiavellian writer Guillaume de La Perrière and his work *Le Miroir politique, contenant diverses manières de gouverner* (1555). Despite characterizing La Perrière's writing as boring compared to that of Machiavelli, Foucault sees great merit in La Perrière's way of conceptualizing government as being concerned with the relationship between men and things (with an emphasis on relationship).

27. As Bröckling et al. point out, such technical means may, for instance, include social engineering strategies embedded in various machines, medial networks, and recording and visualization systems (2011: 12).

28. Foucault's thinking on subjectivation and power relations changed somewhat throughout his career. Whereas his earlier work conceptualized subjects as "docile bodies" shaped by disciplinary processes of power, his later works focused on what he termed "technologies of self," whereby subjects are seen as much more self-sufficient in terms of shaping their conditions of living.

29. David Golumbia (2009) makes a similar argument that computation can be understood as an "ideology that informs our thinking not just about computers, but about economic and social trends."

30. http://www.bbc.co.uk/programmes/b0523m9r

31. As Law & Singleton usefully break the notion of the multiple down: "it is most unlikely that whatever we are looking at is one thing at all. So, for instance, a 'natural' reality such as foot-and-mouth disease is not just seen differently by vets, virologists and epidemiologists (though indeed it is). It is actually a different thing in veterinary, virological and epidemiological practice. It is made or done to be different in these different practices. It is a multiple reality" (2014: 384).

Chapter 3

1. See Wendy H.K. Chun (2011) for more on how the Enlightenment vision connects to software.

2. Secrecy has long been a topic of concern for disciplines such as sociology (most notably, in the works of Simmel, 1906), anthropology (Bellman, 1984), and philosophy (Derrida & Ferraris, 2001). On the relations between secrecy and transparency, see Birchall (2011).

3. The unknown here is simply understood as lack of knowledge or information. For more on how the unknown can be conceptualized further, see, for example, the extant literature on the notion of ignorance (Gross, 2007; McGoey, 2012; Roberts, 2012; Smithson, 2012). Scholars distinguish among different types of ignorance (or lack of knowledge). For example, between known unknowns and unknown unknowns, where the former "denotes knowledge of what is known about the limits of knowledge; there are certain things that we

know that we do not know" while the latter "refers to a total lack of knowledge" (Roberts, 2012: 217).

4. For one of the first discussions on black boxes within science and technology studies, see Callon and Latour (1981), where they conceptualize power as the ability to sit on top of black boxes. For a critical account of "opening up the black box," see Winner (1993). A quick Google Scholar search revealed that over 18,000 articles have been published containing the phrase "opening the black box," including the black boxes of finance, nanotechnology, soil microbial diversity, aid effectiveness, and media effects.

5. Galison exemplifies his notion of antiepistemology by way of one of the most mythical examples of trade secrets, the Coca-Cola formula. As Galison writes, quoting security personal Quist: "the recipe for Coca-Cola Classic has been kept a secret for over one hundred years. It is said that only two Coca-Cola company executives know that recipe [which] is in a safe deposit box in Atlanta, which may be opened only by vote of the company's board of directors...We probably would not know if a national security secret was as well-kept as the secret of Coca-Cola" (2004: 239).

6. Legal debates over algorithmic regulation have largely centered on free speech jurisprudence under the First Amendment. Pasquale and Bracha (2008), for example, argue not only that search engines need to be regulated but, more specifically, their ability to structure search results needs to be regulated, and that the First Amendment does not encompass search engine results. Others disagree, seeing search engines as fully protected by the First Amendment (Volokh & Falk, 2011).

7. Bataille's notion of "non-savoir" has been translated as both unknowing (Bataille & Michelson, 1986) and nonknowledge (Bataille, 2004).

8. At Twitter, they describe their mode of platform development in terms of a "culture of experimentation": https://blog.twitter.com/2015/the-what-and-why-of-product-experimentation-at-twitter-0.

9. There are many resources providing an overview of what a relational materialism entails, its key thinkers and core tenets—for example, Bennett, Cheah, Orlie, Grosz, Coole, & Frost (2010) for an overview on new materialism; Thrift (2007) for an introduction to many of the core issues at stake in a relational ontology; and Latour (2005) for an introduction to actor-network theory. Scholarly debates about these issues also proliferate in special issues of academic journals and within specific academic disciplines (i.e., information systems, education, human geography) that seem to have adapted to a particular strand of relational materialism (i.e., agential realism, new materialism), often with regard to specific concepts (i.e., sociomateriality, material-discursive, assemblage) and thinkers (i.e., Barad, Whitehead, Latour).

10. As Lemke (2015) notes, the term "more-than-human" was coined by Braun and Whatmore (2010: xx). Braun and Whatmore use it as the preferred term over "posthuman." These approaches also emphasize terms such as practice, performance, movement, process, entanglement, relation, materiality and the nonhuman.

11. Prehension is a key concept in Whitehead's metaphysics and refers to the elements, including energies, emotion, purpose, causation, and valuation, that combine (or what Whitehead refers to as concrescence) to produce actual entities (Michael, 2004).

12. For Whitehead, actual entities or occasions become concrete through a process he calls *concrescence,* that is, the "production of novel togetherness" (1978: 21). This insistence of the becoming or thickening of an actual entity from a multiplicity of possibilities (or potentiality) has had an enormous influence on Deleuze's philosophy of the virtual.

13. Lucy Suchman (2007: 283–286) addresses the methodological necessity of making arbitrary analytical cuts in the network. The boundaries drawn and cuts made are never just naturally occurring but constructed for analytical and political purposes.

14. Derived from Austin's (1975) account of the performative function of language as having the power to enact that which it merely seems to state, the notion of performativity has been widely used in critical theory (Butler, 2011), STS (Callon, 1998; Pickering, 1995), and the

sociology of finance (MacKenzie, 2008) as a way to depict the world not as an already existing state of affairs but, rather, as a doing—"an incessant and repeated action of some sort"
(Butler, 1990: 112). The notion of performativity has also played a central role in critical
discussions of software, code and algorithms (see Galloway, 2006a; Hayles, 2005; Introna,
2016; Mackenzie, 2005; Mackenzie & Vurdubakis, 2011).

15. Some scholars would argue that the sociotechnical and sociomateriality are not the same but
    denote different things. The concept of sociomateriality has been particularly important to
    research in information systems and organizational studies. For a discussion on how what
    these terms mean and how they might be distinguished, see Leonardi, Nardi & Kallinikos
    (2013).

16. As with the terms sociotechnical and sociomaterial, the concepts of network, assemblage,
    and hybrids have their own intellectual history that do not necessarily overlap entirely. While
    they all denote a composite term that implies some form of co-constitution between humans
    and the more than human, the term hybrid relates to actor-network theory and the work of
    Bruno Latour in particular, whereas assemblage is more of a Deleuzian concept (although
    applied and used by thinkers affiliated with actor-network theory such as Michael Callon).
    For an understanding of hybrids, see Latour's example of the citizen-gun or gun-citizen that
    he describes on several occasions but, most explicitly, in Latour (1994). Whereas hybrids
    refer to the relations between heterogeneous entities, the notion of assemblage also points to
    the process of assembling, not merely to the existence of a composite entity. In Deleuze and
    Guattari's account, an assemblage is not just a thing but also an ongoing organizing of multi-
    plicities (see Deleuze & Guattari, 1987). Assemblage should not just be understood as a
    gathering of subjectivities and technical objects but, rather, in the sense of its original French
    meaning of *agencement*—a process of assembling rather than a static arrangement (see
    Packer & Wiley, 2013; Callon, 2007). For a good overview of the similarities and differences
    between actor-network theory and the concept of assemblages, see Müller (2015).

17. See DeLanda (2006) for a discussion on these terms and how they differ. The main ontolog-
    ical difference can be found between those who focus on "relations of interiority" and those
    who maintain a focus on "relations of exteriority." The former notion claims that nothing
    exists outside of relations, whereas the latter contends that the parts of an assemblage can
    have intrinsic qualities outside of its associations (Müller, 2015: 31). For Karen Barad, an
    influential philosopher committed to a relational ontology (or agential realism as she calls it)
    "relata do not preexist relations" (2003:815). An agential realist account emphasizes entan-
    glements not as intertwining of separate entities, but rather as relata-within-phenomena that
    emerge through specific intra-actions (ibid.). As Barad puts it, "why do we think that the
    existence of relations requires relata?" (2003: 812). If Barad's ontological commitments con-
    stitute one side of the spectrum, most theorists committed to a relational ontology are either
    less explicit about their metaphysical claims or formulate a theory that attempts to account
    for the relative autonomy of entities *outside* of their relations. In contrast to Barad, Deleuze
    explicitly states that "relations are external to their terms" (Deleuze and Parnet, 2007: 55), mean-
    ing that "a relation may change without the terms changing" (See Delanda, 2006: 11).

18. The US Senate Commerce Committee sent a letter to Facebook CEO Mark Zuckerburg,
    looking for answers on its trending topics section. In the letter, Senator John Thune, chairman
    of the committee, accused Facebook of presenting the feature as the result of an objective
    algorithm while, in reality, human involvement made it much more "subjective."

19. Here, I am borrowing from Bloomfield et al. (2010: 420), who revisit the notion of affor-
    dances and urge researchers to consider the question of *when* an affordance is.

20. Lucy Suchmann makes a similar argument in her book *Human-Machine Reconfiguration* in
    which she turns away from questions of "whether humans and machines are the same or dif-
    ferent to how and when the categories of human or machine become relevant, how relations
    of sameness or difference between them are enacted on particular occasions, and with what
    discursive and material consequences" (2007: 2).

21. As the continuing saga of Facebook's trending topic shows, the figuration of the human-machine relationship is only ever temporarily stabilized. Only two days after Facebook announced that it would replace the human writers with robots, the algorithm started to highlight fake news as part of the trending topic. Without human oversight, the robots were not able to detect that a story featuring the Fox News anchor Megyn Kelly wasn't true. This, of course, caused much outcry again, proving to critics that humans were needed after all. I am including this in a note because of its obvious neverending character. At the time of writing, Facebook might have deployed more humans again to counter the robots gone awry, while in two months' time it might just as well be the other way around.

22. While many scholars who subscribe to a performative notion of ontology claim that reality emerges not just in interactions but *intra*-actions, referencing Barad (2007), I am not committed to making what is essentially a very strong ontological claim. Rather than committing to a view that claims nothing exists outside or external to a relation, which is what Barad's notion of intra-action implies, my view is more in line with Deleuze's notion of assemblage, which assumes a certain autonomy to the terms they relate. See Hein (2016) for a discussion of how compatible Barad and Deleuze are.

23. Thanks to Michael Veale for pointing out these distinctions.

24. Technography has previously been described as an "ethnography of technology" (Kien, 2008), a research strategy aimed at uncovering the constructed nature of technoculture (Vannini & Vannini, 2008), a way to explore artefacts in use (Jansen & Vellema, 2011), or a method "to tease out the congealed social relations embodied in technology" (Woolgar, 1998: 444). Moreover, the notion of technography has been used to describe the "biography of things" (Kahn, 2004) or simply as a synonym for a "technical drawing," for example, within the field of architecture (Ridgway, 2016). My understanding comes closest to that of Woolgar (1998) and of Vannini and Vannini (2008), who describe technography as a general attitude and research strategy aimed at examining the structural aspects of complex techno-cultural layers. However, the way in which I use the term differs from the notion of technography in Woolgar and in Vannini and Vannini in that the descriptions of technology do not necessarily involve a description of situated practices of production and implementation in particular settings. The question is, rather, what can we know about the workings of algorithms without necessarily asking humans or studying particular social settings as an ethnographer would do?

Chapter 4

1. http://newsroom.fb.com/company-info (accessed June, 2017).

2. As Leah Lievrouw (2014) has argued, the tendency for STS and communication scholarship is to privilege the social side. In emphasizing the opposite, this chapter is highly indebted to scholarship on materiality in media studies (Kittler, 1999; Meyrowitz, 1994; McLuhan, 1994), cultural theory (Galloway, 2004; Packer and Crofts Wiley, 2013; Parikka, 2012), sociology, and organization studies (Leonardi et al., 2013; Mackenzie, 2008; Marres, 2012), social media research (Gerlitz and Helmond, 2013; Langlois, 2014; van Dijck, 2013), and software studies (Berry, 2011; Chun, 2011; Fuller, 2008).

3. http://vimeo.com/111171647

4. See Andrew Bosworth's depiction of the Facebook boot camp at Quora (last accessed February 9, 2015): http://www.quora.com/How-does-Facebook-Engineerings-Bootcamp-program-work

5. See FB tech talk "behind the code" in which Facebook engineers discuss the boot camp and the company culture (last accessed February 9, 2015): http://www.livestream.com/fbtechtalks/video?clipId=pla_c1161c6b-dd52-48e7-a8ea-abeb3b198375&utm_source=lslibrary&utm_medium=ui-thumb

6. Throughout the company's history, Facebook has been accused of violating the privacy of its users. There is a rich existing body of literature concerning Facebook and privacy. See, for example, boyd (2008); Debatin, et al. (2009); Hargittai (2010); Tufekci (2008).

7. In Gilles Deleuze's (2006) reading of Foucault, the concept of diagram signifies the function or operationality of power. Deleuze suggests that Foucault is a new cartographer, someone intent on mapping out the relations between forces, to show how power produces new realities.

8. The dimension of subjectivity is key in the writings of Foucault (especially in the later ones). Foucault used the concept of governmentality to analyze everything from the production of orderly and compliant "docile bodies" through pastoral guidance techniques (see Foucault, 1978) to the emergence of liberalism in which notions of freedom are produced so as to replace external regulation by inner production (Bröckling et al., 2011: 5).

9. Many scholars have argued that Bentham's Panopticon and Foucault's adaptation of it in terms of disciplinary power provides a limited model for understanding contemporary forms of surveillance and power (e.g., Boyne, 2000; Green, 1999; Haggerty & Ericson, 2000). One of the more pervasive arguments used against the notion of disciplinary power is what we may call the Deleuzian turn in surveillance studies (Lyon, 2006). In a short piece called the *Postscript on the Societies of Control*, Deleuze argues that discipline has been superseded by something he calls "control." Despite the brevity of Deleuze's essay (only a few pages), the fact that he explicitly connects control to code, automation and networked technology, probably accounts for the main reason scholars find the notion of control to be more useful. However, as Mark G.E. Kelly (2015) points out, much of the arguments voiced against Foucault's notion of discipline have failed to recognize that "discipline is control." It is not the case, as Deleuze suggested, "we are in the midst of a general breakdown of all confinements" (1992: 178). Prisons and schools still persist. Nor is it the case that discipline means confinement in the way that Foucault introduced the notion. As Kelly (2015) suggests, networked technologies such as CCTV and GPS are not evidence that discipline has been surpassed by control, but rather complete the idea of disciplinary power as discipline is essentially about the infinite management of bodies. Others have in turn argued that Foucault moved away from notions of discipline in his later work, focusing instead on notions of biopower, security, and governmentality. Yet, in *Security, Territory, Population* Foucault makes sure to not posit a historical break between discipline and mechanisms of security when he writes: "So, there is not a series of successive elements, the appearance of the new causing the earlier ones to disappear. There is not the legal age, the disciplinary age, and then the age of security. Mechanisms of security do not replace disciplinary mechanisms, which would have replaced juridico-legal mechanisms" (2007: 22). While I can certainly understand the appeal of moving away from a notion of discipline toward a more fluid understanding of control as proposed by Deleuze or the notion of an expansive power indicative of Foucault's security apparatuses, I don't think we have to choose. It is not an either/or; not discipline *or* control; not discipline *or* security. I concur with Foucault when he says that discipline and security are not opposites but part of the same attempts at managing and organizing social spaces. For these reasons I still think the notion of disciplinary power holds great merit for an understanding of the ordering mechanisms of algorithms.

10. https://newsroom.fb.com/news/2013/08/announcing-news-feed-fyi-a-series-of-blogs-on-news-feed-ranking.

11. For more information on the news feed disclosure, see the video broadcasts of the technical sessions of the 2010 Facebook developers conference, especially the session called "Focus on the feed" in which Facebook engineers Ari Steinberg and Ruchi Sanghvi talk about the details of EdgeRank: http://www.livestream.com/f8techniques/video?clipId=pla_5219ce25-53c6-402d-8eff-f3f8f7a5b510

12. While the term "Facebook algorithm" may be somewhat misleading in terms of giving the impression that there is one single Facebook algorithm as opposed to many different algorithms accomplishing different tasks and working in tandem, my reference to the algorithm

in this singular way should be read as an act of convenience on my part. Facebook algorithm is shorter and more commonly used in everyday discourse than EdgeRank or the longer and more precise "news feed ranking algorithm."

13. As exemplified in a *Slate* article about the Facebook news feed: "It doesn't just predict whether you'll actually hit the like button on a post based on your past behavior. It also predicts whether you'll click, comment, share, or hide it, or even mark it as spam. It will predict each of these outcomes, and others, with a certain degree of confidence, then combine them all to produce a single relevancy score that's specific to both you and that post" (Oremus, 2016).

14. *Kairos* refers to the ancient Greek notion of the opportune or the right time to do or say something. For more details on the concept of *kairos*, see, for example, Boer (2013), or Smith (1969).

15. For a detailed description on how trends are defined and algorithmically processed in Facebook, see Li et al. (2013).

16. Daniel Ek, who is the founder of the music streaming site Spotify, which entered into a close partnership with Facebook in 2011, tellingly suggests: "We're not in the music space—we're in the moment space" (Seabrook, 2014).

17. These are just some of the changes made to the news feed as documented by the Facebook News Feed FYI blog (https://newsroom.fb.com/news/category/news-feed-fyi): May 2017, reducing the amount of posts and ads that link to "low-quality web page experiences" by using artificial intelligence to "identify those [web pages] that contain little substantive content and have a large number of disruptive, shocking or malicious ads." January 2017, emphasizing "authentic" content by looking at "signals personal to you, such as how close you are to the person or Page posting." August 2016, reducing the ranking of updates that classify as having clickbait-like headlines. June 2016, posts from friends and family to get top priority followed by posts that "inform" and posts that "entertain." March 2016, prioritizing live videos. June 2015, tweaking the algorithm to take more account of user actions on videos such as turning on sound or making the video full screen as indications of heightened interest. June 2015, taking into account time spent on stories as indicated by users scrolling behavior. April 2015, making posts from friends rank even higher and relaxing previous rules about not showing multiple posts in a row from the same source. September 2014, prioritizing more timely stories, for example as indicated by two people talking about the same issues (i.e., a TV series or a football game). Timeliness, moreover, is indicated by when people choose to like or comment on a post. If more people like a post right after it was published but not a few hours later, the algorithm takes it as an indication that it was more relevant at the time it was posted. What's interesting to note about the blog posts documenting changes is that the posts from 2017 more readily mention artificial intelligence as part of the procedures and techniques for making the news feed more relevant.

18. See chapter 3 for a discussion of the possibilities and challenges of applying a reverse engineering ethos to algorithms.

19. Facebook alternately calls these types of stories aggregate or cluster stories. See Luu (2013) for a description of cluster stories.

20. The most recent feed used to have a counter next to it indicating the number of new stories that had been posted and published by a user's Facebook connections since the last time they had checked the feed. The counter only went as far as 300 new posts, so any number above the limit would just be indicated as "+300." Usually, my most recent feed would reach this limit only after one or two days of not checking.

21. In September 2011, I did this kind of comparison between my "top news" feed before and after checking the most recent feed a couple of times; and, every time, there was a considerable change in the stories displayed between the first and second time I checked.

Chapter 5

1. @Desareon, February 8, 2016.
2. @doughj, February 7, 2016.

3. @YazibelleXO, February 6, 2016.

4. For Raymond Williams, the notion of "structures of feeling" denotes a historically distinct kind of feeling and thinking around a particular quality of social experience and relationship (1977: 130). What defines this social experience is its emergent character as something *felt* but still not fully articulable as such due to its historical unfolding presence in the here-and-now. For Williams, "structures of feelings" became a way of recognizing moments of new experiential impulses and patterns as a way to analyze cultural change and the unruly reality of social life.

5. As Clough and Halley (2007) point out, the social sciences and humanities have seen an "affective turn" in times of ongoing conflict and crisis, a turn that has sought to make analytical sense of what cannot necessarily be explained or made sense of using the language of reason. The study of affect, understood as the study of how bodies are moved, how the world in some way or another affects us and how we, in turn, affect the world, has attracted a number of scholars and thinkers within philosophy, feminist theory, psychology, political science, cultural and social geography, media studies, and critical theory—to name but a few. As suggested by Gregg and Seigworth in their introduction to *The Affect Theory Reader* (2010), two vectors have been particularly pertinent in the turn to affect, both culminating with publications in 1995. On one hand, there was the essay by Sedgwick and Frank called "Shame in the Cybernetic Fold" (1995) and the corresponding book *Shame and Its Sisters* (1995), both of which introduced readers to the psychology of affect developed by Silvan Tomkins. On the other hand, there was an essay by Brian Massumi on the "Autonomy of Affect" (1995), which expanded on Deleuze's Spinozan ethology of bodily capacities. So, if the first vector of affect sets affect apart from previous psychoanalytic conceptions of drives as the primary motivational system in human beings, the second strand concerns the many contemporary reinterpretations of Spinoza's ethico-political writings (Spinoza, 2000)—most notably, by Deleuze (1988, 1990) and his followers. On the most basic level, affect can be understood as the capacity to affect and be affected.

6. Email interview with "Michael," October 3, 2014.

7. Paraphrased from a tweet "Rachel" posted on October 14, 2014.

8. Multiple email interviews and online chats with "Rachel," October 15–26, 2014.

9. On a more general level, the question of how people encounter and make sense of new technology is, of course, one the core questions not only within media studies but also in related fields such as STS and IS research. In media studies, these questions have been extensively discussed within audience and media use research—for instance, through the lens of domestication theory, which focuses on the emotional and symbolic dimensions of communication technologies and how the meanings of technology have to be understood as emergent properties of contextualized audience practices (see Berker, Hartmann & Punie, 2005; Hirsch & Silverstone, 2003; Morley & Silverstone, 1990; Morley, 2003). In science and technology studies, the publication of *The Social Construction of Technological Systems* in 1987 popularized the notion of the social construction of technology, or SCOT, as a way to theorize and analyze technological innovation not as the result of designers but as fundamentally co-constructed in negotiations with users and other stakeholders (see Bijker & Law, 1994; Bijker et al., 2012; Pinch & Bijker, 1984). One of the most influential ideas in terms of understanding the meanings users attribute to technology is the notion that artefacts have "interpretative flexibility," meaning that there is flexibility in the design, use, and interpretation of technology (see Orlikowski, 1992). The idea that technologies do not have fixed meanings or determine use has also been a cornerstone of much research within information systems and organization science—particularly, in fields such as computer-supported cooperative work (CSCW), human-computer interaction (HCI) and social informatics (see, for example, Lamb & Kling, 2003; Kling, 1980; Orlikowski & Gash, 1994; Orlikowski, 2000). One of the earliest accounts of the relationship that people forge with computers is Sherry Turkle's book *The Second Self* (1984) in which she describes the computer as a "marginal object" that defies

easy categorization. A computer, she found, means more to people than merely a physical thing. It is also a metaphysical thing that influences how people think of themselves and others (Turkle, 1984: 16).

10. Film, art and other cultural mediations also lend themselves to the analysis of unknown and hidden aspects of technoculture, an approach that is often used in humanities-oriented media studies that seek to address the experiential dimensions of technologies. See, for example, Hansen (2004) on the phenomenology of new media or, more recently, Hansen (2012) on the micro perception of code and ubiquitous computing. Recently, Lisa Parks and others have also called for a critical study of media infrastructure that focuses on making the materiality of infrastructure more visible by paying attention to images, art and film (Parks, 2007; Parks & Starosielski, 2015; Sandvig, 2013). For an understanding of computers through art and literature, see, for example, Hayles (2010).

11. Depicting algorithms has always been a representational challenge whether it is flowcharts, diagrams, visualizations, introductory computer science textbooks, or commercial depictions (Sandvig, 2015). See also A. Galloway (2011) on the limits of representation in data science.

12. For more on the role of popular imagery as representational practice, see Kirby (2011).

13. Both the names and the exact wording of the tweets have been slightly changed to protect the privacy of the participants in the study reported on in this chapter.

14. Although the term "ordinary people" is both contested and highly ambiguous, the prefix "ordinary" is simply used to denote the aim of the study, which was to try and talk to people who are neither computer specialists nor social media marketers but, on the face of it, have no specialist knowledge of or any obvious vested interest in algorithms.

15. I conducted similar searches for the following platforms and services: Twitter, Instagram, YouTube, Amazon, Google, OkCupid, Tinder, and Spotify. While users tweet about algorithms in connection with all of these platforms, most of the searches have been conducted on Facebook and algorithms, Netflix and algorithms, and Twitter and algorithms because they were the platforms that seemed to solicit the most consistent streams of user responses. The main period of data collection regarding the Twitter searches took place during a nine-month period stretching from October 2014 through June 2015.

16. All 25 participants are pseudonymized, whereas their real age, country of residence, and occupation are disclosed. Australia: Steven (24, graphic designer). Canada: Jolene (22, fashion blogger), Nora (20, student), Larry (23, works in television), Anthony (64, art professor), Richard (41, manual laborer), Alex (age unknown, occupation unknown). Norway: Sarah (33, biologist). Philippines: Louis (20s, former student, current occupation unknown). United Kingdom: Jacob (38, on leave from a university degree). United States: Amber (25, student), Kayla (23, student), Michael (21, Musician), Rachel (24, journalist), Jessa (20s, journalist), Lucas (25, quality assurance engineer), Shannon (45, career counselor), Lena (20s, graduate student), Chris (20, student), Albert (42, works in advertising), Kate (36, former school teacher), Nancy (age unknown, public policy associate), Caitlyn (30s, teacher), Robyn (age unknown, graphic designer). Unknown location, age, and occupation: Tom, John.

17. The participants were recruited from the personal Facebook network of Nora, one of the participants in the Twitter study (see note 16). It was Nora's own interest in the subject matter and offer to distribute a request for interview participants via her own personal Facebook account that helped me recruit new participants. Together, we designed the recruitment request for participants but phrased in the way Nora would normally speak. Nora's status update asked people to contact her privately if they "would be willing to talk to a researcher about your experience with social media, and how it shapes the type of information that you get." Out of the 12 people expressing an interest, 10 ended up engaging in email conversations and face-to-face interviews over Skype during May and June 2016. Once again, the names provided are pseudonyms to protect the privacy of the participants. Due to Nora's

physical locality in a university town in Canada, many of the participants recruited come from a similar geographical and socioeconomic background. They are all in their early twenties, Canadian, engaged in college education, and relatively active on social media (however, none are involved in computer science or similar subjects that would entail knowledge of algorithms).

18. Paraphrased from Jessa's tweet, October 25, 2014.
19. Multiple conversations over email, exchanged between October 27 and November 7, 2014.
20. Paraphrased from Kayla's tweet, September 28, 2014.
21. Based on email interview, October 1, 2014, and online chat on October 2, 2014.
22. Paraphrased from Shannon's tweet published November 17, 2014.
23. Email interview, November 19, 2014.
24. Based on multiple emails exchanged between June 12 and 15, 2015.
25. Interview over Skype, June 2, 2016.
26. Based on an email interview, December 4, 2014, and Lena's tweet, published November 24, 2014.
27. Paraphrased from Albert's tweet published December 29, 2014.
28. Email interview, December 30, 2014.
29. Interview over Skype, May 29, 2016.
30. Based on multiple emails exchanged on November 5, 2014.
31. Based on multiple emails exchanged with Amber on October 1–2, 2014.
32. Paraphrased from Nora's tweet published October 2, 2014.
33. Based on multiple emails exchanged between October 6 and 12, 2014.
34. @RealityTC, February 6, 2016.
35. @RobLowe, February 6, 2016.
36. @Timcast, February 6, 2016.
37. @Polystatos, February 6, 2016.
38. Interview over Skype, June 2, 2016.
39. @etteluap74, March 28, 2016.
40. @CarynWaechter, March 28, 2016.
41. @Monica_xoxx, March 28, 2016.
42. @MrBergerud, March 28, 2016.
43. Interview over Skype, April 10, 2016.
44. Interview with Nora over Skype, April 10, 2016.
45. Interview over Skype, May 29, 2016.
46. Interview over Skype, May 27, 2016.
47. Interview with Melissa over Skype, May 27, 2016.
48. Email interview, February 12, 2015.
49. Email interview, October 12, 2014.
50. Interview over Skype, May 31, 2016.
51. Interview over Skype, May 29, 2016.
52. Email interview, January 19, 2015.
53. Within cognitive psychology, the notion of playful learning has been posited as a core feature of how children learn and develop cognitive skills. Most notably, perhaps, Jean Piaget (2013) formulated a series of developmental stages of play that correspond to the successive stages of cognitive development. Through explorations of an object, the child can obtain the information necessary to navigate functionally in the world of unknowns.
54. In this sense, the algorithmic imaginary bears some resemblance to Cornelius Castoriadis' (1987) notion of the social imaginary—not in terms of seeing it as a culture's ethos but in terms of its epistemological assumptions. Castoriadis thinks "knowing a society means reconstituting the world of its social imaginary significations" (Peet, 2000: 1220). Similarly, we might think of knowing algorithms through the meaning-making and sense-making processes of various actors.

55. I am well aware that talking about the illusionary and the real in the context of the imaginary may create associations with the psychoanalytical theories of Jacques Lacan. However, I am using these terms in a much more pragmatic, everyday sense. For more on Lacan's notion of the imaginary, the symbolic and the real, see Lacan & Fink (2002).
56. Based on multiple emails exchanged on November 5, 2014.

Chapter 6

1. The term "fake news" should be understood as encompassing many related phenomena, which held together refer to various forms of mis- and disinformation, ranging from deliberate misleading content, over parody, through to news that is ideologically opposed (see Tambini, 2017).
2. Although the material turn has long been underway in the social sciences and humanities, I am well aware that many other (often neighboring) fields and areas of studies have not yet fully acknowledged the power of things or adopted a material sensibility. Within the field of journalism studies, the assertion that "materiality matters" is still a relatively novel claim. Although journalism scholars have talked about the role of technology and computers in news-making for decades, "a renewed interest for materiality has emerged in the last few years" (De Maeyer, 2016: 461). For more on the material turn in journalism studies and the role of nonhumans in journalistic practice and products, see, for example, Anderson (2013), De Mayer (2016), Steensen (2016).
3. Scholars have used a variety of different but interrelated concepts to describe this movement toward the algorithmic processing of digital and digitized data, including computational journalism (Diakopoulos, 2015; Karlsen & Stavelin, 2014), data journalism (Fink & Anderson, 2015), data-driven journalism (Parasie, 2015), robot journalism (Carlson, 2015), journalism as programming (Parasie & Dagiral, 2013), and algorithmic journalism (Dörr, 2016). The precise label chosen to describe the intersection between journalism and computing depends, in part, on the specific area of work that is being emphasized (Karlsen & Stavelin, 2014). For example, the terms data journalism and data-driven journalism are most often used to describe an emerging form of storytelling in which journalists combine data analysis with new visualization techniques (Appelgren & Nygren, 2014). Broadly conceived, computational journalism refers to "finding, telling, and disseminating news stories with, by, or about algorithms" (Diakopoulos & Koliska, 2016: 2), and serves as an umbrella term for all kinds of "algorithmic, social scientific, and mathematical forms of newswork" (Anderson, 2013: 1005).
4. Precision journalism was conceived of as "the application of social and behavioral science research methods to the practice of journalism" (Meyer, 2002: 2). Computers and software, Meyer foresaw, would be essential for a new kind of journalism.
5. Although Jeffrey Alexander writes "information will be free," I assume he means "information wants to be free" as this is the iconic phrase attributed to Stewart Brand. Interestingly the first part of the mantra is usually overlooked: "On the one hand information wants to be expensive, because it's so valuable. The right information in the right place just changes your life. On the other hand, information wants to be free, because the cost of getting it out is getting lower and lower all the time. So you have these two fighting against each other" (Doctorow, 2010).
6. The Scandinavian news media context is characterized by what Hallin and Mancini (2004) describe as the "democratic corporatist" model. According to this model, media are marked by a unique "coexistence" that brings together "the polarized pluralist tendency toward more partisan, opinion-oriented journalism, and the liberal tendency toward a more commercialized, news-driven journalism—often assumed to be 'naturally' opposed" (Benson et al., 2012: 22). For more on the Scandinavian context in general, see Syvertsen et al. (2014).

7. The following interviews were conducted for chapter 6. Interviewees disguised by pseudonyms requested anonymity. The gender of anonymous interviewees should not be inferred from their pseudonyms.

1. Hans Martin Cramer, product developer at *Aftenposten*, March 2014, August 2016.
2. Stig Jakobsen, editor-in-chief at *iTromsø*, May 2016.
3. Jens Nicolaisen, digital director at *Jyllandsposten*, February 2015.
4. Ingeborg Volan, director of innovation and newsroom development at *Adresseavisen*, August 2016.
5. Anders Emil Møller, former director of digital development at *Politiken*, March 2014.
6. Johan Koppel Stræde, director of digital development at *Politiken*, September 2016.
7. Espen Sundve, vice president of product management at Schibsted, May 2016.
8. Markus Gustafsson, editor-in-chief at *Omni*, April 2014.
9. Markus Gustafsson, editor-in-chief at *Omni*, March 2015.
10. Henric Englund, software engineer at *Omni*, March 2015.
11. "Clare," editor at *Omni*, March 2015.
12. "Frank," editor at Omni, March 2015.
13. "Emma," editor at *Omni*, March 2015.
14. Catarina Smedshammar, UX designer at *Omni*, March 2015.
15. Alexander Nordström, technical lead at *Omni*, March 2015.
16. Linda Zoumas, product manager at Schibsted Media group, March 2015
17. Christian Gillinger, head of social media at Sveriges Radio, May 2016.
18. Ola Henriksson, web editor and project manager at *Svenska Dagbladet*, June 2016.
19. Jørgen Frøland, project manager for personalization at Polaris Media, August 2016.
20. Geir Larsen, former head of editorial development at VG, March 2014.

8. The informants were selected for their status as experts in the domain of digital and computational journalism, broadly defined. The interviews contained questions about the use of algorithms, data mining and other computational techniques within the respective news organizations, issues and challenges arising from the use of algorithms to support and shape the news, participants' views about the current state of journalism and how they see algorithms as part of it, including the potential for automating and personalizing journalistic practices and products. The interviews averaged at 60 minutes with the shortest being 40 minutes and the longest being 110 minutes. They were taped and subsequently transcribed. The interviews were examined using open coding techniques associated with grounded theory (Corbin & Strauss, 2008). The interview transcripts were subsequently read and analyzed for the specific preoccupations and concerns that the actors were speaking to.

9. For Kristin Asdal and Ingunn Moser this is a move that implies a sensibility toward "contexting," by which they "mean that contexts are being made together with the objects, texts, and issues at stake" (2012: 303).

10. *Aftenposten* is among the 29 titles owned by the Norwegian media house Schibsted. Schibsted Media Platform is Schibsted's new effort to assemble the technology and product teams of all of its titles into a single global technology and product organization.

11. Equipped with the data infrastructure and algorithms delivered by the Norwegian big data analytics company *Cxense* (of which Polaris Media, the company that owns *iTromsø*, is one of the company shareholders), *iTromsø* was the first media outlet in Norway to fully automate its mobile news feed.

12. According to the Columbia Journalism Review, structured journalism is an umbrella term that refers to thinking of journalism as bits and pieces of information that can be mixed and matched in infinite ways (Gourarie, 2015).

13. As I did not explicitly ask for permission to publish their names, all names of the editors I followed and interviewed during my fieldwork at *Omni* are anonymized to protect their privacy.

14. "Event thinking" has emerged as an influential philosophical avenue for contesting the concepts of facts and substance—particularly, as it relates to epistemology and the philosophy of science. Theorists such as Bruno Latour, Isabelle Stengers, Alfred North Whitehead, and Gilles Deleuze have all contributed to bringing the notion of the event to the forefront of process-relational theory. Differences among different theorists aside, the notion of event can be understood as "part of an anti-reductionist project that seeks to describe the relations between actual things, bodies and happenings" (Fraser, 2006: 129). Latour and Stengers both use the notion of event as a way of thinking about science—not in terms of discovery but as an invention of sorts. In *Pandora's Hope* (1999: 305), Latour says he borrows the notion of event from Whitehead as a way to avoid giving all scientific credit to human discoverers, at the expense of objects that typically remain immobile. Similarly, Stengers (2000) conceptualized science as event in the sense that it invents new relations between facts and fiction. In problematizing accepted boundaries, science becomes political in Stengers' account. An entirely different way of conceptualizing the event can be found in Alain Badiou's thinking, which, in many ways, is exactly the opposite of how process-relational philosophers conceptualize the event. For Badiou (2005), events are not premised on contingency but, rather, on a radical break with the past. For more on the notion of event in recent philosophical theory, see Fraser (2006) and Mackenzie (2005).

15. By "different," I do not necessarily mean "all new" or "radically disparate" from how things were before. My intention is not to talk about before and after at all, but to examine how boundaries and relations are enacted in practice. As I hope should be clear by now, I do not mean to suggest that *the* algorithm causes all of this to happen *on its own* or to anthropomorphize the algorithm. To remind readers, any distinction is analytical only, and made with the recognition that these entities necessarily entail each other in practice.

16. The notion of the *pharmakon* I take from Bernhard Stiegler's (2012; 2013) work, where he uses this Greek concept to talk about various technologies as both poison and cure.

Chapter 7

1. Wendy Chun (2016) argues that it is through habits that new media become embedded in our lives. It is not the push to the future characteristic of Big Data that structures lives in the age of smartphones and "new" media, but rather habitual forms of updating, streaming, sharing etc.

2. See also Gillespie (2017); Grimmelmann, J. (2008).

3. A widely used example of platform intervention is how Google responded differently in two cases of "Google bombing," the practice of manipulating Google's algorithms to get a piece of content to the top of the search results for a given topic. While Google chose to intervene and to manually "clean up" its search results when a group of people started a racist campaign against Michelle Obama in 2009 (to make search results for her name yield images of a monkey), the company did not intervene when in the wake of the 2011 terrorist attacks in Norway a campaign was launched urging people to upload pictures of dog droppings, tagging them with the terrorist's name.

4. Claims about heterogeneity and relationality do not automatically imply symmetry or equality. Despite the long-time insistence on symmetries within studies of science and technology, realities are seen as enacted and made through practices. As Pickering suggests with regards to humans and nonhumans, "semiotically, these things can be made equivalent; in practice they are not" (Pickering, 1995: 15). How agency and power manifest in particular practices is therefore an empirical question.

5. Here I am borrowing from Ganaele Langlois, who writes about *meaning machines* and how they "not tightly control what users say, but rather how they come to speak" (2013: 103).

6. In Karen Barad (2007) and Donna Haraway's (2004) terms, we might also say that the "response-ability" is shared. Accordingly, reponsibility and accountability is not so much about taking charge, as it is about the ability to respond to others.

Bibliography

Adams, A., & Sasse, M. A. (1999). Users are not the enemy. *Communications of the ACM, 42*(12), 40–46.

Adams, P., & Pai, C. C. F. (2013). *U.S. Patent No.* 20130179271 A1 ("Grouping and Ordering Advertising Units Based on User Activity"). Retrieved from http://www.google.tl/patents/US20130179271

Agger, B. (2012). *Oversharing: Presentations of self in the internet age.* New York, NY: Routledge.

Ahmed, S. (2000). *Strange encounters: Embodied others in post-coloniality.* London, England: Routledge.

Ahmed, S. (2006). *Queer phenomenology: Orientations, objects, others.* Durham, NC: Duke University Press.

Ahmed, S. (2010). Orientations matter. In J. Bennett, P. Cheah, M.A. Orlie & E. Grosz, E. (Eds.) *New materialisms: Ontology, agency, and politics* (pp. 234–257). Durham, NC: Duke University Press.

Ainsworth, S., & Hardy, C. (2012). Subjects of inquiry: Statistics, stories, and the production of knowledge. *Organization Studies, 33*(12), 1693–1714.

Alexander, J. C. (2015). The crisis of journalism reconsidered: Cultural power. *Fudan Journal of the Humanities and Social Sciences, 8*(1), 9–31.

Alexander, J. C., Breese, E. B., & Luengo, M. (2016). *The crisis of journalism reconsidered.* Cambridge, England: Cambridge University Press.

Allan, G. (1989). *Friendship: Developing a sociological perspective.* New York, NY: Harvester Wheatsheaf.

Altheide, D. L., & Snow, R. P. (1979). *Media logic.* Beverly Hills, CA: Sage.

Amatriain, X. (2013). *Big & personal: Data and models behind Netflix recommendations.* Paper presented at the Proceedings of the 2nd International Workshop on Big Data, Streams and Heterogeneous Source Mining: Algorithms, Systems, Programming Models and Applications, August 11, Chicago, IL.

Amoore, L. (2009). Algorithmic war: Everyday geographies of the War on Terror. *Antipode, 41*(1), 49–69.

Amoore, L. (2013). *The politics of possibility: Risk and security beyond probability.* Durham, NC: Duke University Press.

Ananny, M. (2016). Toward an ethics of algorithms convening, observation, probability, and timeliness. *Science, Technology & Human Values, 41*(1), 93–117.

Anderson, B. (1983). *Imagined communities: Reflections on the origin and spread of nationalism.* London, England: Verso Books.

Anderson, B. (2006). Becoming and being hopeful: towards a theory of affect. *Environment and Planning D: society and space, 24*(5), 733–752.

Anderson, B., Kearnes, M., McFarlane, C., & Swanton, D. (2012). On assemblages and geography. *Dialogues in human geography, 2*(2), 171–189.

Anderson, C. (2013). Towards a sociology of computational and algorithmic journalism. *New Media & Society, 15*(7), 1005–1021.

Anderson, C. W. (2011). Between creative and quantified audiences: Web metrics and changing patterns of newswork in local US newsrooms. *Journalism, 12*(5), 550–566.

Andrejevic, M. (2013). *Infoglut: How too much information is changing the way we think and know.* New York, NY: Routledge.

Angwin, J., Larson, J., Mattu, S., & Kirchner, L. (2016, May 23). Machine bias. *Pro Publica.* Retrieved from https://www.propublica.org/article/machine-bias-risk-assessments-in-criminal-sentencing

Appelgren, E., & Nygren, G. (2014). Data journalism in Sweden: Introducing new methods and genres of journalism into "old" organizations. *Digital Journalism, 2*(3), 394–405.

Aristotle. (2002). *The Nicomachean ethics* (S. Broadie & C. Rowe, Trans.). Oxford, England: Oxford University Press.

Arribas-Ayllon, M., & Walkerdine, V. (2008). Foucauldian discourse analysis. In C. Wiig & W. Stainton-Rogers (Eds.) *The Sage handbook of qualitative research in psychology* (pp. 91–108). London, England: Sage.

Arthur, C. (2012). Facebook's nudity and violence guidelines are laid bare. *The Guardian.* Retrieved from http://www.theguardian.com/technology/2012/feb/21/facebook-nudity-violence-censorship-guidelines.

Asdal, K., & Moser, I. (2012). Experiments in context and contexting. *Science, Technology, & Human Values, 37*(4), 291–306.

Ashby, W. R. (1999). *An introduction to cybernetics.* London, England: Chapman & Hall Ltd.

Austin, J. L. (1975). *How to do things with words.* Oxford, England: Oxford University Press.

Backstrom, L. S. (2013). News Feed FYI: A window into News Feed. *Facebook Business.* Retrieved from https://www.facebook.com/business/news/News-Feed-FYI-A-Window-Into-News-Feed

Badiou, A. (2005). *Being and Event.* London, England: Continuum.

Baki, B. (2015). *Badiou's being and event and the mathematics of set theory.* London, England: Bloomsbury Publishing.

Balkin, J. M. (2016). Information fiduciaries and the first amendment. *UC Davis Law Review, 49*(4): 1183–1234.

Barad, K. (1998). Getting real: Technoscientific practices and the materialization of reality. *Differences: a journal of feminist cultural studies, 10*(2), 87–91.

Barad, K. (2003). Posthumanist performativity: Toward an understanding of how matter comes to matter. *Signs, 28*(3), 801–831.

Barad, K. (2007). *Meeting the universe halfway: Quantum physics and the entanglement of matter and meaning.* Durham, NC: Duke University Press.

Barocas, S., & Selbst, A. D. (2016). Big data's disparate impact. Available at SSRN 2477899.

Barr, A. (2015). Google mistakenly tags black people as gorillas, showing limits of algorithms. Retrieved from http://blogs.wsj.com/digits/2015/07/01/google-mistakenly-tags-black-people-as-gorillas-showing-limits-of-algorithms/

Bartunek, J. M., & Moch, M. K. (1987). First-order, second-order, and third-order change and organization development interventions: A cognitive approach. *The Journal of Applied Behavioral Science, 23*(4), 483–500.

Bataille, G. (2004). *The unfinished system of nonknowledge.* Minneapolis: University of Minnesota Press.

Bataille, G., & Michelson, A. (1986). Un-knowing: laughter and tears. *October, 36,* 89–102.

Bazerman, C. (2002). *The languages of Edison's light.* Cambridge, Mass.: MIT Press.

Beckett, C. (2017). "Fake news": The best thing that's happened to journalism. Retrieved from blogs.lse.ac.uk/polis/2017/03/11/fake-news-the-best-thing-thats-happened-to-journalism/

Beer, D. (2009). Power through the algorithm? Participatory web cultures and the technological unconscious. *New media & society, 11*(6), 985–1002.

Beer, D. (2013). *Popular culture and new media: The politics of circulation.* Basingstoke, England: Palgrave Macmillan.

Bellman, B. L. (1984). *The language of secrecy. Symbols and metaphors in Poro ritual.* Newark, NJ: Rutgers University Press.

Benjamin, S. M. (2013). Algorithms and speech. *University of Pennsylvania Law Review, 161*(1445).

Bennett, J. (2004). The force of things steps toward an ecology of matter. *Political Theory, 32*(3), 347–372.

Bennett, J., Cheah, P., Orlie, M. A., Grosz, E., Coole, D., & Frost, S. (2010). *New materialisms: Ontology, agency, and politics.* Durham, NC: Duke University Press.

Benson, R., Blach-Ørsten, M., Powers, M., Willig, I., & Zambrano, S. V. (2012). Media systems online and off: Comparing the form of news in the United States, Denmark, and France. *Journal of communication, 62*(1), 21–38.

Berker, T., Hartmann, M., & Punie, Y. (2005). *Domestication of media and technology.* Maidenhead, England: McGraw-Hill Education.

Berlant, L. G. (2011). *Cruel optimism.* Durham, NC: Duke University Press.

Bernauer, J. W., & Rasmussen, D. M. (1988). *The final Foucault.* Cambridge, MA: MIT Press.

Berry, D. M. (2011). *The philosophy of software.* London, England: Palgrave Macmillan.

Bijker, W., & Law, J. (1994). *Shaping technology/building society: Studies in sociotechnical change.* Cambridge, MA: MIT Press.

Bijker, W. E., Hughes, T. P., Pinch, T., & Douglas, D. G. (2012). *The social construction of technological systems: New directions in the sociology and history of technology.* Cambridge, MA: MIT Press.

Birchall, C. (2011). Introduction to "secrecy and transparency": The politics of opacity and openness. *Theory, Culture & Society, 28*(7–8), 7–25.

Bissell, D. (2016). Micropolitics of mobility: Public transport commuting and everyday encounters with forces of enablement and constraint. *Annals of the American Association of Geographers, 106*(2), 394–403.

Bloomberg (n.a.) "Room Full of Ninjas: Inside Facebook's Bootcamp". Retrieved from https://www.bloomberg.com/video/inside-facebook-s-engineering-bootcamp-i8gg~WZFR7ywI4nlSgJJKw.html/

Bloomfield, B. P., Latham, Y., & Vurdubakis, T. (2010). Bodies, technologies and action possibilities: When is an affordance? *Sociology, 44*(3), 415–433. doi:10.1177/0038038510362469

Boczkowski, P. J. (2004). The processes of adopting multimedia and interactivity in three online newsrooms. *Journal of Communication, 54*(2), 197–213.

Boer, R. (2013). Revolution in the event: the problem of Kairos. *Theory, Culture & Society, 30*(2), 116–134.

Bogost, I. (2015). The cathedral of computation. *The Atlantic.* Retrieved from http://www.theatlantic.com/technology/archive/2015/01/the-cathedral-of-computation/384300/

Boland, B. (2014). Organic reach on Facebook: Your questions answered. *Facebook for business.* Retrieved from https://www.facebook.com/business/news/Organic-Reach-on-Facebook

Bosworth, A., & Cox, C. (2013). *U.S. Patent No. 8405094 B2* ("Providing a newsfeed based on user affinity for entities and monitored actions in a social network environment"). Retrieved from https://www.google.com/patents/US8402094

Bowker, G. C., & Star, S. L. (2000). *Sorting things out: Classification and its consequences.* Cambridge, MA: MIT Press.

Bowker, G. C., Baker, K., Millerand, F., & Ribes, D. (2010). Toward information infrastructure studies: Ways of knowing in a networked environment. In J. Hunsinger, L. Klastrup, M. Allen (Eds.) *International handbook of internet research* (pp. 97–117). New York, NY: Springer.

boyd, d. (2008). Facebook's privacy trainwreck. *Convergence: The International Journal of Research into New Media Technologies, 14*(1), 13–20.

Boyne, R. (2000). Post-panopticism. *Economy and Society, 29*(2), 285–307.

Bozdag, E. (2013). Bias in algorithmic filtering and personalization. *Ethics and Information Technology, 15*(3), 209–227.

Braidotti, R. (2006). Posthuman, all too human towards a new process ontology. *Theory, Culture & Society, 23*(7–8), 197–208.

Brandom, R. (2016). Leaked documents show how Facebook editors were told to run Trending Topics. *The Verge.* Retrieved from http://www.theverge.com/2016/5/12/11665298/facebook-trending-news-topics-human-editors-bias

Braun, B. & Whatmore, S. J. (2010). The stuff of politics: An introduction. In B. Braun, S Whatmore, & I. Stengers (Eds.) *Political matter: Technoscience, democracy, and public life* (pp. ix–xl) Minneapolis: University of Minnesota Press.

Braverman, I. (2014). Governing the wild: Databases, algorithms, and population models as biopolitics. *Surveillance & Society, 12*(1), 15.

Bröckling, U., Krasmann, S., & Lemke, T. (2011). From Foucaults lectures at the Collège de France to studies of governmentality. In U. Brökling, S. Krasmann & T. Lemke (Eds.) *Governmentality. Current issues and future challenges* (pp. 1–33). New York, NY: Routledge.

Bucher, T. (2013). The friendship assemblage investigating programmed sociality on Facebook. *Television & New Media, 14*(6), 479–493.

Bucher, T. (2016). Database. In B. K. Jensen & R. T. Craig (Eds.), *The international encyclopaedia of communication theory and philosophy* (pp. 489–496). Chichester, England: Wiley-Blackwell.

Buchheit. (2009). Applied philosophy, a.k.a. "hacking." *Paul Buchheit.* Retrieved from http://paulbuchheit.blogspot.com/2009_10_01_archive.html

Burrell, J. (2016). How the machine "thinks": Understanding opacity in machine learning algorithms. *Big Data & Society, 3*(1), 2053951715622512.

Butler, J. (1990). *Gender trouble: Feminism and the subversion of identity.* London: Routledge.

Butler, J. (2011). *Bodies that matter: On the discursive limits of sex.* London: Taylor & Francis.

Callon, M. (1998). *The laws of the markets.* Oxford, England: Blackwell.

Callon, M. (2007). What does it mean to say that economics is performative? In D. Mackenzie, F. Muniesa & L. Siu (Eds.) *Do economists make markets?* (pp. 311–357). Princeton, NJ: Princeton University Press.

Callon, M., & Latour, B. (1981). Unscrewing the big Leviathan: How actors macro-structure reality and how sociologists help them to do so. In K. Knorr-Cetina & A. V. Cicourel (Eds.) *Advances in social theory and methodology: Toward an integration of micro-and macro-sociologies* (pp. 277–303). London, England: Routledge.

Callon, M., & Law, J. (2005). On qualculation, agency, and otherness. *Environment and Planning D: Society and Space, 23*(5), 717–733.

Callon, M., & Muniesa, F. (2005). Peripheral vision economic markets as calculative collective devices. *Organization Studies, 26*(8), 1229–1250.

Candela. (2016). Session with Joaquin Quiñonero Candela. *Quora.* Retrieved from https://www.quora.com/session/Joaquin-Quiñonero-Candela/1

Carlson, M. (2015). The robotic reporter: Automated journalism and the redefinition of labor, compositional forms, and journalistic authority. *Digital Journalism, 3*(3), 416–431.

Castoriadis, C. (1987). *The imaginary institution of society.* Cambridge, MA: MIT Press.

Cathcart, W. (2016). Creating value for news publishers and readers on Facebook. *Facebook for developers.* Retrieved from: https://developers.facebook.com/videos/f8-2016/creating-value-for-news-publishers-and-readers-on-facebook/

Chadwick, A. (2013). *The hybrid media system: Politics and power.* New York, NY: Oxford University Press.

Chaykowski, K. (2016, September 14). Facebook news feed head: Trending topics is "better" without human editors. *Forbes.* Retrieved from http://www.forbes.com/sites/kathleenchaykowski/2016/09/14/facebooks-head-of-news-feed-trending-topics-is-better-without-human-editors-despite-fake-news/#73e85459243f

Chen, D. Y., Grewal, E. B., Mao, Z., Moreno, D., Sidhu, K. S., & Thibodeau, A. (2014). *U.S. Patent No. 8856248 B2* ("Methods and systems for optimizing engagement with a social network"). Washington, DC: U.S. Patent and Trademark Office.

Cheney-Lippold, J. (2011). A new algorithmic identity: Soft biopolitics and the modulation of control. *Theory, Culture & Society, 28*(6), 164–181.

Cheney-Lippold, J. (2016). Jus algoritmi: How the National Security Agency remade citizenship. *International Journal of Communication, 10,* 22.

Christian, B. (2012). The A/B test: Inside the technology that's changing the rules of business. *Wired.* Retrieved from http://www.wired.com/2012/04/ff_abtesting/

Chun, W. H. K. (2011). *Programmed visions: Software and memory.* Cambridge, MA: MIT Press.

Chun, W. H. K. (2016). *Updating to Remain the Same: Habitual New Media.* Cambridge, MA: MIT Press.

Citron, D. K., & Pasquale, F. A. (2014). The scored society: Due process for automated predictions. *Washington Law Review, 89,* 1–33.

Clerwall, C. (2014). Enter the robot journalist: Users' perceptions of automated content. *Journalism Practice, 8*(5).

Clough, P. T., & Halley, J. (Eds.). (2007). *The affective turn: Theorizing the social.* Durham, NC: Duke University Press.

Codd, E. F. (1970). A relational model of data for large shared data banks. *Communications of the ACM, 13*(6), 377–387.

Coddington, M. (2015). Clarifying journalism's quantitative turn: A typology for evaluating data journalism, computational journalism, and computer-assisted reporting. *Digital Journalism, 3*(3), 331–348.

Cohen, J. E. (2016). The regulatory state in the information age. *Theoretical Inquiries in Law, 17*(2).

Cohen, S., Hamilton, J. T., & Turner, F. (2011). Computational journalism. *Communications of the ACM, 54*(10), 66–71.

Coleman, G. (2014). *Hacker, hoaxer, whistleblower, spy: The many faces of Anonymous.* London, England: Verso.

Condliffe, J. (2015). You're using neural networks every day online—Here's how they work. *Gizmodo.* Retrieved from http://gizmodo.com/youre-using-neural-networks-every-day-online-heres-h-1711616296

Cooren, F., Fairhurst, G., & Huët, R. (2012). Why matter always matters in (organizational) communication. In P. M. Leonardi, B. A. Nardi, & J. Kallinikos (Eds.), *Materiality and organizing: Social interaction in a technological world* (pp. 296–314). Oxford, England: Oxford University Press.

Corasaniti, N., & Isaac, M. (2016). Senator demands answers from Facebook on claims of "trending" list bias. Retrieved from http://www.nytimes.com/2016/05/11/technology/facebook-thune-conservative.html?_r=0

Corbin, J., & Strauss, A. (2008). Basics of qualitative research. London: Sage.

Cormen, T. H. (2013). *Algorithms unlocked.* Cambridge, MA: MIT Press.

Cotter, C. (2010). *News talk: Investigating the language of journalism*: Cambridge University Press.

Couldry, N. (2012). *Media, society, world: Social theory and digital media practice.* Cambridge, England: Polity.

Couldry, N., Fotopoulou, A., & Dickens, L. (2016). Real social analytics: a contribution towards a phenomenology of a digital world. *The British Journal of Sociology, 67*(1), 118–137.

Ctrl-Shift (2015). The data driven economy: Toward sustainable growth. Report commissioned by Facebook.

Cutterham, T. (2013). Just friends. Retrieved from http://thenewinquiry.com/essays/just-friends/

Davidson, J., Liebald, B., Liu, J., Nandy, P., & Van Vleet, T. (2010). *The YouTube video recommendation system.* Paper presented at the Proceedings of the fourth ACM conference on Recommender systems. Barcelona, Spain.

De Mayer, J. (2016). Adopting a 'Material Sensibility' in Journalism Studies. In T. Witschge, C.W. Anderson, D. Domingo & A. Hermida (Eds.) The SAGE Handbook of Digital Journalism (pp. 460–476). London, England: Sage.

De Vries, K. (2010). Identity, profiling algorithms and a world of ambient intelligence. *Ethics and Information Technology, 12*(1), 71–85.

Debatin, B., Lovejoy, J. P., Horn, A. K., & Hughes, B. N. (2009). Facebook and online privacy: Attitudes, behaviors, and unintended consequences. *Journal of Computer-Mediated Communication, 15*(1), 83–108.

DeLanda, M. (2006). *A new philosophy of society: Assemblage theory and social complexity.* London, England: Bloomsbury

Deleuze, G. (1988). *Spinoza: Practical philosophy.* San Francisco, CA: City Lights Books.

Deleuze, G. (1990). *Expressionism in philosophy: Spinoza.* New York, NY: Zone Books.

Deleuze, G. (1992). Postscript on the societies of control. *October, 59,* 3–7.

Deleuze, G. (2006). *Foucault.* London, England: Routledge.

Deleuze, G., & Guattari, F. (1987). A thousand plateaus. Minneapolis: University of Minnesota Press.

Deleuze, G., & Parnet, C. (2007). *Dialogues II.* New York, NY: Columbia University Press.

Derrida, J. (2005). *Politics of friendship* (Vol. 5). New York, NY: Verso.

Derrida, J., & Ferraris, M. (2001). *A Taste for the secret,* trans. Giacomo Donis. Cambridge, England: Polity.

Desrosières, A., & Naish, C. (2002). *The politics of large numbers: A history of statistical reasoning.* Cambridge, MA: Harvard University Press.

Deuze, M. (2012). *Media life.* Cambridge, England: Polity.

Dewandre, N. (2015). The human condition and the black box society. *Boundary 2.* Retrieved from https://www.boundary2.org/2015/12/dewandre-on-pascal/#authorbio

Diakopoulos, N. (2014). Algorithmic accountability reporting: On the investigation of black boxes. Tow Center for Digital Journalism, Columbia University, New York, NY.

Diakopoulos, N. (2015). Algorithmic Accountability: Journalistic investigation of computational power structures. *Digital Journalism, 3*(3), 398–415.

Diakopoulos, N., & Koliska, M. (2017). Algorithmic transparency in the news media. *Digital Journalism, 5*(7), 809–828.

Doctorow, C. (2010). Saying information wants to be free does more harm than good. Retrieved from https://www.theguardian.com/technology/2010/may/18/information-wants-to-be-free

Domingo, D. (2008). Interactivity in the daily routines of online newsrooms: Dealing with an uncomfortable myth. *Journal of Computer-Mediated Communication, 13*(3), 680–704.

Domingos, P. (2015). *The master algorithm: How the quest for the ultimate learning machine will remake our world.* New York, NY: Basic Books.

Dörr, K. N. (2016). Mapping the field of algorithmic journalism. *Digital Journalism, 4*(6), 700–722.

Dourish, P. (2014). NoSQL: The shifting materialities of database technology. *Computational Culture* (4).

Driscoll, K. (2012). From punched cards to "big data": A social history of database populism. *communication+ 1, 1*(1), 4.

Duggan, M., Ellison, N., Lampe, C., Lenhart, A., & Madden, M. (2015). *Social media update 2014.* Retrieved from Pew Research Center: http://www.pewinternet.org/files/2015/01/PI_SocialMediaUpdate20144.pdf

Eilam, E. (2005). *Reversing: Secrets of reverse engineering.* Indianapolis, IN: John Wiley & Sons.

Elmer, G. (2004). *Profiling machines: Mapping the personal information economy.* Cambridge, MA: MIT Press.

Ensmenger, N. (2012). The digital construction of technology: Rethinking the history of computers in society. *Technology and Culture, 53*(4), 753–776.

Eslami, M., Rickman, A., Vaccaro, K., Aleyasen, A., Vuong, A., Karahalios, K., ... Sandvig, C. (2015). *"I always assumed that I wasn't really that close to [her]": Reasoning about invisible algorithms in the news feed.* Paper presented at the Proceedings of the 33rd Annual SIGCHI Conference on Human Factors in Computing Systems, New York, NY.

Espeland, W. N., & Sauder, M. (2007). Rankings and reactivity: How public measures recreate social worlds. *American Journal of Sociology, 113*(1), 1–40.

Espeland, W. N., & Stevens, M. L. (2008). A sociology of quantification. *European Journal of Sociology, 49*(03), 401–436.

Facebook (2011). How news feed works. Retrieved from https://web.archive.org/web/20110915091339/http://www.facebook.com/help?page=408

Facebook (2012). Form 1 Registration Statement. Retrieved from https://www.sec.gov/Archives/edgar/data/1326801/000119312512034517/d287954ds1.htm

Facebook (2013). How does my News Feed determine which content is most interesting? Retrieved from http://web.archive.org/web/20130605191932/https://www.facebook.com/help/166738576721085

Facebook (2014). #AskMark: Why do you wear the same shirt every day?. Retrieved from https://vimeo.com/111171647

Facebook. (2015). How does News Feed decide which stories to show? *Facebook Help Center.* Retrieved from https://www.facebook.com/help/166738576721085

Facebook. (2016). Search FYI: An update to trending. Retrieved from http://newsroom.fb.com/news/2016/08/search-fyi-an-update-to-trending

Facebook (2018). What kinds of posts will I see in News Feed? Facebook Help Center. Retrieved from https://www.facebook.com/help/166738576721085

Farias, G., Dormido-Canto, S., Vega, J., Rattá, G., Vargas, H., Hermosilla, G., Alfaro, L. & Valencia, A. (2016). Automatic feature extraction in large fusion databases by using deep learning approach. *Fusion Engineering and Design, 112,* 979–983.

Fattal, A. (2012). Facebook: Corporate hackers, a billion users, and the geo-politics of the "social graph." *Anthropological Quarterly, 85*(3), 927–955.

Faubion, J. D. (1994). Michel Foucault power: Essential works of Foucault 1954–1984 (Vol. 3): London, England: Penguin.

Fink, K., & Anderson, C. W. (2015). Data journalism in the United States: Beyond the "usual suspects." *Journalism Studies, 16*(4), 467–481.

Firstround (2014). "80% of Your Culture is Your Founder". Retrieved from http://firstround.com/review/80-of-Your-Culture-is-Your-Founder/

Flach, P. (2012). *Machine learning: the art and science of algorithms that make sense of data.* Cambridge, England: Cambridge University Press.

Flanagan, M., & Nissenbaum, H. (2014). *Values at play in digital games.* Cambridge, MA: MIT Press.

Flynn, J. (2004). Communicative power in Habermas's theory of democracy. *European Journal of Political Theory, 3*(4), 433–454.

Foucault, M. (1977). *Discipline and punish: The birth of the prison.* New York, NY: Vintage.

Foucault, M. (1978). *The history of sexuality: An introduction. Vol. 1.* New York, NY: Vintage.

Foucault, M. (1980). *Power/knowledge: Selected interviews and other writings, 1972–1977.* New York, NY: Harvester Wheatsheaf.

Foucault, M. (1982). The subject and power. *Critical Inquiry, 8*(4), 777–795.

Foucault, M. (1988). *Politics, philosophy, culture: Interviews and other writings, 1977–1984.* New York, NY: Routledge.

Foucault, M. (1990). *The history of sexuality: An introduction, volume I.* Trans. Robert Hurley. New York, NY: Vintage Books.

Foucault, M. (1993). About the beginning of the hermeneutics of the self: Two lectures at Dartmouth. *Political Theory, 21*(2), 198–227.

Foucault, M. (1994). Polemics, politics, and problematizations. In P. Rabinow (Ed.), *Ethics: Subjectivity and truth* (pp. 111–119). New York, NY: The New Press.

Foucault, M. (2007). *Security, population, territory: lectures at the Collège de France 1977–78.* Trans. G. Burchell. New York, NY: Palgrave Macmillan.

Foucault, M. (2008). The birth of biopower: Lectures at the College de France, 1978–1979. Trans. Graham Burchell. New York, NY: Palgrave Macmillan.

Foucault, M. (2010). What is enlightenment? In P. Rabinow (Ed.), *The Foucault reader* (pp. 32–50). New York, NY: Vintage Books.

Foucault, M. (2012). *The history of sexuality, vol. 2: The use of pleasure.* New York, NY: Vintage.

Foucault, M. (2015). *On the Punitive Society: Lectures at the Collège de France, 1972–1973.* Basingstoke, England: Palgrave McMillan.

Foucault, M., & Rabinow, P. (1997). *Ethics: subjectivity and truth: the essential works of Michel Foucault, 1954–1984* (Vol. 1). New York, NY: The New Press.

Fraser, M. (2006). Event. *Theory, Culture & Society, 23*(2–3), 129–132.

Fuchs, C. (2012). The political economy of privacy on Facebook. *Television & New Media, 13*(2), 139–159.

Fuller, M. (2008). *Software studies: A lexicon.* Cambridge, MA: MIT Press.

Galison, P. (1994). The ontology of the enemy: Norbert Wiener and the cybernetic vision. *Critical Inquiry, 21*(1), 228–266.

Galison, P. (2004). Removing knowledge. *Critical Inquiry, 31*(1), 229–243.

Galloway, A. R. (2004). *Protocol: How control exists after decentralization.* Cambridge, MA: MIT Press.

Galloway, A. R. (2006a). Language wants to be overlooked: On software and ideology. *Journal of Visual Culture, 5*(3), 315–331.

Galloway, A. R. (2006b). *Gaming: Essays on algorithmic culture.* Minneapolis: University of Minnesota Press.

Galloway, A. (2011). Are some things unrepresentable? *Theory, Culture & Society, 28*(7–8), 85–102.

Gans, H. J. (1979). *Deciding what's news: A study of CBS evening news, NBC nightly news, Newsweek, and Time.* Evanston, IL: Northwestern University Press.

Garcia, M. (2017). In quest for homepage engagement, newsrooms turn to dreaded "A" word. Retrieved from https://www.cjr.org/analysis/news-algorithm-homepage.php

Ge, H. (2013). News Feed FYI: More Relevant Ads in News Feed. Retrieved from https://newsroom.fb.com/news/2013/09/news-feed-fyi-more-relevant-ads-in-news-feed/

Gehl, R. W. (2014). *Reverse engineering social media.* Philadelphia, PA: Temple University Press.

Gerlitz, C., & Helmond, A. (2013). The like economy: Social buttons and the data-intensive web. *New media & society, 15*(8), 1348–1365.

Gerlitz, C., & Lury, C. (2014). Social media and self-evaluating assemblages: on numbers, orderings and values. *Distinktion: Scandinavian Journal of Social Theory, 15*(2), 174–188.

Gibson, E. J. (1988). Exploratory behavior in the development of perceiving, acting, and the acquiring of knowledge. *Annual Review of Psychology, 39*(1), 1–42.

Gillespie, T. (2011). Can an algorithm be wrong? Twitter Trends, the specter of censorship, and our faith in the algorithms around us. *Culture Digitally.* Retrieved from http://culturedigitally.org/2011/10/can-an-algorithm-be-wrong/

Gillespie, T. (2014). The Relevance of Algorithms. In T. Gillespie, P. Boczkowski, & K. Foot (Eds.), *Media technologies: Essays on communication, materiality, and society* (pp. 167–194). Cambridge, MA: MIT Press.

Gillespie, T. (2016a). Algorithm. In B. Peters (Ed.), *Digital keywords: A vocabulary of information society and culture* (pp. 18–30). Princeton, NJ: Princeton University Press.

Gillespie, T. (2016b). #trendingistrending: when algorithms become culture. In R. Seyfert & J. Roberge (Eds.) *Algorithmic cultures: Essays on meaning, performance and new technologies* (pp. 52–75). New York, NY: Routledge.

Gillespie, T. (2017). Algorithmically recognizable: Santorum's Google problem, and Google's Santorum problem. *Information, Communication & Society, 20*(1), 63–80.

Gillespie, T., Boczkowski, P., & Foot, K. (2014). *Media Technologies: Essays on Communication, Materiality, and Society.* Cambridge, Mass: MIT Press.

Goel, V. (2014). Facebook tinkers with users' emotions in news feed experiment, stirring outcry. *New York Times.* Retrieved from http://www.nytimes.com/2014/06/30/technology/facebook-tinkers-with-users-emotions-in-news-feed-experiment-stirring-outcry.html

Goffey, A. (2008). Algorithm. In M. Fuller (Ed.), *Software studies: A lexicon.* Cambridge, MA: MIT Press.

Golumbia, D. (2009). *The cultural logic of computation.* Cambridge, MA: Harvard University Press.

Gomez-Uribe, C. A., & Hunt, N. (2015). The Netflix recommender system: Algorithms, business value, and innovation. *ACM Transactions on Management Information Systems (TMIS), 6*(4), 13.

Goode, L. (2009). Social news, citizen journalism and democracy. *New Media & Society, 11*(8), 1287–1305.

Goodman, N. (1985). *Ways of worldmaking.* Indianapolis, IN: Hackett Publishing.

Gourarie, C. (2015). "Structured journalism" offers readers a different kind of story experience. Retrieved from https://www.cjr.org/innovations/structured_journalism.php

Grauer, Y. (2016). ACLU Files Lawsuit On Behalf of Researchers and Journalists Seeking To Uncover Discrimination Online. *Forbes.* Retrieved from http://www.forbes.com/sites/ygrauer/2016/06/30/aclu-files-lawsuit-on-behalf-of-researchers-and-journalists-seeking-to-uncover-discrimination-online/#1edfbf306b92

Green, S. (1999). A plague on the panopticon: surveillance and power in the global information economy. *Information, Communication & Society, 2*(1), 26–44.

Gregg, M. (2007). Thanks for the Ad(d): Neoliberalism's compulsory friendship. Retrieved from http://www.onlineopinion.com.au/view.asp?article = 6400

Gregg, M., & Seigworth, G. J. (2010). *The affect theory reader.* Durham, NC: Duke University Press.

Grier, D. (1996). The ENIAC, the verb "to program" and the emergence of digital computers. *IEEE Annals of the History of Computing, 18*(1), 51–55.

Griffith, E. (2016). Why huge growth and profits weren't enough for Facebook's investors this quarter. *Fortune.* Retrieved from http://fortune.com/2016/11/02/facebook-earnings-investors-growth/

Grimmelmann, J. (2008). The Google dilemma. *New York Law School Law Review, 53,* 939–950.

Gross, M. (2007). The unknown in process dynamic connections of ignorance, non-knowledge and related concepts. *Current Sociology, 55*(5), 742–759.

Grosser, B. (2014). What do metrics want? How quantification prescribes social interaction on Facebook. *Computational Culture* (4).

Gubin, M., Kao, W., Vickrey, D., & Maykov, A. (2014). *U.S. Patent No.* 8768863 ("Adaptive ranking of news feed in social networking systems"). Retrieved from https://www.google.com/patents/US20140258191

Hacking, I. (1990). *The taming of chance.* Cambridge, England: Cambridge University Press.

Hacking, I. (1991). How should we do the history of statistics? In G. Burchell, C. Gordon, & P. Miller (Eds.), *The Foucault effect–studies in governmentality* (pp. 181–195). London, England: Harvester Wheatsheaf.

Hacking, I. (1999). Making up people. In M. Biagioli & P. Galison (Eds.), *The science studies reader* (pp. 161–171). New York, NY: Routledge.

Hacking, I. (2006). *The emergence of probability: A philosophical study of early ideas about probability, induction and statistical inference.* Cambridge, England: Cambridge University Press.

Hacking, I. (2007). *Kinds of people: Moving targets. Proceedings of the British Society: 151,* 285–318.

Hacking, I. (2015). Biopower and the avalanche of printed numbers. In V. W. Cisney & N. Morar (Eds.), *Biopower: Foucault and beyond* (pp. 65–81). Chicago, IL: University of Chicago Press.

Haggerty, K. D., & Ericson, R. V. (2000). The surveillant assemblage. *The British Journal of Sociology, 51*(4), 605–622.

Haigh, T. (2001). Inventing information systems: The systems men and the computer, 1950–1968. *Business History Review, 75*(01), 15–61.

Hallin, D. C., & Mancini, P. (2004). *Comparing media systems: Three models of media and politics.* Cambridge, England. Cambridge University press.

Hallinan, B., & Striphas, T. (2016). Recommended for you: The Netflix Prize and the production of algorithmic culture. *New Media & Society, 18*(1), 117–137.

Hamilton, B. (2010). Bootcamp: Growing culture at Facebook. *Facebook engineering.* Retrieved from https://www.facebook.com/notes/facebook-engineering/bootcamp-growing-culture-at-facebook/249415563919

Hamilton, K., Karahalios, K., Sandvig, C., & Eslami, M. (2014). *A path to understanding the effects of algorithm awareness.* Paper presented at the CHI'14 Extended Abstracts on Human Factors in Computing Systems, April 26–May 1, Toronto, Canada.

Hamilton, J. T., & Turner, F. (2009). *Accountability through algorithm, Developing the field of computational journalism.* Paper presented at the Center for Advanced Study in the Behavioral Sciences Summer Workshop. Duke University in association with Stanford University.

Hansen, M. B. (2004). *New philosophy for new media*. Cambridge, MA: MIT Press.

Hansen, M. B. (2012). *Bodies in code: Interfaces with digital media*. New York, NY: Routledge.

Haraway, D. (1991). Simians, cyborgs, and women: New York, NY: Routledge.

Haraway, D. J. (2004). *The Haraway reader*. East Sussex, England: Psychology Press.

Hardin, R. (2003). If it rained knowledge. *Philosophy of the Social Sciences, 33*(1), 3–24.

Harding, S. (1996). Feminism, science, and the anti-enlightenment critiques. In A. Garry & M. Pearsall (Eds.) *Women, knowledge, and reality: Explorations in feminist philosophy* (pp. 298–320). New York, NY: Routledge.

Hardy, Q. (2014). The Monuments of Tech. *New York Times*. Retrieved from http://www.nytimes .com/2014/03/02/technology/the-monuments-of-tech.html

Hargittai, E. (2010). Facebook privacy settings: Who cares? *First Monday, 15*(8).

Hayles, N. K. (2005). *My mother was a computer: Digital subjects and literary texts*. Chicago, IL: University of Chicago Press.

Hays, R. B. (1988). Friendship. In S. Duck, D. F. Hay, S. E. Hobfoll, W. Ickes, & B. M. Montgomery (Eds.), *Handbook of personal relationships: Theory, research and interventions* (pp. 391–408). Oxford, England: John Wiley.

Heath, A. (2015). Spotify is getting unbelievably good at picking music—here's an inside look at how. *Tech Insider*. Retrieved from http://www.techinsider.io/inside-spotify-and-the-future-of-music-streaming

Hecht-Nielsen, R. (1988). Neurocomputing: picking the human brain. *Spectrum, IEEE, 25*(3), 36–41.

Hein, S. F. (2016). The new materialism in qualitative inquiry: How compatible are the philosophies of Barad and Deleuze? *Cultural Studies? Critical Methodologies, 16*(2), 132–140.

Helberger, N., Kleinen-von Königslöw, K., & van der Noll, R. (2015). Regulating the new information intermediaries as gatekeepers of information diversity. *Info, 17*(6), 50–71.

Helm, B. W. (2010). *Love, friendship, and the self: Intimacy, identification, and the social nature of persons*. Cambridge, England: Cambridge University Press.

Hermida, A., Fletcher, F., Korell, D., & Logan, D. (2012). Share, like, recommend: Decoding the social media news consumer. *Journalism Studies, 13*(5–6), 815–824.

Hill, D. W. (2012). Jean-François Lyotard and the inhumanity of internet surveillance. In C. Fuchs, K. Boersma, A. Albrechtslund, & M. Sandoval (Eds.), *Internet and surveillance: The challenges of Web* (Vol. 2, pp. 106–123). New York, NY: Routledge.

Hirsch, E., & Silverstone, R. (2003). *Consuming technologies: Media and information in domestic spaces*. London, England: Routledge.

Hirschfeld, L. A. (2001). On a folk theory of society: Children, evolution, and mental representations of social groups. *Personality and Social Psychology Review, 5*(2), 107–117.

Hoel, A. S., & Van der Tuin, I. (2013). The ontological force of technicity: Reading Cassirer and Simondon diffractively. *Philosophy & Technology, 26*(2), 187–202.

Hromkovič, J. (2015). Alan Turing and the Foundation of Computer Science. In G. Sommaruga & T. Strahm (Eds.) *Turing's Revolution* (pp. 273–281). Cham, Germany: Springer

Hull M (2011) Facebook changes mean that you are not seeing everything that you should be seeing. Retrieved from http://www.facebook.com/notes/mark-hull/please-read-facebook-changes-mean-that-you-are-not-seeing-everything-that-you-sh/10150089908123789.

Hutchby, I. (2001). Technologies, texts and affordances. *Sociology, 35*(2), 441–456.

Ingold, T. (1993). The temporality of the landscape. *World Archaeology, 25*(2), 152–174.

Ingold, T. (2000). *The perception of the environment: essays on livelihood, dwelling and skill*. East Susses, England: Psychology Press.

Ingold, T. (2011). *Being alive: Essays on movement, knowledge and description*. London, England: Routledge.

Introna, L., & Wood, D. (2004). Picturing algorithmic surveillance: The politics of facial recognition systems. *Surveillance & Society, 2*(2/3).

Introna, L. D. (2011). The enframing of code agency, originality and the plagiarist. *Theory, Culture & Society, 28*(6), 113–141.

Introna, L. D. (2016). Algorithms, governance, and governmentality on governing academic writing. *Science, Technology & Human Values, 41*(1), 17–49.

Introna, L. D., & Nissenbaum, H. (2000). Shaping the Web: Why the politics of search engines matters. *The Information Society, 16*(3), 169–185.

Jansen, K., & Vellema, S. (2011). What is technography? *NJAS-Wageningen Journal of Life Sciences, 57*(3), 169–177.

Johnson, M. (1993). *Moral imagination: Implications of cognitive science for ethics.* Cambridge, England: Cambridge University Press.

Johnson-Laird, P. N., & Oatley, K. (1992). Basic emotions, rationality, and folk theory. *Cognition & Emotion, 6*(3–4), 201–223.

Juan, Y. F., & Hua, M. (2012). Contextually relevant affinity prediction in a social networking system. *U.S. Patent Application No. 12/978,265, US 2012/0166532 A1.* Retrieved from https://www.google.com/patents/US20120166532

Juniper, J., & Jose, J. (2008). Foucault and Spinoza: Philosophies of immanence and the decentred political subject. *History of the Human Sciences, 21*(2), 1–20.

Jurgenson, N., & Rey, P. (2012). Comment on Sarah Ford's "Reconceptualization of privacy and publicity." *Information, Communication & Society, 15*(2), 287–293.

Just, N., & Latzer, M. (2017). Governance by algorithms: Reality construction by algorithmic selection on the internet. *Media, Culture & Society, 39*(2), 238–258.

Kacholia, V. (2013). News feed FYI: Showing more high quality content. *Facebook: News feed FYI.* Retrieved from https://newsroom.fb.com/news/2013/08/news-feed-fyi-showing-more-high-quality-content/

Kaerlein, T. (2013). Playing with personal media: On an epistemology of ignorance. *Culture Unbound. 5,* 651–670.

Kahn, D. (2004). A musical technography of John Bischoff. *Leonardo Music Journal, 14,* 75–79.

Karlsen, J., & Stavelin, E. (2014). Computational journalism in Norwegian newsrooms. *Journalism Practice, 8*(1), 34–48.

Karppi, T., & Crawford, K. (2016). Social media, financial algorithms and the hack crash. *Theory, Culture & Society, 33*(1), 73–92.

Kaun, A., & Stiernstedt, F. (2014). Facebook time: Technological and institutional affordances for media memories. *New Media & Society, 16*(7), 1154–1168.

Kelly, M. G. (2015). Discipline is control: Foucault contra Deleuze. *New Formations, 84*(84–85), 148–162.

Kempton, W. (1986). Two theories of home heat control. *Cognitive Science, 10*(1), 75–90.

Kendall, T., & Zhou, D. (2010). *U.S. Patent No. 20100257023 A1* ("Leveraging Information in a Social Network for Inferential Targeting of Advertisements"). Washington, DC: U.S. Patent and Trademark Office.

Keyani, P. (2014). Evolving culture and values. Understanding the tradeoffs. Growth through failure. The importance of leadership and open communication. *InfoQ.* Retrieved from http://www.infoq.com/presentations/facebook-culture-growth-leadership

Kien, G. (2008). Technography= technology+ ethnography. *Qualitative Inquiry, 14*(7), 1101–1109.

Kincaid, J. (2010). EdgeRank: The Secret Sauce That Makes Facebook's News Feed Tick. Retrieved from http://techcrunch.com/2010/04/22/facebook-edgerank/

King, R. (2013). Facebook engineers explain News Feed ranking algorithms; more changes soon. *ZDNet.* Retrieved from http://www.zdnet.com/article/facebook-engineers-explain-news-feed-ranking-algorithms-more-changes-soon

Kirby, D. A. (2011). *Lab coats in Hollywood: Science, scientists, and cinema.* Cambridge, MA: MIT Press.

Kirchner, L. (2015, September 6). When discrimination is baked into algorithms. *The Atlantic.* Retrieved from http://www.theatlantic.com/business/archive/2015/09/discrimination-algorithms-disparate-impact/403969/

Kitchin, R. (2017). Thinking critically about and researching algorithms. *Information, Communication & Society, 20*(1), 14–29.

Kitchin, R., & Dodge, M. (2005). Code and the transduction of space. *Annals of the Association of American geographers, 95*(1), 162–180.

Kitchin, R., & Dodge, M. (2011). *Code/space: Software and everyday life*. Cambridge, MA: MIT Press.

Kittler, F. A. (1999). *Gramophone, film, typewriter*. Stanford, CA: Stanford University Press.

Klein, E. (2016). Facebook is going to get more politically biased, not less. *Vox*. Retrieved from http://www.vox.com/2016/5/13/11661156/facebook-political-bias

Kling, R. (1980). Social analyses of computing: Theoretical perspectives in recent empirical research. *ACM Computing Surveys (CSUR), 12*(1), 61–110.

Knight, W. (2015, September 22). The hit charade. *MIT Technology Review*. Retrieved from https://www.technologyreview.com/s/541471/the-hit-charade/

Knobel, C., & Bowker, G. C. (2011). Values in design. *Communications of the ACM, 54*(7), 26–28.

Knorr-Cetina, K. (1999). *Epistemic cultures: How scientists make sense*. Cambridge, MA: Harvard University Press.

Knuth, D. E. (1984). Literate programming. *The Computer Journal, 27*(2), 97–111.

Knuth, D. E. (1998). *The art of computer programming: Sorting and searching* (Vol. 3). London, England: Pearson Education.

Kroll, J. A., Huey, J., Barocas, S., Felten, E. W., Reidenberg, J. R., Robinson, D. G., & Yu, H. (2016). Accountable algorithms. *University of Pennsylvania Law Review, 165*, 633–706.

Kushner, S. (2013). The freelance translation machine: Algorithmic culture and the invisible industry. *New Media & Society, 15*(8), 1241–1258.

Lacan, J., & Fink, B. (2002). *Ecrits: A selection*. New York, NY: WW Norton.

LaFrance, A. (2015). Not even the people who write algorithms really know how they work. *The Atlantic*. Retrieved from http://www.theatlantic.com/technology/archive/2015/09/not-even-the-people-who-write-algorithms-really-know-how-they-work/406099/

Lamb, R., & Kling, R. (2003). Reconceptualizing users as social actors in information systems research. *Mis Quarterly, 27*(2), 197–236.

Langlois, G. (2014). *Meaning in the age of social media*. New York, NY: Palgrave Macmillan.

Langlois, G., & Elmer, G. (2013). The research politics of social media platforms. *Culture Machine, 14*, 1–17.

Lash, S. (2007). Power after hegemony cultural studies in mutation? *Theory, Culture & Society, 24*(3), 55–78.

Latour, B. (1994). On technical mediation. *Common knowledge, 3*(2), 29–64.

Latour, B. (1999). *Pandora's hope: Essays on the reality of science studies*. Cambridge, MA: Harvard University Press.

Latour, B. (2004). Why has critique run out of steam? From matters of fact to matters of concern. *Critical Inquiry, 30*(2), 225–248.

Latour, B. (2005). *Reassembling the social: An introduction to actor-network-theory*. Oxford, England: Oxford University Press.

Law, J. (1999). After ANT: Complexity, naming and topology. *The Sociological Review, 47*(S1), 1–14.

Law, J. (2002). *Aircraft stories: Decentering the object in technoscience*. Durham, NC: Duke University Press.

Law, J. (2004a). *After method: Mess in social science research*. London, England: Routledge.

Law, J. (2004b). Matter-ing: Or how might STS contribute?." Centre for Science Studies, Lancaster University, draft available at http://www. heterogeneities. net/publications/Law2009TheGreer-BushTest. pdf, accessed on December 5th, 2010, 1–11.

Law, J., & Singleton, V. (2014). ANT, multiplicity and policy. *Critical policy studies, 8*(4), 379–396.

Lazer, D., Kennedy, R., King, G., & Vespignani, A. (2014). The parable of Google flu: Traps in big data analysis. *Science, 343*(6176), 1203–1205.

Lemke, T. (2001). "The birth of bio-politics": Michel Foucault's lecture at the Collège de France on neo-liberal governmentality. *Economy and Society, 30*(2), 190–207.

Lemke, T. (2012). *Foucault, governmentality, and critique*. Boulder, CO: Paradigm.

Lemke, T. (2015). New materialisms: Foucault and the 'government of things'. *Theory, Culture & Society, 32*(4), 3–25.

Lenglet, M. (2011). Conflicting codes and codings: How algorithmic trading is reshaping financial regulation. *Theory, Culture & Society, 28*(6), 44–66.

Leonardi, P. M., Nardi, B. A., & Kallinikos, J. (2012). *Materiality and organizing: Social interaction in a technological world*. Oxford, England: Oxford University Press.

Levy, S. (2010). *Hackers*. Sebastopol, CA: O'Reilly Media.

Lewis, S. C. (2015). Journalism in an era of big data: Cases, concepts, and critiques. *Digital Journalism, 3*(3), 321–330.

Lewis, S. C., & Usher, N. (2013). Open source and journalism: Toward new frameworks for imagining news innovation. *Media, Culture & Society, 35*(5), 602–619.

Lewis, S. C., & Usher, N. (2016). Trading zones, boundary objects, and the pursuit of news innovation: A case study of journalists and programmers. *Convergence, 22*(5), 543–560.

Lewis, S. C., & Westlund, O. (2015). Big Data and Journalism: Epistemology, expertise, economics, and ethics. *Digital Journalism, 3*(3), 447–466.Li, J., Green, B., & Backstrom, L. S. (2013). *U.S. Patent No. 9384243 B2* ("Real-time trend detection in a social network"). Washington, DC: U.S. Patent and Trademark Office.

Lievrouw, L. (2014). Materiality and media in communication and technology studies: An unfinished project. In T. Gillespie, P. Boczkowski, & K. Foot (Eds.), *Media technologies: Essays on communication, materiality, and society* (pp. 21–51). Cambridge, MA: MIT Press.

Linden, C. G. (2017). Decades of automation in the newsroom: Why are there still so many jobs in journalism? *Digital Journalism, 5*(2), 123–140.

Lowrey, W. (2006). Mapping the journalism–blogging relationship. *Journalism, 7*(4), 477–500.

Luu, F. (2013). *U.S. Patent No.* 20130332523 A1 ("Providing a multi-column newsfeed of content on a social networking system"). Retrieved from https://www.google.com/patents/US20130332523

Lyon, D. (2006). *Theorizing surveillance*. London, England: Routledge.

Mackenzie, A. (2002). *Transductions: Bodies and machines at speed*. London, England: Continuum.

Mackenzie, A. (2005). Problematising the technological: the object as event? *Social Epistemology, 19*(4), 381–399.

Mackenzie, A. (2006). *Cutting code: Software and sociality*. New York, NY: Peter Lang.

Mackenzie A (2007) Protocols and the irreducible traces of embodiment: The Viterbi Algorithm and the mosaic of machine time. In R. Hassan and R.E. Purser RE (Eds.) *24/7: Time and Temporality in the Network Society (pp. 89–106)*. Stanford, CA: Stanford University Press.

Mackenzie, A. (2015). The production of prediction: What does machine learning want? *European Journal of Cultural Studies, 18*(4–5), 429–445.

Mackenzie, A., & Vurdubakis, T. (2011). Codes and codings in crisis signification, performativity and excess. *Theory, Culture & Society, 28*(6), 3–23.

MacKenzie, D. (2008). *Material markets: How economic agents are constructed*. Oxford, England: Oxford University Press.

Mager, A. (2012). Algorithmic ideology: How capitalist society shapes search engines. *Information, Communication & Society, 15*(5), 769–787.

Mahoney, M. S. (1988). The history of computing in the history of technology. *Annals of the History of Computing, 10*(2), 113–125.

Manovich, L. (1999). Database as symbolic form. *Convergence: The International Journal of Research into New Media Technologies, 5*(2), 80–99.

Manovich, L. (2001). *The language of new media*. Cambridge MA: MIT Press.

Mansell, R. (2012). *Imagining the internet: Communication, innovation, and governance*. Oxford, England: Oxford University Press.

Marres, N. (2012). *Material participation: technology, the environment and everyday publics*. Basingstoke, England: Palgrave Macmillan.

Marres, N. (2013). Why political ontology must be experimentalized: On eco-show homes as devices of participation. *Social Studies of Science, 43*(3), 417–443.

Marwick, A. E. (2013). *Status update: Celebrity, publicity, and branding in the social media age*. New Haven, CT: Yale University Press.

Massumi, B. (1995). The autonomy of affect. *Cultural Critique* (31), 83–109.

Matheson, D. (2004). Weblogs and the epistemology of the news: some trends in online journalism. *New Media & Society, 6*(4), 443–468.

Maturana, H. R., & Varela, F. J. (1987). *The tree of knowledge: The biological roots of human understanding*. Boston, MA: Shambhala Publications.

McCormack, D. P. (2015). Devices for doing atmospheric things. In P. Vannini (Ed.), *Non-Representational methodologies. Re-Envisioning research*. New York, NY: Routledge.

McGoey, L. (2012). The logic of strategic ignorance. *The British Journal of Sociology, 63*(3), 533–576.

McKelvey, F. (2014). Algorithmic media need democratic methods: Why publics matter. *Canadian Journal of Communication, 39*(4).

McLuhan, M. (1994). *Understanding media: The extensions of man*. Cambridge, MA: MIT Press.

Mehra, S. K. (2015). Antitrust and the robo-seller: Competition in the time of algorithms. *Minnesota Law Review, 100*, 1323.

Meyer, P. (2002). *Precision journalism: A reporter's introduction to social science methods*. Lanham, MD: Rowman & Littlefield.

Meyer, R. (2014). Everything we know about Facebook's secret mood manipulation experiment. *The Atlantic*. Retrieved from http://www.theatlantic.com/technology/archive/2014/06/everything-we-know-about-facebooks-secret-mood-manipulation-experiment/373648/

Meyrowitz, J. (1994). Medium theory. In S. Crowley & D. Mitchell (Eds.) *Communication Theory Today (pp. 50–77)*. Stanford, CA: Stanford University Press.

Michael, M. (2004). On making data social: Heterogeneity in sociological practice. *Qualitative Research, 4*(1), 5–23.

Miller, C. H. (2015, July 9). When algorithms discriminate. *New York Times*. Retrieved from http://www.nytimes.com/2015/07/10/upshot/when-algorithms-discriminate.html?_r=0

Miller, P., & Rose, N. (1990). Governing economic life. *Economy and Society, 19*(1), 1–31.

Minsky, M., & Papert, S. (1969). *Perceptrons*. Cambridge, MA: MIT Press.

Mirani, L. (2015). Millions of Facebook users have no idea they're using the internet. *Quartz*. Retrieved from http://qz.com/333313/milliions-of-facebook-users-have-no-idea-theyre-using-the-internet

Miyazaki, S. (2012). Algorhythmics: Understanding micro-temporality in computational cultures. *Computational Culture* (2). Retrieved from: http://computationalculture.net/algorhythmics-understanding-micro-temporality-in-computational-cultures/

Mol, A. (1999). Ontological politics. A word and some questions. *The Sociological Review, 47*(S1), 74–89.

Mol, A. (2002). *The body multiple: Ontology in medical practice*: Durham, NC: Duke University Press.

Mol, A. (2013). Mind your plate! The ontonorms of Dutch dieting. *Social Studies of Science, 43*(3), 379–396.

Morley, D. (2003). *Television, audiences and cultural studies*. London, England: Routledge.

Morley, D., & Silverstone, R. (1990). Domestic communication—technologies and meanings. *Media, Culture & Society, 12*(1), 31–55.

Moser, I. (2008). Making Alzheimer's disease matter. Enacting, interfering and doing politics of nature. *Geoforum, 39*(1), 98–110.

Müller, M. (2015). Assemblages and actor-networks: Rethinking socio-material power, politics and space. *Geography Compass, 9*(1), 27–41.

Murray, J. (2012). Cybernetic principles of learning. In. N. Seel (Ed) *Encyclopedia of the Sciences of Learning* (pp. 901–904). Boston, MA: Springer.

Napoli, P. M. (2014). On automation in media industries: Integrating algorithmic media production into media industries scholarship. *Media Industries, 1*(1). Retrieved from: https://quod.lib.umich.edu/m/mij/15031809.0001.107/—on-automation-in-media-industries-integrating-algorithmic?rgn=main;view=fulltext

Napoli, P. M. (2015). Social media and the public interest: Governance of news platforms in the realm of individual and algorithmic gatekeepers. *Telecommunications Policy, 39*(9), 751–760.

Narasimhan, M. (2011). Extending the graph tech talk. Retrieved from http://www.facebook.com/video/video.php?v=10150231980165469

Naughton, J. (2016). Here is the news—but only if Facebook thinks you need to know. *The Guardian.* Retrieved from http://www.theguardian.com/commentisfree/2016/may/15/facebook-instant-articles-news-publishers-feeding-the-beast

Newton, C. (2016). Here's how Twitter's new algorithmic timeline is going to work. *The Verge.* Retrieved from http://www.theverge.com/2016/2/6/10927874/twitter-algorithmic-timeline

Neyland, D., & Möllers, N. (2017). Algorithmic IF...THEN rules and the conditions and consequences of power. *Information, Communication & Society, 20*(1), 45–62.

Nielsen, R. K. (2016). The many crises of Western journalism: A comparative analysis of economic crises, professional crises, and crises of confidence. In J. C. Alexander, E. B. Breese, & M. Luengo (Eds.), *The crisis of journalism reconsidered* (pp. 77–97)ᵃ Cambridge, England: Cambridge University Press.

Nielsen, R. K., & Schrøder, K. C. (2014). The relative importance of social media for accessing, finding, and engaging with news: An eight-country cross-media comparison. *Digital Journalism, 2*(4), 472–489.

Nunez, M. (2016). Former Facebook workers: We routinely suppressed Conservative news. *Gizmodo.* Retrieved from http://gizmodo.com/former-facebook-workers-we-routinely-suppressed-conser-1775461006

Obama, B. (2009). *Freedom of Information Act.* Retrieved from https://www.usitc.gov/secretary/foia/documents/FOIA_TheWhiteHouse.pdf

Ohlheiser, A. (2016). Three days after removing human editors, Facebook is already trending fake news. *The Washington Post.* Retrieved from https://www.washingtonpost.com/news/the-intersect/wp/2016/08/29/a-fake-headline-about-megyn-kelly-was-trending-on-facebook/?utm_term=.d7e4d9b9bf9a

Olazaran, M. (1996). A sociological study of the official history of the perceptrons controversy. *Social Studies of Science, 26*(3), 611–659.

Oremus, W. (2016). Who controls your Facebook feed. *Slate.* Retrieved from http://www.slate.com/articles/technology/cover_story/2016/01/how_facebook_s_news_feed_algorithm_works.html

Orlikowski, W. J. (1992). The duality of technology: Rethinking the concept of technology in organizations. *Organization Science, 3*(3), 398–427.

Orlikowski, W. J. (2000). Using technology and constituting structures: A practice lens for studying technology in organizations. *Organization Science, 11*(4), 404–428.

Orlikowski, W. J., & Gash, D. C. (1994). Technological frames: Making sense of information technology in organizations. *ACM Transactions on Information Systems (TOIS), 12*(2), 174–207.

Orlikowski, W. J., & Scott, S. V. (2008). 10 Sociomateriality: Challenging the separation of technology, work and organization. *The Academy of Management Annals, 2*(1), 433–474.

Orlikowski, W. J., & Scott, S. V. (2015). Exploring material-discursive practices. *Journal of Management Studies, 52*(5), 697–705.

Owens, E., & Vickrey, D. (2014). News feed FYI: Showing more timely stories from friends and pages. *Facebook News Feed FYI.* Retrieved from https://newsroom.fb.com/news/2014/09/news-feed-fyi-showing-more-timely-stories-from-friends-and-pages/

Packer, J., & Wiley, S. B. C. (2013). *Communication matters: Materialist approaches to media, mobility and networks.* New York, NY: Routledge.

Papacharissi, Z. (2015). *Affective publics: Sentiment, technology, and politics.* New York, NY: Oxford University Press.

Parasie, S. (2015). Data-driven revelation? Epistemological tensions in investigative journalism in the age of "big data." *Digital Journalism, 3*(3), 364–380.

Parasie, S., & Dagiral, E. (2013). Data-driven journalism and the public good: "Computer-assisted-reporters" and "programmer-journalists" in Chicago. *New Media & Society, 15*(6), 853–871.

Parikka, J. (2012). New materialism as media theory: Medianatures and dirty matter. *Communication and Critical/Cultural Studies, 9*(1), 95–100.

Pariser, E. (2011). *The filter bubble: What the Internet is hiding from you.* London, England: Penguin UK.

Parks, L. (2007). *Around the antenna tree: The politics of infrastructural visibility.* Paper presented at the ACM SIGGRAPH 2007 art gallery. San Diego, USA.

Parks, L., & Starosielski, N. (2015). *Signal traffic: Critical studies of media infrastructures.* Urbana: University of Illinois Press.

Pasick, A. (2015). The magic that makes Spotify's Discover Weekly playlists so damn good. *Quartz.* Retrieved from http://qz.com/571007/the-magic-that-makes-spotifys-discover-weekly-playlists-so-damn-good/

Pasquale, F. (2015). *The black box society.* Cambridge, MA: Harvard University Press.

Pasquale, F. A., & Bracha, O. (2008). Federal search commission? Access, fairness and accountability in the law of search. *Cornell Law Review, 93, 1149–1210.*

Passoth, J.-H., Peuker, B., & Schillmeier, M. (2012). *Agency without actors? New approaches to collective action.* London, England: Routledge.

Pavlik, J. (2000). The impact of technology on journalism. *Journalism Studies, 1*(2), 229–237.

Peet, R. (2000). Culture, imaginary, and rationality in regional economic development. *Environment and Planning A, 32*(7), 1215–1234.

Perel, M., & Elkin-Koren, N. (2017). Black box tinkering: Beyond transparency in algorithmic enforcement. *Florida Law Review, 69, 181–221.*

Peters, C., & Broersma, M. J. (2013). *Rethinking journalism: Trust and participation in a transformed news landscape.* London, England: Routledge.

Piaget, J. (2013). *Play, dreams and imitation in childhood.* London, England: Routledge.

Pickering, A. (1995). *The mangle of practice: Time, agency, and science.* Chicago, IL: University of Chicago Press.

Pinch, T. J., & Bijker, W. E. (1984). The social construction of facts and artefacts: Or how the sociology of science and the sociology of technology might benefit each other. *Social Studies of Science, 14*(3), 399–441.

Plantin, J.-C., Lagoze, C., Edwards, P. N., & Sandvig, C. (2016). Infrastructure studies meet platform studies in the age of Google and Facebook. *New Media & Society,* 1461444816661553.

Poole, E. S., Le Dantec, C. A., Eagan, J. R., & Edwards, W. K. (2008). *Reflecting on the invisible: understanding end-user perceptions of ubiquitous computing.* Paper presented at the Proceedings of the 10th international conference on Ubiquitous computing, September 11–14, Seoul, Korea.

Popper, B. (2015). Tastemaker. *The Verge.* Retrieved from http://www.theverge.com/2015/9/30/9416579/spotify-discover-weekly-online-music-curation-interview.

Power, M. (1999). *The audit society: Rituals of verification.* Oxford, England: Oxford University Press.

Power, M. (2004). Counting, control and calculation: Reflections on measuring and management. *Human Relations, 57*(6), 765–783.

Rabinow, P. (1994). *Essential works of Foucault 1954–1984.* London, England: Penguin Books.

Rabinow, P. (2009). *Anthropos today: Reflections on modern equipment.* Princeton, NJ: Princeton University Press.

Rader, E., & Gray, R. (2015). Understanding user beliefs about algorithmic curation in the Facebook news feed. *CHI 2015,* Seoul, Republic of Korea.

Rajchman, J. (1988). Foucault's art of seeing. *October,* 89–117.

Rancière, J. (2004). *The politics of aesthetics: The distribution of the sensible.* London, England: Continuum.

Ridgway, S. (2016). *Architectural projects of Marco Frascari: The pleasure of a demonstration.* London, England: Routledge.

Rieder, B. (2017). Scrutinizing an algorithmic technique: The Bayes classifier as interested reading of reality. *Information, Communication & Society, 20*(1), 100–117.

Roberge, J., & Melançon, L. (2017). Being the King Kong of algorithmic culture is a tough job after all Google's regimes of justification and the meanings of Glass. *Convergence: The International Journal of Research into New Media Technologies, 23*(3), 306–324.

Roberts, J. (2012). Organizational ignorance: Towards a managerial perspective on the unknown. *Management Learning, 44*(3), 215–236.

Rodgers, S. (2015). Foreign objects? Web content management systems, journalistic cultures and the ontology of software. *Journalism, 16*(1), 10–26.

Rodrigues, F. (2017). Meet the Swedish newspaper editor who put an algorithm in charge of his homepage. Retrieved from http://www.storybench.org/meet-swedish-newspaper-editor-put-algorithm-charge-homepage/

Rose, N. (1999). *Powers of freedom: Reframing political thought.* Cambridge, England: Cambridge University Press.

Rosen, J. (2005). Bloggers vs. journalists is over. Retrieved from http://archive.pressthink.org/2005/01/21/berk_essy.html

Rosenberry, J., & St John, B. (2010). *Public journalism 2.0: The promise and reality of a citizen engaged press.* London, England: Routledge.

Rubinstein, D. Y., Vickrey, D., Cathcart, R. W., Backstrom, L. S., & Thibaux, R. J. (2016). Diversity enforcement on a social networking system newsfeed: Google Patents.

Sandvig, C. (2013). The internet as an infrastructure. In *The Oxford handbook of internet studies* (pp. 86–108). Oxford, England: Oxford University Press.

Sandvig, C. (2015). Seeing the sort: The aesthetic and industrial defense of "the algorithm." *Journal of the New Media Caucus.* Retrieved from http://median.newmediacaucus.org/art-infrastructures-information/seeing-the-sort-the-aesthetic-and-industrial-defense-of-the-algorithm/

Sandvig, C., Hamilton, K., Karahalios, K., & Langbort, C. (2014). Auditing algorithms: Research methods for detecting discrimination on internet platforms. Presented at *Data and Discrimination: Converting Critical Concerns into Productive Inquiry.* May 22, Seattle, USA.

Sauder, M., & Espeland, W. N. (2009). The discipline of rankings: Tight coupling and organizational change. *American Sociological Review, 74*(1), 63–82.

Schmidhuber, J. (2015). Deep learning in neural networks: An overview. *Neural Networks, 61*, 85–117.

Schubert, C. (2012). Distributed sleeping and breathing: On the agency of means in medical work. In J. Passoth, B. Peuker & M. Schillmeier (Eds.) *Agency without actors: New approaches to collective action* (pp. 113–129). Abingdon, England: Routledge.

Schultz, I. (2007). The journalistic gut feeling: Journalistic doxa, news habitus and orthodox news values. *Journalism Practice, 1*(2), 190–207.

Schultz, A. P., Piepgrass, B., Weng, C. C., Ferrante, D., Verma, D., Martinazzi, P., Alison, T., & Mao, Z. (2014). *U.S. Patent No. 20140114774 A1* ("Methods and systems for determining use and content of pymk based on value model"). Washington, DC: U.S. Patent and Trademark Office.

Schütz, A. (1946). The well-informed citizen: An essay on the social distribution of knowledge. *Social Research, 13* (4), 463–478.

Schutz, A. (1970). *Alfred Schutz on phenomenology and social relations.* Chicago, IL: University of Chicago Press.

Seabrook, J. (2014). Revenue Streams. *The New Yorker.* Retrieved from https://www.newyorker.com/magazine/2014/11/24/revenue-streams

Seaver, N. (2013). Knowing algorithms. *Media in Transition, 8*, 1–12.

Sedgwick, E. K., & Frank, A. (1995). Shame in the cybernetic fold: Reading Silvan Tomkins. *Critical Inquiry, 21*(2), 496–522.

Simmel, G. (1906). The sociology of secrecy and of secret societies. *The American Journal of Sociology, 11*(4), 441–498.

Simon, J. (2015). Distributed epistemic responsibility in a hyperconnected era. In L. Floridi (Ed.), *The Onlife Manifesto* (pp. 145–159). Heidelberg, Germany: Springer.

Simondon, G. (1980). On the Mode of Existence of Technical Objects, Trans. N. Mellanphy, London: University of Western Ontario.

Simondon, G. (1992). The genesis of the individual. *Incorporations, 6,* 296–319.

Simondon, G. (2011). On the mode of existence of technical objects. *Deleuze Studies, 5*(3), 407–424.

Slack, J. D., & Wise, J. M. (2002). Cultural studies and technology. In L. Lievrouw & S. Livingstone (Eds.), *The handbook of new media* (pp. 485–501). London, England: Sage.

Smith, J. E. (1969). Time, times, and the "right time"; Chronos and kairos. *The Monist, 53*(1), 1–13.

Smithson, M. (2012). *Ignorance and uncertainty: Emerging paradigms.* Berlin, Germany: Springer Science & Business Media.

Snider, L. (2014). Interrogating the algorithm: Debt, derivatives and the social reconstruction of stock market trading. *Critical Sociology, 40*(5), 747–761.

Sommaruga, G., & Strahm, T. (Eds.). (2015). *Turing's revolution: The impact of his ideas about computability.* Heidelberg, Germany: Birkhäuser Springer.

Spinoza, B. (2000). *Ethics.* Ed. Trans. GHR Parkinson. Oxford, England: Oxford University Press.

Star, S. L., & Ruhleder, K. (1996). Steps toward an ecology of infrastructure: Design and access for large information spaces. *Information Systems Research, 7*(1), 111–134.

Statt, N. (2016). Facebook denies systemic bias in Trending Topics but changes how they are chosen. *The Verge.* Retrieved from http://www.theverge.com/2016/5/23/11754812/facebook-trending-topics-changes-political-bias-senate-inquiry.

Steensen, S. (2016). What is the matter with newsroom culture? A sociomaterial analysis of professional knowledge creation in the newsroom. *Journalism,* 1464884916657517.

Stengers, I. (2000). *The invention of modern science.* Minneapolis: University of Minnesota Press.

Stewart, K. (2007). *Ordinary affects.* Durham, NC: Duke University Press.

Stiegler, B. (2012). Relational ecology and the digital pharmakon. *Culture Machine, 13,* 1–19.

Stiegler, B. (2013). *What makes life worth living: On pharmacology.* New York, NY: John Wiley & Sons.

Stocky, T. (2016). Status update. Retrieved from https://www.facebook.com/tstocky/posts/10100 853082337958?pnref=story

Strathern, M. (2000a). The tyranny of transparency. *British Educational Research Journal, 26*(3), 309–321.

Strathern, M. (2000b). *Audit cultures: Anthropological studies in accountability, ethics, and the academy.* London, England: Routledge.

Strauss, C. (2006). The imaginary. *Anthropological Theory, 6*(3), 322–344.

Striphas, T. (2015). Algorithmic culture. *European Journal of Cultural Studies, 18*(4–5), 395–412.

Suchman, L. (2004). "Figuring personhood in sciences of the artificial". Department of Sociology, *Lancaster University.* Retrieved from https://www.scribd.com/document/88437121/Suchman-Figuring-Personhood

Suchman, L. (2007). *Human-machine reconfigurations: Plans and situated actions.* Cambridge, England: Cambridge University Press.

Sullivan, B. (2016). "I just got really mad": The Norwegian editor tackling Facebook on censorship. Retrieved from https://motherboard.vice.com/en_us/article/i-just-got-really-mad-the-norwegian-editor-tackling-facebook-on-censorship-aftenposten

Sundve, E. (2017). The future of media? This is Schibsted's «next generation news experience». Retrieved from https://www.medier24.no/artikler/the-future-of-media-this-is-schibsted-s-next-generation-news-experience/365323

Surden, H. (2014). Machine learning and law. *Washington Law Review, 89,* 87–217.

Sweeney, L. (2013). Discrimination in online ad delivery. *Queue, 11*(3), 10.

Syvertsen, T., Enli, G., Mjøs, O. J., & Moe, H. (2014). *The media welfare state: Nordic media in the digital era.* Ann Arbor: University of Michigan Press.

Taigman, Y., Ming, Y., Ranzato, M., & Wolf, L. (2014). *DeepFace: Closing the gap to human-level performance in face verification.* Paper presented at the conference Computer Vision and Pattern Recognition IEEE, June 23–28, Columbus, OH.

Tambini, D. (2017). Fake news: public policy responses.

Taylor, C. (2004). *Modern social imaginaries*. Durham, NC: Duke University Press.

Thomas, W. (2015). Algorithms: From Al-Khwarizmi to Turing and beyond. In G. Sommaruga & T. Strahm (Eds.), *Turing's revolution: The impact of his ideas about computability* (pp. 29–42). Heidelberg, Germany: Birkhäuser Springer.

Thompson, J. B. (2005). The new visibility. *Theory, Culture & Society, 22*(6), 31–51.

Thrift, N. (2005). *Knowing capitalism*. London, England: Sage.

Thrift, N. (2007). *Non-representational theory: Space, politics, affect*. London, England: Routledge.

Thurman, N. (2015). Journalism, gatekeeping and interactivity. In S. Coleman & D. Freelon (Eds.) *Handbook of digital politics* (pp. 357–376). Cheltenham, England: Edward Elgar.

Thurman, N., Schifferes, S., Fletcher, R., Newman, N., Hunt, S., & Schapals, A. K. (2016). Giving Computers a Nose for News: Exploring the limits of story detection and verification. *Digital Journalism, 4*(7), 838–848.

Townley, B. (1993). Foucault, power/knowledge, and its relevance for human resource management. *Academy of Management Review, 18*(3), 518–545.

Trottier, D., & Lyon, D. (2012). Key features of social media surveillance. In C. Fuchs, K. Boersma, A. Albrechtslund, & M. Sandoval (Eds.), *Internet and Surveillance: The Challenges of Web 2.0 and Social Media* (pp. 89–105). New York, NY: Routledge.

Tsoukas, H. (1997). The tyranny of light: The temptations and the paradoxes of the information society. *Futures, 29*(9), 827–843.

Tufekci, Z. (2008). Can you see me now? Audience and disclosure regulation in online social network sites. *Bulletin of Science, Technology & Society, 28*(1), 20–36.

Tufekci, Z. (2015). Algorithmic harms beyond Facebook and Google: Emergent challenges of computational agency. *Colorado Technology Law Journal, 13*(2), 203–218.

Turitzin, C. (2014). News Feed FYI: What happens when you see more updates from friends. *News Feed FYI*. Retrieved from http://newsroom.fb.com/news/2014/01/news-feed-fyi-what-happens-when-you-see-more-updates-from-friends

Turkle, S. (1984). *The second self: Computers and the human spirit*. Cambridge, MA: MIT Press.

van Dalen, A. (2012). The algorithms behind the headlines: How machine-written news redefines the core skills of human journalists. *Journalism Practice, 6*(5–6), 648–658.

van Dijck, J. (2012). Facebook as a tool for producing sociality and connectivity. *Television & New Media, 13*(2), 160–176.

van Dijck, J. (2013). The culture of connectivity: A critical history of social media: Oxford University Press.

van Dijck, J., & Poell, T. (2013). Understanding social media logic. *Media and Communication, 1*(1), 2–14.

Vannini, P. (2015). *Non-representational methodologies: Re-envisioning research*. London, England: Routledge.

Vannini, P., & Vannini, A. (2008). Of walking shoes, boats, golf carts, bicycles, and a slow technoculture: A technography of movement and embodied media on Protection Island. *Qualitative Inquiry, 14*(7), 1272–1301.

Verran, H. (2001). *Science and an African logic*. Chicago, IL: University of Chicago Press.

Volokh, E., & Falk, D. M. (2011). Google: First amendment protection for search engine search results. *Journal of Law, Economics, & Policy, 8*, 883–900.

Von Hilgers, P. (2011). The history of the black box: The clash of a thing and its concept. *Cultural Politics, 7*(1), 41–58.

Vu, H. T. (2014). The online audience as gatekeeper: The influence of reader metrics on news editorial selection. *Journalism, 15*(8), 1094–1110.

Wade, B. W., & Chamberlin, D. D. (2012). IBM relational database systems: The early years. *IEEE Annals of the History of Computing, 34*(4), 38–48.

Walsh, B. (2014). Google's flu project shows the failings of big data. Retrieved from http://time.com/23782/google-flu-trends-big-data-problems.

Wang, J., Burge, J., Backstrom, L. S., Ratiu, F., & Ferrante, D. (2012). *U.S. Patent No. 20120041907 A1* ("Suggesting connections to a user based on an expected value of the suggestion to the social networking system"). Washington, DC: U.S. Patent and Trademark Office.

Wardrip-Fruin, N. (2009). *Expressive processing: Digital fictions, computer games, and software studies.* Cambridge, MA: MIT Press.

Wash, R. (2010). *Folk models of home computer security.* Paper presented at the Proceedings of the Sixth Symposium on Usable Privacy and Security, July 14–16, Redmond, WA.

Webb, D. (2003). On friendship: Derrida, Foucault, and the practice of becoming. *Research in Phenomenology, 33,* 119–140.

Weiss, A. S., & Domingo, D. (2010). Innovation processes in online newsrooms as actor-networks and communities of practice. *New Media & Society, 12*(7), 1156–1171.

Welch, B., & Zhang, X. (2014). News Feed FYI: Showing better videos. *News Feed FYI.* Retrieved from http://newsroom.fb.com/news/2014/06/news-feed-fyi-showing-better-videos/

Weltevrede, E., Helmond, A., & Gerlitz, C. (2014). The politics of real-time: A device perspective on social media platforms and search engines. *Theory, Culture & Society, 31*(6), 125–150.

Whitehead, A. N. (1978). *Process and reality: An essay in cosmology* Ed. David Ray Griffin and Donald W. Sherburne, NY: Free Press.

Wiener, N. (1948). *Cybernetics: Control and communication in the animal and the machine.* New York, NY: Technology Press & Wiley.

Wilf, E. (2013). Toward an anthropology of computer-mediated, algorithmic forms of sociality. *Current Anthropology, 54*(6), 716–739.

Williams, R. (1977). *Marxism and literature.* Oxford, England: Oxford University Press.

Williams, R. (1985). *Keywords: A vocabulary of culture and society.* Oxford, England: Oxford University Press.

Williams, R. (2005). *Television: Technology and cultural form.* New York, NY: Routledge.

Williams, S. (2004). *Truth, autonomy, and speech: Feminist theory and the first amendment.* New York: New York University Press.

Williamson, B. (2015). Governing software: networks, databases and algorithmic power in the digital governance of public education. *Learning, Media and Technology, 40*(1), 83–105.

Wing, J. M. (2006). Computational thinking. *Communications of the ACM, 49*(3), 33–35.

Winner, L. (1986). *The whale and the reactor: A search for limits in an age of high technology.* Chicago, IL: University of Chicago Press.

Winner, L. (1993). Upon opening the black box and finding it empty: Social constructivism and the philosophy of technology. *Science, Technology, and Human Values, 18*(3): 362–378.

Wirth, N. (1985). *Algorithms+ data structures= programs.* Englewood Cliffs, NJ: Prentice Hall.

Woolgar, S. (1998). A new theory of innovation? *Prometheus, 16*(4), 441–452.

Woolgar, S., & Lezaun, J. (2013). The wrong bin bag: A turn to ontology in science and technology studies? *Social Studies of Science, 43*(3), 321–340.

WSJ. (2015, October 25). Tim Cook talks TV, cars, watches and more. *Wall Street Journal.* Retrieved from http://www.wsj.com/articles/tim-cook-talks-tv-cars-watches-and-more-1445911369

Yusoff, K. (2009). Excess, catastrophe, and climate change. *Environment and Planning D: Society and Space, 27*(6), 1010–1029.

Ziewitz, M. (2016). Governing algorithms myth, mess, and methods. *Science, Technology & Human Values, 41*(1), 3–16.

Zimmer, M. (2008). The externalities of search 2.0: The emerging privacy threats when the drive for the perfect search engine meets Web 2.0. *First Monday, 13*(3). Retrieved from http://firstmonday.org/article/view/2136/1944

Zuckerberg, M. (2014). "Today is Facebook's 10th anniversary". Retrieved from https://www.facebook.com/zuck/posts/10101250930776491

Zuckerberg, M., Bosworth, A., Cox, C., Sanghvi, R., & Cahill, M. (2012). *U.S. Patent No. 817128* ("Communicating a newsfeed of media content based on a member's interactions in a social network environment"). Retrieved from https://www.google.com/patents/US8171128

Zuiderveen Borgesius, F. J., Trilling, D., Moeller, J., Bodó, B., De Vreese, C. H., & Helberger, N. (2016). Should we worry about filter bubbles? *Internet Policy Review. Journal on Internet Regulation, 5*(1). Retrieved from https://policyreview.info/articles/analysis/should-we-worry-about-filter-bubbles

Index

Printed in the USA/Agawam, MA
January 8, 2021

767989.015